OCTAVIA E. BUTLER

MODERN MASTERS OF SCIENCE FICTION

Edited by Gary K. Wolfe

Science fiction often anticipates the consequences of scientific discoveries. The immense strides made by science since World War II have been matched step by step by writers who gave equal attention to scientific principles, human imagination, and the craft of fiction. The respect for science fiction won by Jules Verne and H. G. Wells was further increased by Isaac Asimov, Arthur C. Clarke, Robert Heinlein, Ursula K. Le Guin, Joanna Russ, and Ray Bradbury. Modern Masters of Science Fiction is devoted to books that survey the work of individual authors who continue to inspire and advance science fiction.

A list of books in the series appears at the end of this book.

OCTAVIA E. BUTLER

Gerry Canavan

UNIVERSITY OF
ILLINOIS PRESS
Urbana, Chicago, and Springfield

Library of Congress Control Number: 2016950188
ISBN 978-0-252-04066-5 (hardcover)
ISBN 978-0-252-08216-0 (paperback)
ISBN 978-0-252-09910-6 (e-book)

For John Barberet, who got me started,
and Priscilla Wald, who got me going

CONTENTS

ILLUSTRATIONS

Our thanks to the Huntington Library and to Writer's House for permission to use these images. The listed codes reflect their location within the Huntington's manuscript collection.

Acknowledgments

Like some supercharged Oankali mating ritual, this book has many parents. I dedicate the book to the two teachers who first introduced me to Octavia Butler's work. John Barbaret taught *Parable of the Sower* in a "utopias" course my freshman year of college at Case Western Reserve University, one of the classes that was most important in setting me on the long path toward graduate school in literature and beyond. My friend and advisor, the incomparable Priscilla Wald, taught *Dawn* in her amazing "Human Being after Genocide" course at Duke University early in my time there, which was probably the most important semester in my development as a scholar. I devoured *Dawn* (and then *Adulthood Rites*, and then *Imago*) over a single weekend in time for class that Monday, and then set about tracking down, by the end of the summer, every other novel Butler had published. Priscilla, we still don't agree about whether the Oankali are saviors or monsters—but that's okay.

I'd also like to thank the countless other people I've talked with about Butler's work over the years, including good friends at Duke, Marquette University, the International Conference for the Fantastic in the Arts, the Science Fiction Research Association, the Eaton Conference, the Society for Utopian Studies, on Facebook, Tumblr, Twitter, and elsewhere. There are far too many people to name, but I'm especially grateful to Fredric Jameson, Kate Hayles, Eric Carl Link, Darko Suvin, Ben Robertson, Rebekah Sheldon, Brent Bellamy, Ayana Jamieson, Ritch Calvin, Rebecca Evans, Fran McDonald, Melody Jue, Lisa Klarr, Ryan Vu, Ramzi Fawaz, Isiah Lavender III, Lisa Yaszek, Mark Bould, Sherryl Vint, David Higgins, Malisa Kurtz, Grace Dillon, Aaron Bady, Lili Loofbourow, Brian Attebery, John Rieder, De Witt Douglas Kilgore, Phil Wegner, Jad Smith, Justin Roby, Alexis Lothian, Kathryn Allen, Sarah Juliet Lauro, Jeffrey Hicks, Josh Pearson, Maya Sullivan, Tony Manno, John Brick,

Kathryn Hendrickson, Thomas Moore, Rob Latham, Steve Shaviro, Annalee Newitz, Eileen Klein, Rebecca J. Holden, Nisi Shawl, Conseula Francis, Nalo Hopkinson, Kim Stanley Robinson, Julie Gay, and Neil Easterbrook. (Alas, this only scratches the surface!) I'm especially grateful to Neil for the introduction to Willis Regier, my first editor at University of Illinois Press, and Marika Christofides, his successor, both of whom were incredible to work with and instrumental in seeing this book through to completion, as well as to the anonymous readers who provided very helpful feedback. I'm grateful also to Sarah Nagel, Alexandra Levick, Ernestine Walker, and Merrilee Heifetz for granting permission for the photographs we include in this volume and for the republication of "Lost Races of Science Fiction" as an appendix, as well as for their guidance on other important matters.

This book owes a debt to the encouragement, support, and collaboration of my home department at Marquette, including my colleagues Kris Ratcliffe, John Su, Leah Flack, Angela Sorby, C. J. Hribal, Diane Hoeveler, Marques Redd, Tol Foster, Al Rivero, Amy Blair, Rebecca Nowacek, Heather Hathaway, Brittany Pladek, Sarah Wadsworth, and Jodi Melamed, among many others. I also owe a debt to the many students who have participated in class and office-hour discussions on *Dawn*, *Kindred*, *Fledgling*, and *Parable of the Sower* over the past few years, and who opened my eyes to many new nuances, puzzles, Easter eggs, and intricacies in the texts.

My research at the Huntington Library (San Marino, California)—and consequently this entire book—was made financially possible by generous research grants from Marquette and by a John Brockway Huntington Foundation fellowship from the Huntington itself. I would also like to thank the library staff at the Huntington for their tireless retrieval of box after box for my perusal.

A Faculty Development Award from Marquette University supported the republishing of Butler's essay "Lost Races of Science Fiction"; this is the first time the essay has appeared in print since its 1980 publication in *Transmission*.

Portions of this book have previously appeared in modified, abbreviated, or extended form in *Science Fiction Studies*, *The Los Angeles Review of Books*, *Paradoxa 25: "Africa SF," Disability in Science Fiction: Representations of Technology as Cure*, and *The Next Generation: Emerging Voices in Utopian Studies*. I'm very grateful to those editors and publishers, both for the opportunity to work out some of these ideas and for their willingness to allow me to reprint some of that text here.

My most extravagant thanks as always to my spouse, Jaimee Hills, who really moved heaven and earth to make the time for me to write all this, and to Zoey and Connor, who put up with two long research trips to California when they were too young to effectively protest. Thanks also to my mom and dad and brother and everyone else who has gotten an earful from me about Octavia Butler at some point in the past few years.

Finally, my thanks to OEB, whom I felt as if I knew a little bit even before I ghoulishly read all her secret journals and private letters. You went away much too soon. You're missed.

CHRONOLOGY

1947   Octavia Estelle Butler is born in Pasadena, California
ca. 1959   Begins writing science fiction after watching *Devil Girl from Mars* on television
1960   Begins submitting stories to science fiction magazines; swindled out of $61 by
           fraudulent literary agent
1965   Graduates high school
1966   Wins Pasadena City College literary contest
1967   Wins fifth place in national *Writer's Digest* short story contest
1968   Graduates from Pasadena City College with an associate's degree in history;
           enrolls in California State University, Los Angeles
1969   Enrolls in UCLA Extension creative writing workshop; subsequently enrolls in
           Screen Writers Guild of America Open Door Workshop, led by Harlan Ellison
1970   Attends Clarion Science Fiction Writers Workshop in Clarion, Pennsylvania,
           where the teachers include Joanna Russ, Samuel R. Delany, Fritz Leiber, and
           Damon Knight; sells "Childfinder" to Harlan Ellison for *The Last Dangerous
           Visions* (which is never published)
1971   "Crossover"
1976   *Patternmaster*; temporarily moves to Maryland to research *Kindred*
1977   *Mind of My Mind*
1978   *Survivor*
1979   *Kindred*; "Near of Kin"
1980   *Wild Seed* (shortlisted for "retrospective" James Tiptree Jr. Award, 1995); "Lost
           Races of Science Fiction"; approached by Martin Greenberg regarding ultimately
           failed *Black Futures* anthology; Guest of Honor at feminist science fiction
           convention WisCon in Madison, Wisconsin
1982   Visits Finland and the Soviet Union with a group of other science fiction writers
           (including Joe Haldeman, Forrest Ackerman, and Roger Zelazny)
1983   "Speech Sounds" (Hugo Award, 1984)
1984   *Clay's Ark*; "Bloodchild" (Hugo, Locus, and Nebula Awards, 1984–1985)
1985   Research trip to Peru with UCLA study group (research for Xenogenesis trilogy);
           begins teaching at Clarion West (and later Clarion East as well)
1987   *Dawn*; "The Evening and the Morning and the Night" [II] (Nebula nominee, 1987)
1988   *Adulthood Rites*; "Birth of a Writer" (republished as "Positive Obsession" in
           Bloodchild [1996])
1989   *Imago*

1993	*Parable of the Sower* (Nebula nominee, 1994)
1995	Awarded John D. and Catherine T. MacArthur Foundation Fellowship
1996	Death of Butler's mother; *Bloodchild* short story collection (first edition)
1997	Receives honorary PhD from Kenyon College
1998	*Parable of the Talents* (Nebula winner, 1999); *"Devil Girl from Mars:* Why I Write Science Fiction" delivered at "Media in Transition" forum at MIT
1999	Moves to Seattle
2000	*Lilith's Brood* (Xenogenesis trilogy omnibus edition and rebranding); Lifetime Achievement Award in Writing from the PEN American Center; Guest of Honor at the International Conference for the Fantastic in the Arts
2003	"Amnesty"; "The Book of Martha"
2005	*Fledgling*; *Bloodchild* second edition including "Amnesty" and "The Book of Martha"
2006	Butler dies in Seattle, Washington, following a fall near her home
2007	*Seed to Harvest* (Patternist omnibus edition, minus *Survivor*)
2010	Inducted into Science Fiction Hall of Fame
2012	Solstice Award from the Science Fiction Writers of America
2014	"A Necessary Being" and "Childfinder" published in *Unexpected Stories*

OCTAVIA E. BUTLER

BEGINNING AT THE END

"I am a 34-year-old writer who can remember being a 10-year-old writer and who expects someday to be a 70-year-old writer," writes Octavia E. Butler in the short autobiographical author's note she updated year after year and decade after decade between 1981 and the publication of her final novel, *Fledgling*, in 2005. By and large the nearly forty separate versions of this "Brief Conversation with Octavia Butler" that can be found in the Huntington Library's archival collection of her papers are strikingly identical to one another: "I'm also comfortably asocial—a hermit in the middle of Seattle—a pessimist if I'm not careful, a feminist, a black, a former Baptist, an oil-and-water combination of ambition, laziness, insecurity, certainty, and drive." But over the course of her life the details did shift around a bit. In the earliest versions she still describes herself as a student, as well as a "quiet egotist," both of which quickly fall away in later versions; "usually hopeful" makes a very late appearance as a self-description for the first time in 2004; there is her big move away from the Los Angeles area to Seattle in 1999; the moment when "a black" becomes, instead, "African American." As she entered her forties, she decided to give herself another ten years, expecting now to someday be an 80-year-old writer.[1]

But it didn't happen. Octavia E. Butler died on February 24, 2006, after a fall near her home; she was only 58. The loss sent shockwaves of grief radiating across the myriad communities of writers, academics, and science fiction fans who had been touched by her life and work. At the time of her death she had become a legend in her field, one of the best writers of her generation, and an inspiration to the generation of writers that followed her; an inevitable part of any all-time best-of list of science fiction writers; a fixture on English, Women's Studies, Queer Theory, African American Studies, and Postcolonial Theory college syllabi; a winner of the Hugo, Nebula, and Locus awards, as well as a lifetime achievement award from the PEN American Center; an admired public intellectual; and even an officially certified genius, though like most awardees she preferred the less florid "John D. and Catherine T. MacArthur Foundation Fellow." She was never, perhaps, quite the household name she had once hoped to be—but she was widely and very deeply beloved.

Butler left behind a stunning literary legacy of twelve novels and nine short stories that have been pored over by scholars and fans since the first novel, *Patternmaster*, was published in 1976—to say nothing of the thousands of pages of unpublished work that first became available at the Huntington in November 2013. Her fiction exemplifies the complex insights of the Afrofuturist school of science fiction, which notes (as writer and musician Greg Tate has put it) that "black people live the estrangement that science fiction writers imagine."[2] If we are interested in stories about brutal invaders who come in technologically advanced ships from far away, who kidnap, murder, rape, and enslave, we do not need to look to outer space; that is already Earth's actual history, and is the case in the world where Butler's characters have (often quite unhappily) been condemned to live. Writing in a genre that since its inception had been, as she put it, "nearly all white, just as until recently, it's been nearly all male,"[3] Butler's transformative importance in the history of science fiction can hardly be overstated. She stood for decades as science fiction's sole prominent black female voice, broadening the outlook of the field in ways that are still being felt today. She sometimes told the story of the white editor who "didn't think that blacks should be included in science fiction stories because they changed the character of the stories [. . .] you could use an alien instead and get rid of all this messiness and all those people that we don't want to deal with."[4] After Butler, this level of arrogant dismissal would be almost unthinkable in science fiction. Her novels—like those of Samuel R. Delany, Ursula K. Le Guin, Joanna Russ, and James Tiptree Jr. (Alice Sheldon), other titans of the field with whom she is commonly paired—are all corrections of that fundamental error, the recovery of the "nightmare of history" whose memory has been erased from the everyday life of the privileged. With those fellow travelers and others, she showed that the genre was capable of better, and of more. Butler's creative and critical work demonstrates that science fiction was never *really* a straight, white, male genre, despite its pretensions to the contrary; blackness, womanhood, poverty, disability, and queerness were always there, under the surface, the genre's hidden truth. She proved that the speculations of science fiction could no longer afford to ignore the fraught questions of identity and difference that have transformed global society across all levels in the postwar period. She made science fiction "messy"—or, rather, showed how messy it had always been. The future never belonged to just one tiny fraction of the human race.

Butler's science fictions typically pit power against justice and leave both utterly transformed. These are stories born from her own subaltern position in American society: "I began writing about power," she once told Carolyn S. Davidson, "because I had so little."[5] In Butler's novels power acts as it always does, rapaciously inflicting itself upon those without; it is the task of the powerless to turn the tables, or else survive in the gaps. Nearly every story in her oeuvre considers the inevitable struggle for dominance that occurs when two "alien" forms of life, with different capabilities, and different needs, encounter each other for the first time. These themes have made Butler a rare crossover figure between the "science fiction" and "literature" sections of the bookstore, as well as made her an inevitable reference in critical theory. Scholars and philosophers have frequently turned to her novels as fodder for thought experiments, philosophical speculations, and political analogies, perhaps nowhere more famously than in Donna Haraway's 1985 "Cyborg Manifesto" and related works, which helped launch a new wave of feminism using an interpretation of Butler's Oankali as a key analytical example.

But the politics of Butler's stories are never kneejerk or obvious, either; Butler is a deeply ambiguous thinker. Readers of her notes and journals in the Huntington are soon greeted by the strange shorthand *aop* that she used ubiquitously throughout her life, standing in for "as opposed to"—male aop female, white aop black, healing aop killing. It seemed very difficult for Butler to think of anything without immediately thinking also of its opposite(s) and of how all supposed opposites are dialectically intertwined. This extends even to the level of her plots: very commonly, almost characteristically, she would wind up writing the opposite of the narrative she originally set out to write.

Consequently, there are no easy answers, no manifestos or utopias to be found within her pages. Frequently her heroes turn sour, or become suspect, or seem to cross unthinkable lines of ethics and integrity in the name of survival. Just as frequently as they fight back, her characters choose not to resist their invaders, but to aid them—or fall in love with them, or merge entirely with them. In biological terms, her most frequent metaphor is not individualistic competition but mutual interdependence: symbiosis. We need the Other to live (whether we like it or not). In "The Monophobic Response," Butler ultimately concludes that fantasies of "aliens" are ultimately borne out of this palpable "need" for otherness, an unquenchable desire for the union of differences that seem innate and insurmountable.[6] That interplay of attraction and revulsion is the source of what is simultaneously most utopian and most disturbing about her stories. In Butler's fiction the violence of power is always matched by an erotics of power, an unexpected dimension of domination that retains an inescapable hold on her characters despite the fact that they did not choose it, do not want it, and often suffer grievously for it.

In the Pattternist series (1976–1984) the alien encounter comes between ordinary human beings and the superpowered posthuman mutants who ultimately supplant and enslave them—a nightmarish vision that draws from an adolescent Octavia's somewhat disturbing fantasy to "live forever and breed people."[7] In her short stories we similarly see human beings struggling to survive in the gaps and interstices of power, whether they be living as breeding stock for powerful alien overlords (as in her widely anthologized "Bloodchild"), living in the aftermath of an alien invasion (as in her late story "Amnesty"), or living with serious, even catastrophic disability (as in "The Evening and the Morning and the Night" [II] and "Speech Sounds"). In the Xenogenesis series (1987–1989, later renamed "Lilith's Brood"), my favorite of her works, a human race that has just destroyed itself through cataclysmic nuclear war is given a second chance through the intervention of the alien Oankali, gene traders from the stars, who fiercely desire the infinite mutability of our cancers—and who won't take no for an answer. In the Parables series (1993–1998), a world ruined by neoliberal privatization and ecological collapse is given hope by the empathic capabilities of a woman whose psychological dysfunction allows her quite literally to feel another's pain—a capacity that makes her at once highly empathetic and extremely dangerous. In *Fledgling* (2005), Butler turned to the horror genre with a science-fictional take on vampire mythology, re-imagining the vampire and her victim as a sexually charged union of symbiotic *un*equals. And in *Kindred* (1979), perhaps her most mainstream, "literary" novel, the time-travel fantasy so popular in science fiction is deconstructed through its spellbinding use of a nonwhite, nonmale protagonist, for whom the past is a site not of nostalgia or desire but of horror and abiding dread.

When she died, fans of Butler's work were eagerly anticipating the release of at least two sequels, the long-awaited *Parable of the Trickster* and the planned sequel to her most recent novel, *Fledgling*; instead, there would be no more.

FUROR SCRIBENDI

When Butler was approached in the late 1990s with the idea of writing a memoir, she began one cursory attempt with a strong declaration of her life's purpose, declaring writing not only "the love of [her] life," and the reason she was alive, but the reason she *wanted* to be alive.[8] In two short autobiographical essays published in *Bloodchild*, she describes this overawing devotion to her craft as a "positive obsession" and as a "furor scribendi" (a madness for writing).[9] Forget talent, forget inspiration, she says in the second of these; writing is about habit, about persistence. Writing was a holy thing for Butler, a constant and daily devotion. When she was still working day jobs—miserable, grinding work she hated—she would get up at two or three in the morning and write. She kept up the practice long after she no longer had to. She wrote through a lonely childhood, through discouragement from family and teachers, through a decade and a half of mounting rejection slips, through bankruptcy, through too many years after that of being underpaid and disrespected on the midlist. She wrote. When she wasn't writing—when she was stuck, or when she was blocked, or later in her life when her medication seemed to interfere with her creativity—she was miserable. She was only really happy when she was writing.

With so much writing—constant writing, endless ideas—it is perhaps surprising that she published comparatively few novels and stories. Other authors highlighted in the Modern Masters of Science Fiction series published dozens of books over the course of their lives; Butler published only twelve novels and one collection of short stories. Now that her papers at the Huntington Library have been opened to scholars, we can begin to see where all that writing time went. Butler was not only a writer but a *rewriter*, and a re-rewriter, and a re-re-rewriter, almost to the point of compulsion. She was also a brutal self-critic, above and beyond the ruthless requirements of a literary marketplace that was not always ready for her and her ideas. Among the Huntington's thousands of files, we consequently find myriad alternative versions of her familiar stories and novels, some keeping only character names but transplanting them to entirely different narrative situations, others telling the same story with new twists and turns. She wrote the first three Patternist books for nearly two decades between the ages of fifteen (when she first got the idea) and twenty-nine (when she finally sold *Patternmaster*); there were at least three *Kindred*s; two or three *Dawn*s; at least four *Sower*s . . .

And those are only the alternate versions of the published novels. Butler also composed several unpublished and/or unfinished novels that can be found and read at the Huntington as well; two versions of a novel called *Blindsight* (about a blind faith healer/cult leader with the power of psychokinesis) and several long but ultimately unfinished attempts at a novel called *Paraclete* (about a woman with the power to *literally* write truth). Other potential novels are even more fragmentary, though still intriguing. There are unpublished short stories and essays, and unfinished sequels like *Doro-Jesus* and *Parable of the Trickster* and *Fledgling II*, only partially finished or fragmentary, which she would work on for a while and then put aside, or transform as the kernel of a plot event in some other text. Add these to her notebooks and letters; multiple, overlapping journals and travel notebooks; bound commonplace books and outlines and scrap paper—all of which also wound up in boxes at the Huntington—and a fuller picture of her life's work begins to come into focus. While her published work will naturally always take precedence, there is a sense in which it is really only the very tip of a vast iceberg. Butler had a totemic relationship with her writing; she seems to have endeavored to keep every scrap of paper she had ever written on, on the grounds, perhaps, that someday she might need it for a story. (For ideas developed beyond the level of scrap paper, even keeping the original wasn't enough; in one of Butler's unfinished memoirs, she recalled with horror the briefcase she lost in the mid-1970s containing half a novel, after which she made sure she had *more* than one copy of everything, just in case.[10])

One of the crucial things the Huntington archive reveals about Butler's work is her intense fidelity to the stories she wrote as a child. The early Patternist novels have often been neglected by her scholars, because they are so early and so raw, because they seem to be missing crucial parts of the overall narrative arc that would make them most satisfying (especially a proper ending), and because in at least one prominent case (*Survivor*) Butler explicitly disavowed the book, prevented its republication, and begged everyone not to read it. But when we look at her work through the lens of what we find in the archive, we see that the Patternist stories are overwhelmingly crucial, in two senses. First, as we will see, nearly everything she writes, with only a few exceptions, is ultimately derived from the Patternist milieu in one way or the other. One of her first two sales, "Childfinder," to Harlan Ellison in 1971 for his *The Last Dangerous Visions* anthology (which was only published posthumously in *Unexpected Stories* in 2014), is set in an embryonic version of the Patternist milieu. The earliest versions of *Kindred* explicitly take place in the Patternist universe, as do some versions of her failed novel *Blindsight*. The Oankali originate in the 1970s in the Patternist milieu as a "Missionary" story, following a different group of off-world settlers on a different planet. The first story Butler titled "The Evening and the Morning and the Night" is a Missionary story—never published—and when Butler did publish a very different story with that name a decade later, she openly worried that it might still be too much like a Patternist story.[11] "Bloodchild" could very easily *be* a Missionary story, with only one or two slight sentences differentiating it from that future history, as Butler also acknowledged with private frustration.[12] Even "Speech Sounds" concerns widespread cognitive impairment and "mutes" (this time, *literally* mutes) in the wake of a global plague—almost like an after-the-credits sequence from *Clay's Ark*, which she was writing and circulating for publication at the same time. Whenever her creativity lagged, she began toying with the idea of returning to the Patternists, in one form or another.

Perhaps most unexpectedly, the earliest 1989 version of the Parable books (and the ongoing plan for her never-completed *Parable of the Trickster*) was initially intended to take place entirely off-world, as a kind of re-do correcting the mistakes she had made in *Survivor*—and multiple versions of the unfinished *Trickster* unexpectedly inject a Doro-like "body jumper" who is able to survive her own murder through Patternist-style psychic powers. This addition would have completely changed the "mundane SF" setting of the published Parable books in ways Butler's readers would likely have found very frustrating to their suspension of disbelief—that she considered doing it anyway suggests the extent of the hold the Patternist stories still had on her imagination. Her larger outline for the Parables books, coupled with her 1970s journals, reveals that the Earthseeders are actually just an updated version of the future-history interplanetary saga she had always planned to write about the Missionaries. And more or less everything she writes after the late 1990s—*Fledgling*, *Paraclete*, "Amnesty," "The Book of Martha"—spirals out of the uncompleted fragments of *Trickster*, and thus out of *Patternmaster/Mind of My Mind/Survivor* milieu by association.

Second, but related, is the overarching importance of the Doro-Mary dyad in Butler's imagination, and the extent to which she wrote and rewrote this charged relationship across her fictions. Over and over again Butler imagines an intense, cold, powerful, and attractive man who is usually a borderline-abusive gaslighter—and then imagines a powerful female survivor as his associate-prisoner-competitor-lover (and typically all of them at once). This is not to say that her plots or her characters are all somehow the same—but it is to say that they are very much in close conversation with one another, and best read in terms of one another. She was always returning to Doro somehow, in some new body or shape.

The Huntington archive also allows us to trace the development of Butler's thought through her countless drafts in ways that make clearer her sometimes idiosyncratic take on her own work. The violence of Oankali sexual practices—their disturbing rejection of human norms about consent—looks quite different when considered through the lens of the inescapably powerful polyamorous triad in the unpublished *Blindsight* from which it was first derived. We can similarly view the Oankali more clearly when we see that in the original versions of the stories they *were* slavers, and monsters—whom Butler (like her Lilith) came to see quite differently over the course of prolonged contact—or see the tortured sadness of "Childfinder" and view the Patternist books with new insight when perceived through the revulsion for childhood in unpublished stories like "Good-by," from 1965. We can likewise reconstruct Butler's great unfinished project, the crafting of a feminist utopia, mostly in its *absence* from the published texts. The topic had interested her since the 1970s, when such books were very popular, and served as a formative inspiration for many of her greatest novels. One might say that Butler saw not race but *men*—masculinity, not just on the level of ideology but on the level of biology—as the real problem to be solved. But most of the strongest feminist-utopian elements of her novels, explicitly planned in her sketches and personal notes for composition, fell out of these books as she wrote them, making them a thread running across her career that can best be seen only from the perspective of the cutting-room floor.

In the archives—in the scenes Butler cuts from the novels, in the work she abandoned, in the stories she outlined but never began—we can see distinctly the lifelong tension between Butler's desire to write what she always called a YES-BOOK (a universally loved best-seller) versus the NO stories she felt driven to tell despite her ambition for sales and for fame. The Huntington archives make clear that Butler typically edited her writing in order to make it more optimistic. The drafts, consistently, are much more brutal and unforgiving than the published works, often filled with much more extreme violence and resulting in unhappier outcomes (a surprising fact, given how gruesome and disturbing the *published* books can be). Butler honed and developed a personal theory of bestsellerdom, articulated in her personal notes and pep talks across her career, that preoccupied her as a writing strategy yet one she was unable to ever quite put into practice: she sought endlessly to write what she called YES-BOOKS, but felt they always seemed to collapse into NO-BOOKS instead. (YES-BOOKS, she thought, were best-sellers—NO-BOOKS sold, alas, the way her actual books did.) We might perhaps say that her published works tend to be MAYBE books, somewhere between YES and NO—but in her drafts the form of the NO-BOOK is allowed to flower fully, precisely because they were never hammered into what she saw as final, publishable, salable shape.

Separated from the market's mandatory optimism, her drafts express the excess, or the remainder, of "YES."[13]

So much has already been written on Butler. The *MLA International Bibliography* lists hundreds of articles and book chapters on her novels; an updated Octavia Butler bibliography in an issue of *Utopian Studies* (current only to 2008) spans thirty pages. But the constraints of scholarly publishing have left few scholars with the opportunity to consider Butler's work in its entirety: not just this or that story, or this or that novel, but all of it, everything at once. This entry in the Modern Masters of Science Fiction series is an opportunity to do that work. *Octavia E. Butler* thus takes a somewhat different approach than much of the (excellent) existing scholarship on Butler, seeking to trace her career biocritically and holistically, primarily through references to the Huntington archive: her false starts, her alternative, abandoned drafts, her frustrations and her triumphs. I proceed through her life, as Butler once imagined she would in her own unfinished memoirs, by focusing in each chapter on the major works she was composing at that time: the early Patternist books (chapter 2), *Kindred* (chapter 3), *Blindsight*, *Clay's Ark*, and the short stories (chapter 4), the Xenogenesis and Parables books (chapters 5 and 6, respectively), and *Fledgling* (chapter 7). This book seeks to take as its organizing principle the full totality of Butler's work, as it exists both in print and in the Huntington, using as much of that material as I was able to access and process during my research trips to San Marino, and strives to draw from it a full appreciation of Butler's staggering creative genius. In writing this book I have relied much less on scholars of her work than I expected when I set out, tending to focus instead on Butler's own personal analysis and sharp sense of self-critique. I have found that Butler is often as fascinating a thinker and as exhilarating a writer in what she did not publish as in what she did, and I endeavor (as best as I can) to bring to life the incredible richness of those little-seen pages in my own writing.

But my reliance on the archive carries with it a number of significant challenges that I want to be transparent about. First, there is the inevitable issue of copyright: the unpublished material in the Huntington is naturally protected by its copyright, and so I am able to quote from it only very sparingly in accordance with the limited principles of scholarly fair use. I have done my best to capture the spirit of the material, even when I am unable to rely on Butler's wonderful writing directly. Where Butler's unedited or unfinished work in the archive contains obvious spelling or grammatical errors—she would be, I think, the first to admit she was an utterly atrocious speller—I have simply corrected them.

Second, related to that there is the question of how to properly represent the partial, unfinished, and unedited material of a writer who very jealously guarded her public presentation, and who was very concerned about being made to look silly, foolish, uneducated, or unsophisticated in print. I have sought to honor Butler's choices in such matters, even as I bring to light some work she ultimately did not seek to publish during her life, and in doing so I have endeavored to respect her position as one of, I believe, the truly greatest writers of the second half of the twentieth century, both in and out of the science fiction genre. I sincerely hope I have succeeded.

Third, there is the technical question of tracing my access to this material. I have opted to use the Huntington's OEB coding of categorization for my own citation of her papers, based off the library's five-hundred-page finding aid (which can be accessed online as a PDF at http://www.oac.cdlib.org, via the Online Archive of California website). Where it seems necessary, I have included contextualizing information in the footnote to explain what sort of document I am talking about.

Finally, there is the fraught question of ethics in this kind of archival research, particularly with regard to an author who died suddenly and unexpectedly (and who was thus unable to personally "prune" her papers before they were turned over to the librarians). Butler wanted us to see this work—one can find in the Huntington even the directives she left for her heirs asking that this bequest be honored[14]—but she didn't organize it or box it up herself. These sorts of unmanaged archives can thus pose very difficult problems for a scholar. Butler's journals and private letters reveal both the highs and the lows of her career (sometimes in very stark terms); they also reveal the highs and lows of her personal life. As her friends recount in the many memorials and testimonials that followed her death (in the pages of *Science Fiction Studies*, in the edited collection *Strange Matings*), Butler was prone to depression, to self-loathing, and to brutal and agonized self-talk. It is hard to know, from outside, whether she was especially disposed to journaling when she felt this way, or if instead, sadly, she felt like this a disproportionate amount of the time—nor does it seem remotely appropriate from my position as a scholar to attempt to psychologize her life based on her journals, to imagine some origin point in her biology or personal history for the persistent sense of isolation, inferiority, and unhappiness with which she wrestled, or to speculate about what sorts of things might have been left unsaid. In these pages I have tried, as best I can, to let Butler speak and argue for herself, in a manner I hope she would have understood if not always approved. I hope that future scholars using her archive will think carefully about these issues and make similar choices about the genuine ethical problems posed by this kind of archival scholarly research; it is certainly not easy, knowing where to step back and where to draw a line, but it is important. I have tried—at times, struggled—as best I can to remain on the proper side of the line and to eschew voyeurism, vulturism, and graverobbing. And where I have overstepped my bounds, or misstepped, or abused the generous gift of her personal papers that she left for her critics and her acolytes and her fans, the fault is certainly and exclusively my own.

CHAPTER 1

CHILDFINDER (1947–1971)

Published Works

"Crossover" (1971)
"Childfinder" (completed 1971, published 2014)

Octavia Estelle Butler was born June 22, 1947, in Pasadena, California, to Laurice and Octavia M. Butler. She'd had four brothers, all of whom died before she was born. Though she talked about this aspect of her biography in interviews only rarely, the fact of these lost siblings hung over her life, as did the very early loss of her father, who died while she was still a toddler. "I often wonder what kind of person I would have been if my brothers had lived," she told Charles Rowell in 1997. "I wonder what kind of person I would have been if they had lived and if I had had more of the society of kids when I was a kid. But, anyway, since I didn't have that, I made my own society in the books [I read] and in the stories that I told myself."[1] As for her father, his absence haunted her, too, both in her sense that she felt she grew up not understanding a male perspective and in her fascination across her fiction with parents "not being able to raise their own children."[2]

She was raised primarily by her mother and grandmother, in a household where money was often quite tight. Butler and her mother were close—being able to help her mother financially following her MacArthur award in 1995 was one of the high points of Butler's life—though like many parents and children, they were able to become significantly closer only once they no longer lived under the same roof.[3] She considered her mother (and her grandmother, and her great-grandmother) as inspirations for surviving the harsh world of poverty and racial prejudice into which they were thrust; she spoke poignantly of the sense of inferiority that had always plagued her mother, who was pulled out of school at age ten to work. This respect was a hard-learned lesson, one that came too late. Butler recalled with shame looking down on her mother's work as a housecleaner when she was young, and hurting her mother badly with her scorn, something she deeply regretted as an adult: "I didn't have to leave school when I was ten, I never missed a meal, always had a roof over my head, *because* my mother was willing to do demeaning work and accept humiliation." Many of Butler's most-beloved heroines would be women quite like her mother, women who struggled and compromised not because they were "frightened or timid or cowards" but who made the best of no-win situations because "they were heroes."[4] Her mother's support was crucial in other ways as well: somehow finding the money for her daughter's first typewriter or her trip to the Clarion science fiction writers' workshop, even as Octavia M. was unable to quite affirm or approve (or understand) her daughter's choice to pursue writing as a career.

Her mother called her "Junie," but she was "Estelle" to nearly everyone else—a name that lived on even when she became known internationally as "Octavia," represented in the middle initial she insisted be included in her name in all her publications. Looking back on her childhood from the perspective of adulthood, Butler would describe herself as solitary and lonely; extremely, almost cripplingly shy; and a dreamer. From as young as age four she spent a great deal of time alone telling herself stories; she began writing them down, she said, only when she discovered that she was beginning to forget some of her favorites.[5] Her earliest stories were animal fantasies, usually about horses who could change their shape and "made fools of the men who came to catch [them]."⁶ (In an 1970s interview with Jeffrey M. Elliot, intended for *Negro History Bulletin* but published, partially, elsewhere, she describes one origin for these fugitive horses: an early trip to a carnival where she realized the ponies were being terribly abused.⁷) But the focus of her writing changed completely in her adolescence, the night she watched a late-night B-movie called *Devil Girl from Mars*. "I saw it when I was about 12 years old," she told an audience at MIT in 1994, "and it changed my life." Butler's characteristically ironic and self-deprecating narrative of her thought process watching this movie concedes an early understanding of SF as a degraded genre, filled with plot holes and clichés:

> As I was watching this film, I had a series of revelations. The first was that "Geez, I can write a better story than that." And then I thought, "Gee, anybody can write a better story than that." *(Laughter/Applause)* And my third thought was the clincher: "Somebody got paid for writing that awful story." *(Applause)* So I was off and writing, and a year later I was busy submitting terrible pieces of fiction to innocent magazines.⁸

And so she began, writing that night the first of the short stories that would dominate her teenage imagination and would ultimately come to make up the spine of her Patternist universe.

In her MIT talk (and in others like it) Butler sought to differentiate the raw narrative *badness* of *Devil Girl from Mars*'s plotting with the free space of the imagination opened up in the 1960s by the possibility of new worlds and new histories. As she told an interviewer in 2006: "I was attracted to science fiction because it was so wide open. I was able to do anything and there were no walls to hem you in and there was no human condition that you were stopped from examining."⁹ This wide-open horizon, she says elsewhere, was so attractive to her in part because of her sense that, as a "little 'colored' girl in that era of conformity and segregation [. . .] my real future looked bleak." In response the young Octavia "fantasized living impossible, but interesting lives—magical lives in which I could fly like Superman, communicate with animals, control people's minds"—all three of which would later go on to structure key moments of pleasure in the otherwise bleak Patternist series.¹⁰

Crucially—and characteristically—the *adult* Butler came to understand this sense of unconstrained possibility quite dialectically; she suggests in the MIT talk that throughout the 1960s both science fiction and "science" more generally were hopelessly imbricated in the neocolonial politics of the nation-state, from *Devil Girl*'s Mars-Needs-Men! send-up of imperial fantasy to a Space Race inseparably bound up in Cold War paranoia about "those evil Russians." Still, the dreams of empire and widespread national paranoia were good for something; it at least made the wide-ranging speculations of SF "OK [. . .] because prior to this, there had been the idea that comic books and science fiction could rot your brains."[11] She especially adored *The Twilight Zone* and *Star Trek*, with a crush on William Shatner secretly recorded in her diaries using codenames (a common practice for her);[12] the Huntington even has among its papers a *Star Trek* fan fiction composed sometime between her late teens and the sale of her first novel,[13] and she watched *Star Trek* avidly as an adult when the franchise returned to TV in the late 1980s and 1990s.

But Butler's early fantasies were most strongly influenced by the reading she did at home and at the library. She was a voracious reader, especially of science fiction, ecstatically consuming whatever she could get her hands on. First it was the stories she found in magazines at the grocery store, like *Amazing* and *Fantastic* and *Galaxy*; she would purchase a magazine or two if she had the money, or simply read the stories as her mother shopped if she did not.[14] As soon as she was allowed out of the "romper room" of children's literature at the library, she turned to novels. She read Heinlein, Sturgeon, Herbert, Asimov, Bradbury, all the well-known writers of Golden Age SF, and internalized their assumptions about the universe and about human potentiality; many of her later stories would retain the traces of these writers, even as she added new favorites like John Brunner, Ursula K. Le Guin, and Suzy McKee Charnas. An avid collector of comics, she was especially fascinated by texts about supermen, including the original, Superman himself;[15] she also adored the animal stories of Felix Salten, especially *Bambi's Children*, a book she admired and thought about across her life.

A particular early favorite, not so well-known today as some of the other names, was Zenna Henderson, whose works thematically reflected Butler's intense sense of being different, and alienated, from the people around her;[16] many years later, struggling with her drafts of *Parable of the Trickster*, she would recall a slogan from Henderson's novels, "Different is dead." She would buy used copies of Henderson's *Pilgrimage* (1961) and give them to her friends, in search of someone to discuss the books with—"loaning them," she told Veronica Mixon in an *Essence* interview in 1979, to friends she thought "might be susceptible." She felt Henderson's novels appealed almost universally to young girls; she would later try the same trick with *Dune*, she said, with much less success.[17] Henderson's novels were focused primarily on "The People," mostly beneficent aliens with telekinetic and telepathic abilities who live in secret exile among human beings on Earth after a catastrophe destroyed their home world; it isn't hard to see their impact on her stories of the much more sinister Patternists (who, though biologically human, live in hiding in mainstream society) as well as the "Missionaries" of *Survivor* (who flee to other planets after the catastrophe of the Patternists destroys human civilization on Earth).

The earliest versions of these stories—available now in the Butler archives at the Huntington, in the very composition notebooks she wrote them in decades ago—typically concerned a young girl (plainly a stand-in for young Estelle herself) who is visited by a UFO from Mars in the middle of the night and taken around the solar system by the ship's occupant, the dashing and romantic "Flash." Most of these stories revolve around the adventures of "Flash" and the girl, renamed "Silver Star," though the reader of her later books is immediately drawn to the presence of a character named "Doro," the shifty and duplicitous "first protector of Sol."[18] In these early stories Butler worked out many of the assumptions about telepathy, and about power, that would ultimately drive the Patternist books she would begin to publish nearly two decades later; while the setting shifts from the solar system to a post-apocalyptic Earth, many of the characters were retained without significant changes, including not just Doro but also Coransee, Flash himself (renamed Teray in the published *Patternmaster*) and Silver Star (who ultimately becomes the healer Amber in *Patternmaster*, as well as the Ur-template for any number of other Butler heroines to come). (In a quiet suggestion of her lifelong fidelity to these childhood fantasies, in the early 2000s her private email address would be butler8star@qwest.net.)[19] Almost literally everything Butler would ever write spiraled out of those early stories, which can be networked together into a singular whole, almost into a kind of Butlerian "mythos" (something like the supernarrative frameworks used by Asimov and Lovecraft). Butler constantly adapted and remixed her own fiction, especially to rescue material that didn't work in its original context.

Nor are the stories purely juvenile, despite her age and relative unsophistication. In many cases they explored dark and disturbing—and certainly *adult*—themes. Early on in the Flash series (1961, when Butler is fourteen) she writes of Silver Star being wed to Flash in a sadomasochistic Martian marriage ceremony that seems to involve extreme subjugation, even literal enslavement (including branding with a ceremonial knife). In a strong anticipation of several of her later novels, the character seems utterly in thrall to Flash, perhaps even being manipulated in some way by his powers and unable to freely or fully consent; the character's first impulse is to run, until she hears his spoken command to stop resisting.[20] It is perhaps not surprising that when Butler listed her own early influences, she frequently included alongside Golden Age science fiction writers "some interesting pornography I found in someone's trash"—or that she recalls being accused of receiving adult help with her writing because she wrote about such adult topics: "In other words, I sometimes wrote dirty stories."[21] In another early fragment, this one from around 1967—seemingly an experiment in erotic writing—she describes a truly horrifying world of legalized sex slavery, narrated nonchalantly and with extremely explicit language in the first person by a girl whose entry into this world begins at age six, after an attack by her male babysitter; in still another, "Hope", circa 1960, a young girl in a concentration camp during the Holocaust is forced to trade sex for the lives of her family members.[22] Writing was an extremely erotic practice for Butler across her life—she saw her sex drive and her writing drive as very tightly linked[23]—and from these early stories we can already see the extent to which the erotic, as a category, would be for her bound up very tightly with domination, submission, and the sometimes very radical blurring of consent. Much of what we get in the published work actually turns out to be a somewhat sanitized version of her original ideas, especially when we trace those ideas back through the decades to their earliest articulation in her juvenilia; the unpublished stories and expurgated drafts often take an even darker approach to these scenarios, particularly with regard to their erotic (or outright sadomasochistic) content.

These stories were also tremendously influential to Butler's sense of self. In her journals from her teenage years (and well into her twenties) she frequently speaks to herself using terms from these stories and from the other science fiction she read. Borrowing from her Flash stories the idea of a divided self, she would often write to herself as "Shaar" or "Shaari" or "Mishaari" (other renamings of the Silver Star character) and speak of the people around her as if they were mere humans, different from herself and her kind. Commonly in her journals she writes as if the Shaar stories were all actually true, mingling the events in the stories with events in her real life as if there were no difference between the two; she would keep this private habit up in her personal journals for decades. Even as it faded, her sense of a multiple or divided self would not: her journals and story notes are typically in the form of first-person narratives written by her own characters, or self-interviews with imaginary interlocutors, or exhortations to herself to "remember" or "recall" or "consider" different propositions from her fictions.

She was similarly fascinated by the pseudosciences of telepathy and ESP, which her love of science fictional "superman" stories had encouraged her to think of as plausible. These themes appear ubiquitously in her juvenilia and early work as well, not only in the proto-Patternist stories but also in such works as "Evolution" (dated July 31, 1962), which depicts the emergence of an angel-like group of mutants in the fallout of a nuclear war, or "To the Victor," a story about psychic dueling, written under the pen name Karen Adams, which won the Pasadena City College Literary Contest in 1965 (the first bit of money Butler ever made from her writing).[24] She even wrote of working to develop her own psi powers; she took a self-hypnosis class in high school and used variations on the techniques she learned there in self-affirmation regimens for the rest of her life. Countless examples of this practice, too, can be found included among her papers at the Huntington, intermingled among her notebooks and drafts: "You will write every day"; "You will write a great book"; "You will become a bestselling author"; and on and on. (These daily affirmations would later begin to take the form of tiny poems, from which she would borrow for the interstitial poetry in the Parables books.) Butler's interest in self-hypnosis would also encourage her to develop personal mantras, like "So be it; see to it," or "Every day in every way," or "Contract!" which punctuate dozens of her diary entries and daily affirmation exercises.

Other mantras, described in her personal journals and often combined with the Shaar fantasy, included "intensify" or "110," a "call for help or strength" to be used "only in dire emergency, physical or mental." (The 110, it should be noted, is the highway a person might use to drive away from Pasadena.)[25] The Huntington also includes an example of a lengthy "Hypnotic Essay" from the late 1960s or early 1970s, which instructs the intended reader (presumably Butler herself) to read the essay and believe everything that is written in it; the paper then exhorts its readers that they will no longer doubt themselves, or be afraid, or feel shame over things that have happened to them in their past.[26] In a 1966 college term paper (for which she received an A+) she describes a summer class on self-hypnosis that taught her to write with total focus, and even to control her allergies.[27] She was similarly fascinated with self-help and self-improvement seminars, retyping or copying by hand word for word various motivational texts from people like Napoleon Hill as a way of internalizing their lessons.[28] She would make contracts with herself (particularly with regard to making her daily word count), insisting on their total inviolability even as she violated them time and time again. Her practices of self-hypnosis and self-affirmation informed more than the Parables books: the Patternists, the Oankali, double-DGD-carriers, and the Ina all have hypnotic powers of command, and one of the manuscripts left unfinished by her death (*Paraclete*) concerns precisely this fantasy of a woman whose written words become literal truths.

Even as a teenager Butler was sending out her stories for publication; she decided quite early that she would be a writer. (One of her earlier memories of her writing career, in fact, was being bilked for $61.20 by a fraudulent literary agent in 1960.[29]) Her family, while indulgent of her interest in writing, were not especially supportive of her desire to make this her career. While her mother bought Estelle her first typewriter, which she would continue to use well into the 1970s, neither her mother nor her aunts believed her writing goals had any future. They implored her to take up a career with more practical basis that could support her, a secretary (as her mother wished) or a nurse (as her aunt pleaded). "Honey," she remembers her aunt telling her one night when Butler was thirteen, "Negroes can't be writers."[30] All of her family members encouraged her to seek practical employment, though Butler would have none of it. She faced similar opposition from unsupportive teachers, including perhaps most famously the college writing professor who "finally asked in exasperation, 'Can't you write anything normal?'"[31]

Butler's problems with her teachers were compounded by a learning disability she characteristically described as "a bit dyslexic," though she was not formally diagnosed as a child and only learned what dyslexia was much later in life. As a child, she told interviewers, she often felt stupid; she devoted herself to self-education to keep up with her classmates,[32] developing autodidactic practices that would serve her well when researching her fiction later on. She was a voracious reader, but a very slow one: she learned better from audiotapes and had very fond memories of her mother reading to her at night. She was a slow writer, too, and by her own admission a very poor speller; she struggled to carefully proofread her work across her career, fearing embarrassment, and frequently told fans who wrote her for writing advice to get a grammar book and take a writing class. But in the end she did not see her dyslexia as a major impediment in her life—it just required her to learn and work differently from other people. The only thing dyslexia ever really kept her from doing, she would say later, was learning how to drive.[33]

Her extreme shyness was another matter. Here Butler did feel that her social anxiety held her back—and not only from career opportunities but from connection to other people, and even romance. ("Shyness," she writes in "Positive Obsession," "is shit. It isn't cute or feminine or appealing. It's shit.") Her worst memories of childhood revolved around her shame of being so shy:

> I memorized required reports and poems for school, then cried my way out of having to recite. Some teachers condemned me for not studying. Some forgave me for not being very bright. Only a few saw my shyness.
> "She's so backward," some of my relatives said.
> "She's so nice and quiet," tactful friends of my mother said.[34]

She was a sensitive child as well as shy, deeply affected by comments from friends and family as well as by global events (especially the political assassinations that dominated the 1960s, which she attempted to process at length in her personal diaries).

In her self-hypnosis, personal journals, and daily affirmation practices she often brutally berated herself for her shyness and sensitivity. This was a lifelong struggle for her, and she was very hard on herself. As she grew in prominence, she would carefully prepare her speeches and even rehearse small talk for conventions; one document in the Huntington archive is an exhaustive list of personal rules for making public appearances palatable, ranging from "use only words whose meaning [and] pronunciation you're sure of" to avoiding "boasting" and "babble," to "If you know people, speak to them or wave—even if you only *think* you know them"—even "relax" and "find a bathroom after lunch."[35] For most of her career she steadfastly refused to read from her books in public out of fear of embarrassment or error, instead delivering small lectures and then taking questions; she loosened this prohibition on public readings only fairly late in her career.

She never felt at home in her body, either: she spoke and wrote often of how big she was (and was from a young age); in her own aborted memoir she describes the embarrassment of being mistaken for her friends' mothers as a young teenager. ("I wanted to disappear. Instead, I grew six feet tall."[36]) She always hated being photographed; later in life, when she became prominent enough to make demands on her publishers, she would insist that photographs of her not appear on any of her books.[37] When she fantasized about money, particularly in her teens and twenties, she thought in part about the dental surgery and electrolysis she was convinced she needed, alongside travel, schooling, and independence. Her characters would frequently look masculine, or be mistaken for men, or masquerade as men, or even change genders; this was built on her own experience of her looks and deep voice, which caused her to experience social rejection from a young age and even be attacked with homophobic slurs. Although Butler was not a lesbian or bisexual (both popular misconceptions), she wondered for a while if she might be, if that could be the single cause that might explain her loneliness. In the end, though, she determined she was just "a hermit": "I enjoy my own company more than I enjoy most other people's."[38] But if she was truly a hermit she was an uneasy one; she was, always, deeply lonely, and deeply aware of her loneliness, even as she credited it as a driver of her inexhaustible creativity. Across her life, writing functioned as an alternative to romance, but it did not solve the problem fully, or eliminate her desire for the romantic companion she longed for but was never able to find.

In 1969 Butler took a class through a Screen Writers Guild of America "Open Door" Workshop—a program intended as outreach to black and Latino writers in L.A.—run by Harlan Ellison. It was an event that would prove pivotal in her career. Ellison, already a successful and well-known writer of SF, became both friend and mentor to Butler, supporting her entry to the first Clarion Science Fiction Writers' Workshop, held in Clarion, Pennsylvania, in 1971; alongside Ellison, the legendary Samuel R. Delany would be one of her teachers there. (Ellison even loaned her some money to go; she borrowed the rest from relatives.) The trip changed Butler's life. She had never been outside California before, or really outside the Pasadena area except for a short time when she lived with her grandmother near the Mojave Desert; now she was suddenly seeing the rest of the country through the window of a Greyhound bus. She kept a travel journal and meticulously recorded everything that happened to her on her days-long trip across the country.

When she got to Clarion, though, she was frustrated, both by her inability to connect with the other students and by her inability to write at the level she wanted (or with the ferocious speed Ellison insisted upon, demanding a story a night from his workshop writers). She wrote sad letters to her mother at home, then apologized for writing them; she asked both her mother and friends to write her back quickly, so she could at least know "there were still Negroes somewhere in the world."[39] But over the course of the two weeks she acclimated, making friends she would keep for the rest of her life (such as Vonda McIntyre, who would also become a well-known science fiction writer).

Clarion was also the place Butler made her first sales. One of these stories, "Crossover," was published in the *Clarion Journal*. The story—about a blue-collar woman with a bad job and a worse relationship history—is barely SF, if at all, and Butler personally did not regard it as one of her better stories. But the story is nonetheless interesting for the troubling world of hopelessness, addiction, and (perhaps) incipient psychosis it suggests.

The other story, "Childfinder," was much more promising. This story Butler sold to Ellison himself for the upcoming third volume of his *Dangerous Visions* anthologies of cutting-edge, New Wave science fiction. The story draws from the proto-Patternist milieu she had developed in her teens, but it contains elements that differ in important ways from the series as it would eventually be published at the end of the 1970s. We are prepped to think of "Childfinder" as science fiction from the story's opening words, which appear to be an encyclopedia entry on "Psi" and "Psi people" looking back on the development of psionic powers from some point in the future (a technique perhaps borrowed from Asimov's interstitial *Encyclopedia Galactica* entries in the Foundation series). The writer of the encyclopedia entry speaks of Psi as something all his readers are familiar with, and speculates on how novel and exciting it "must have" been to have different peoples suddenly possess "opportunities to understand each other." But then a sour note is struck: "Such abilities could bridge age-old divisions of race, religion, nationality, etc. as could nothing else. Psi could have put the human race on the road to utopia." Could have—not did.

"Childfinder" is the story of Barbara, a black woman living in a rundown house in a town that stands in for Pasadena (even the address given, 855 South Madison, is a Pasadena address). "Away from the organization," reads the first line of the story, giving us a sense that this is a story about someone who is on the run. We soon begin to suspect what sort of organization it is:

> Not that I minded the place really. I'd lived in worse. And I killed every damn rat and roach on the premises before I moved in. Besides, there was this kid next door. Young, educable, with the beginnings of a talent she was presently using for shoplifting. A pre-telepath.[40]

As the story develops, we discover that the narrator has inserted herself into this child's life as a mentor, trying to draw her out of her shell by giving her books to read. In the scene we witness, Barbara and Valerie discuss a book about Harriett Tubman that Barbara has recommended. The point is not necessarily the content of the book; Barbara wants primarily to break the ten years of "failure conditioning" that characterizes the young lives of special people in a world that doesn't value them, especially black kids like Valerie.[41] But Tubman is not some arbitrarily selected historical figure, either; we soon discover that Barbara (like so many of Butler's later black heroines) is a Harriet Tubman figure herself.

When Valerie leaves, she sees a white woman strolling toward Barbara's house; she knows from bitter experience that white people come into her neighborhood only for evictions and "equally savory kinds of business."[42] The white woman condescendingly asks Valerie what she's doing with such a big book, and Valerie quickly makes herself scarce rather than engage. Barbara discovers that her flight is at an end; the organization has tracked her down. She is confronted by the woman, Eve, someone higher up in the hierarchy of the organization who has come to apologize and return her to the fold. Eve tells Barbara she should come back and asks her to bring the psychic children she has found with her; Barbara points out that these are "the same kids you wouldn't even consider before I left." Eve says they now know they were wrong—"Come back now and we will listen"—but Barbara replies that she doesn't need the organization at all anymore.

Now we begin to see why Psi only "could have" led to utopia, and perhaps why it did not:

> "So the others are right. You're forming an opposing organization."
>
> "We won't oppose you unless we have to."
>
> "A segregated black-only group [. . .] Don't you see, you're setting yourself up for the same troubles that plague the normals?"

But Barbara believes she has the upper hand: "No. Until you get another childfinder, I don't think they'll be quite the same. More like reversed."[43] And Barbara is confident that they won't get another childfinder soon: she's already found two potential white childfinders and crippled their minds to prevent them from opposing her and her group.

Barbara discovers that Eve has brought three "psychic brawlers" with her in order to restrain her and bring her back to the organization whether she likes it or not—but before they can do anything, the brawlers are laid low by members of Barbara's own group, who have psychically sensed her distress and come to her aid. This wasn't part of Barbara's plan, and she must fight with her own charges to allow the organization's people to wake up and take her. *They know me, Jordan,* she thinks at her group. *I can't hide from them. They can find me wherever I am and they can use me to find you.*[44] Her group refuses this call, saying they can fight the white Psis now and win—but Barbara tells them that they need to survive until they are strong enough, and that letting her go is the only way that can happen.

Barbara's plan was never to survive this encounter; she is the first of Butler's many protagonists who are not able to raise their own (in this case, metaphorical) children:

So in a couple minutes, as soon as Jordan let Eve and her friends regain consciousness, I was going to forget everything I knew about pre-psi kids and finding them. Thinking about it, thinking about forgetting, thinking about erasing the thing that had become as important to me as breathing, brought my fear back full force. [. . .] I almost envied those white kids I'd crippled. They never knew what they were losing.

But the stakes were too high, not only for the personal survival of the psychic teens in her group, but also "because they were going to settle a lot of scores for me and a few million other people . . . someday."[45] "Childfinder" is in this way an early articulation of the interest in reproductive futurity[46] that will dominate many of Butler's novels; because the future can only exist if there are people to live in it, many of her "survivor" heroines are forced to make terrible compromises and endure unthinkable hardships in the name of children, in hopes that at least *some* future will exist.

Up to this point "Childfinder" seems to fit comfortably in the "revenge" mode of Afrofuturist science fiction—stories in which nonwhite people come into the power to inflict upon whites some fraction of the horrors that whites have inflicted upon everyone else across modern history. The clear echoes of Butler's beloved superhero comics present in the story are no accident; Barbara reads a bit like a black version of Professor X who has finally decided to work with the Brotherhood of Evil Mutants, who thinks maybe the mutant nationalists have a point after all. Barbara's increasingly powerful black-only counter-organization will, she hopes, gain sufficient power to destroy the white psychics—and then they will take over the world. But, true to the subversions and unexpected reversals that would define Butler's career, the story doesn't really endorse that position either. Instead, as one of the men on the floor begins to wake and Barbara prepares to obliterate her own mind, the narrative switches back into the text from the encyclopedia:

> Historians believe that an atmosphere of tolerance and peace would be a natural outgrowth of a psionic society.
>
> Records of the fate of the psis are sketchy. Legend tells us that they were all victims of a disease to which they were particularly vulnerable. Whatever the cause, we may be sure that this is one civilization that was destroyed by purely external forces.[47]

The implication in the intervening narrative is that this authoritative-sounding voice from the future is exactly wrong about what eliminated the Psis, and that it was a much more internal, much more *banal* disease of the mind rather than the body. In a clever inversion of the famous "Principles of Newspeak" appendix to George Orwell's *1984*, whose past-tense discussion of the Airstrip One language suggests that we might yet hope for the eventual end of Big Brother's reign despite the bleak ending of Winston Smith's personal story, the quotes from *Psi: History of a Vanished People* point to the unhappy events of "Childfinder" as the ultimate seed of destruction for the entire nascent Psi project. The last words of the story are no less chilling when we understand the racism of our moment could persist even after the transformation of the human into incredible, god-like superbeings; we find that the book this academic text has come from is titled *Psi: History of a Vanished People*. Racism survives even the radically new historical conditions that ought to have made it completely obsolete, poisoning the future too.

In her afterword to the story, intended to be published alongside it in *The Last Dangerous Visions*, Butler speaks forlornly of the story as a warning akin to the warnings her aunts and grandmother would give her and her cousins as they played: "Get along out there! No fighting!" But Butler does not possess the failed optimism of her older relatives: "I know no one's listening." "After a few years of watching the human species make things unnecessarily difficult for itself," she writes, "I have little hope that it will do anything more than survive and continue its cycle of errors."[48]

The unspooling of these events contains many of the important themes that would come to define Butler's later writing: the persistence of race and racism, even in progressive, future-facing communities; the lengths a person will go to survive; the extremes a mother will endure to protect her children; how terrible power is, and how intoxicating it is to wield. It is especially interesting to see how this early story compares to the later Patternist books, discussed in the next chapter, which similarly seem to side with the villains of Butler's beloved superhero comics rather than their nominal heroes—but which "solve" the racial crisis of "Childfinder" by making *all* the psychics black superheroes and thereby allow the prophesied revenge narrative to actually come to pass after all.

Ellison was completely unrestrained in his praise both for the story and for Butler herself as a writer, assuring her that the publication of this story would not only pay her a significant sum in royalties but would immediately put her on the map as a science fiction writer, making her career in one fell swoop.[49] He believed she had not only great talent but also a highly marketable new perspective in a changing publishing landscape; he encouraged her to "use" her background to her advantage and "write black!"[50] He used the same argument in the letters to editors he would write on her behalf.[51] Of course she liked the first part, but she was frustrated by the second—not only because the advice to use her background seemed to her to detract from or delegitimize her talent, but because she wrote SF precisely to *escape* the world of race and gender oppression she saw around her. It would not be the last time she would experience an unhappy tension between being a *science fiction* writer and a *black* writer.

Nor did Butler's political leanings fit easily into black politics of the late 1960s and 1970s; she did not feel at home either in King's conciliatory liberalism or in the more radical, more separatist Black Power movements that were its chief challenger. She was deeply suspicious of both approaches, a suspicion that can be strongly felt in the multiple drafts of a screenplay she wrote for Ellison's workshop about a fictional militant black-nationalist organization called DARE. In some of the versions the leader of the group, Jather, is exposed as a dangerous liar, hypocrite, and fraud; in others, the main character becomes his eager lover.[52] Butler would recount later the way that her writing fantastic stories was seen as a "betrayal" by some of her contemporaries in the 1960s and 1970s, as in their minds only "writing [. . .] utter reality" counted as "contributing to the struggle."[53] Of course, she saw things differently.

As her career developed, Butler famously and repeatedly refused attempts to reduce her books to commentary on contemporary racial politics. "So many critics have read this as a story about slavery, probably just because I am black," she would later say of "Bloodchild." "The only places I am writing about slavery is where I actually say so."[54] When a student writes to her in 1988 asking if Butler is "trying to consciously make a feminist or racial statement" in her work, the author's handwritten annotation in the margins of the letter is striking and definitive: "No. Story."[55] To Butler, story always came first and foremost. Her rejection of analogical readings of her work can sometimes be quite hard to swallow, however; "Bloodchild," for instance, seems quite clearly to be about a relationship of slavery, regardless of whether Butler personally saw it in those terms—and indeed, as we will see, neoslavery fantasy (what Isiah Lavender has called "meta-slavery"[56]) of one sort of another can be found in every single one of her novels, and in most of her short stories as well.

Butler, for her part, was completely carried away by Ellison. She nursed a fierce crush on him that seems not to have been reciprocated, or perhaps even taken notice of[57]—though they were, for a time, quite close. (He also bought her a typewriter, her second, to replace the one her mother had purchased for her years before.[58]) But as the years dragged on Butler began to despair of "Childfinder" ever seeing print. She and the other writers received yearly updates from Ellison on the project, always promising that despite the recent bumps in the road, the book would soon see publication. Ellison even sent the writers an advance on their royalties as consideration for their time and patience. The delay wore on their friendship; Butler's letters to Ellison grew both rarer and shorter. Thinking much later in her life of Harlan as one possible model for a character in the *Parable of the Trickster*, she would dyspeptically describe the character as "bright and decent" but "defensive [. . .] oversensitive [. . .] startlingly unforgiving [. . .]," someone who breaks promises.[59] Still, she never stopped thinking of Ellison as a close friend, and missed their closeness as they grew apart—and she used her relationship with him as her personal model for mentorship, both in her fictions and in her very generous relationship with the fans who approached her asking for help with their writing.

In fact, *The Last Dangerous Visions* never materialized—ever. As of 2016 it remains unpublished. "Childfinder" saw print only in the posthumous publishing of two of Butler's stories as the e-book *Unexpected Stories* in 2014, making it oddly both the first and the last of Butler's published fiction. Meanwhile, while "Childfinder" sat unpublished, Butler's rocket ship to instant fame sat uselessly on its launch pad; not only did *The Last Dangerous Visions* completely fail to make her famous, she found herself unable even to follow up on the meager success of "Crossover." Despite writing constantly, she would not sell another story for nearly six years.

CHAPTER 2

PSYCHOGENESIS (1971–1976)

Published Works

Patternmaster (1976)
Mind of My Mind (1977)
Survivor (1978)

Significant Unpublished Work

"The Evening and the Morning and the Night" [I] (1970s)

Any optimism that Butler felt about her writing as she returned from Clarion evaporated as *The Last Dangerous Visions*—the book that was supposed to make her career—languished, and her subsequent stories accumulated rejection after rejection. At times she felt like the only thing that Clarion had gotten her was additional debt, as she struggled to pay back the loans she had undertaken from friends and family to attend the workshop in the first place. Her letters from this period to her Clarion friends evince a preoccupation with the sales side of the business: who is selling, who isn't, who has given up, who has moved into other kinds of work. The letters typically ended with a sign-off in the same mold: not "Goodbye," but "Good sales."

Moving out of her mother's house into the rental she would live in for the next two decades gave her independence but also a new and crushing loneliness: her journal entries in the seventies and across the next decades of her life often speak of her desire for companionship and love, with repeated resolutions to meet more people and find a partner that seem never to have borne fruit. In one long sequence from the mid-1970s—characteristic of Butler's journals from the period in that it seems to slide freely between actual and invented experiences—she describes a lonely woman who decides to give lesbianism a try in the face of repeated negative experiences with men. But the ambition doesn't hold; the woman simply prefers men, despite everything that is bad about them.[1]

By now Butler's writing had firmly settled into what, upon the sales of her first novels at the end of the 1970s, would become the Patternist milieu. These stories, growing out of the intersection of her childhood fantasies about visitations from UFOs and her high-school fascination with psychics and psi-powers, were clustered around three major historical moments, each of which would be the focus of one of her first three novels. In stories set in the far future—the setting for her first published novel, *Patternmaster* (1976)— we find a world totally transformed by the emergence of psychics who have enslaved the nonpsychic, or mute, portion of the human race. In an SF version of the present that is not unlike "Childfinder" (the subject of her second novel, *Mind of My Mind* [1977]), we see the history of this situation unfold as two competing groups of psychics, each led by a charismatic leader, battle for supremacy as their "race" approaches its destiny. And somewhere between these two future-historical narrative poles we have the stories of interstellar exploration that Butler called her "Missionary" stories, like her first-completed and third-published novel, *Survivor* (1978): the stories of unaltered humans who are allowed by the Earthbound Patternists to travel off-world to explore the galaxy and ensure the survival of the human race.

Butler's intense fidelity to this vision of the future, as has already been noted, is utterly remarkable: nearly everything she writes before the publication of *Patternmaster* fits somehow within the Patternist milieu, and the earliest drafts of every novel she writes until the Parable books of the 1990s originate somewhere within this world as well, the terms of which she first established in her early teens. Understanding the Patternist series is thus crucial not only for tracing Butler's early development as a writer and thinker but also for understanding the totality of her work. Often overlooked in favor of Butler's superior later books, the Patternist novels establish structures and themes that loom very large across Butler's oeuvre—the pliability of the human body, the cruelty of the mind, the endurance of the soul—while also highlighting her trademark fascination with power: its seductiveness, and its misuse.

Extant versions of the Patternmaster series in the Huntington archive— some of them quite fragmentary, others significantly developed—date back to Butler's early teen years. "When I got the idea for *Patternmaster*," she told an interviewer, "I was twelve, but I had no idea how to write a novel. I tried, but it was quite a few years before I was able to write it. When I got the idea for *Mind of My Mind*, I was 15. When I got the idea for *Survivor*, I was 19."[2] As we will see, the stories derive quite directly from the "superman" archetype in science fiction that was so popular during Butler's adolescence, as well as from the similar superhero and supervillain stories she consumed as an avid comics reader. She was workshopping Patternist stories in college and at her Open Door classes with Harlan Ellison and Sid Stebel, and she brought the stories with her to Clarion in 1970; they were to an overwhelming extent her primary creative outlet in those early years.

At different points in her development the stories would have different levels of interconnection and independence, but generally speaking the vision of the future she imagined through the stories was remarkably consistent from her teen years through the publication of the five Patternist novels we have: *Patternmaster* (1976), *Mind of My Mind* (1977), *Survivor* (1978), *Wild Seed* (1980), and *Clay's Ark* (1984). Mentally, Butler categorized the stories in the following general schema:

- "Prepattern" stories (like *Wild Seed*) that predate the development of the psionic network in the story (first called *Psychogenesis*) that is eventually published as *Mind of My Mind*—these stories revolve around the African body-swapping Trickster figure Doro, whose millennia-long breeding project culminates in the Pattern, which subsequently destroys him;

- "Midpattern" stories about the emergence of the Pattern and the early days of the Patternists as a secret conspiracy of telepaths living hidden among normal human society, eventually emerging from the shadows and taking over the world (though "Childfinder," as discussed, departs in significant ways from the typical Patternist "canon");
- Stories about "Missionaries," unaltered, untelepathic human beings who leave Planet Earth in spaceships; in some versions of the meta-narrative this is because they are fleeing from the Patternist takeover, while in other versions (as in *Survivor*) they are doing this at the behest of the ruling Patternists, whose too-close psychic bond renders them incapable of leaving Earth themselves;
* Stories about the collapse of civilization following the return of one of the Mission ships, *Clay's Ark*, whose crew has been infected with a highly contagious virus that turns them into monsters popularly called Clayarks;
- Late Pattern stories about the post-apocalyptic equilibrium that is eventually established in the far future following the destructive emergence of the Clayarks, with the Patternists (now living in a strict feudal hierarchy) safely controlling some areas and the wild Clayarks controlling others, with normal humans living as the "mute" slaves of the Patternists (*Patternmaster*).

While periodically Butler would imagine the stories as not necessarily relying on one another, the key elements of the interconnected world can be traced quite far into her early and juvenile stories, often filling in gaps left by the actual published stories. The intriguing "Good-by," from 1965, for instance, explores in depth a subject that is only touched on in the published Patternist novels: the difficult transitional metamorphosis that young psychics enter as they gain their full powers in their teen years, as well as the inability of adult psychics to be around *any* children, including their own (and the consequent need for "mutes" to act as surrogate caretakers). In "Good-by" the young telepaths are told—almost *threatened*—that once they have come fully into their powers, they will be allowed to look into the horrifying mind of a child to see the "crude, megalomaniacal" desires lurking within. (And the unfiltered, unconscious imagination of a child, we are told, is "even worse" than their conscious thoughts.)[3] An intense zombie-apocalypse story fragment from around 1967 titled "Pattern—The Falling Civilization," in contrast, is a post-*Clay's Ark* story. It sees a high school transformed into a refugee camp terrorized by the Clayarks (then called Cla-arks) following the events of the novel *Clay's Ark*, which is published more than fifteen years later. The Cla-arks are bad, but the nightmarish concentration camp seems little better; the first day sees ten Cla-arks executed, alongside "one suspected Cla-ark."[4]

Butler's ambition was to use the Missionary stories to tell multiple stories of interstellar colonization, à la the long-running future-history "saga" series of Golden Age SF writers she admired, such as Heinlein and Asimov. Each story would center on the fate of a single starship launched by a doomed human species on a dying Earth, each charged to consider itself "the last vestige of humanity" so that the stakes of each story are the survival of the human species as such.[5] Some of the stories would end horribly (as with "The Evening and the Morning and the Night [I]," discussed below); some would involve the human Missionaries being enslaved by aliens,[6] while in others they would be the enslavers;[7] still others would end with at least mixed success (as does *Survivor*). The idea would always animate Butler; until the end of her life she was still thinking of writing Missionary stories, transformed now into the "Destiny" of the Earthseed cultists in the Parables book, which were always intended to spawn four or more books about different extraplanetary colonies that would either succeed or fail through their ability or inability to adapt to their new circumstances (see chapter 6).

But despite the promise of these stories, and her strong commitment to them, they simply would not sell. Butler, despairing, even developed a plan to shift her writing output entirely, making extensive notes and plans to write "CF" ("commercial fiction") instead of "SF." She pored over magazines where commercial fiction was published, attempting to distill the essence of the genre and its typical narrative strategies into a form she could copy—replicating, perhaps, the sort of intense study she had undertaken of SF as a teenager, albeit in a more deliberate and systematic way.[8] She began several of these stories, but the plan never came together as she hoped; most of her romances prominently feature disturbing or grotesque elements that were out of sync with the sentimentality of the typical magazine romance—like "Quiet Love," about the tensions involving parental nonacceptance of the protagonist's deaf-mute boyfriend,[9] or "Addict," in which the female protagonists are not lovestruck doves but serial killers.[10] She looked into technical writing and multilevel marketing, trying to find some way to sustain herself outside the clerk, temp, and manual-labor work that were making her miserable and keeping her poor; for a time she considered giving up writing altogether and transitioning to photography, believing perhaps she would have more luck in that field.[11] But none of the alternatives ever really took root—and she was rarely happier than when she was laid off from one of her dead-end jobs, because the time on unemployment would give her free time to rededicate herself to writing.[12]

Butler was frustrated: her journals from the 1970s circle around her persistent feeling that she is "getting nowhere";[13] she berates herself for her laziness, for her inability to change. She was acutely aware that she did not "fit" in the science fiction marketplace as it was constituted at the time; she mourns the death of John W. Campbell in 1971—whose reactionary political notions, particularly regarding race, were already notorious—by saying she had always hoped to "sell that old man a story [. . .] as a kind of private joke."[14] Not long after that she fantasizes about doing "something quietly vindictive" to another editor, Ed Ferman, who rejected "The Evening and the Morning and the Night [I]," and notes forlornly that her stories seem to be the wrong kind of "interracial story": "neither militant nor moderate nor anything else I can think of other than human."[15] She frequently experimented with pen names in her submissions, attempting, it seems, to mask her gender or her race or both—Lynn Guy, Jerry Anderson, O. E. Butler, and so forth—though in the end she only ever published under her own name. Her writing habits were indistinguishable from her fierce, thwarted desire to sell: throughout the 1970s and until the end of her life, her first notes for a project were, almost always, the advertising copy for the back of the book.

"HALFWAYITIS"

Butler's 1970s journals reflect a growing pessimism both global and intensely personal; she suggests in one notable 1972 entry that the project of civilization may be akin to the trajectory of an uncontrolled, novice downhill skier, almost certain to end in a "dramatic lethal crash,"[16] while a disturbing 1974 essay ruminates on what will happen "if I do suicide," imagining that it won't be a planned event but rather she will simply find herself "in a place where it would be easy to die."[17] (One cannot help but think here of her fictional consummate survivors like Lilith, Lauren Olamina, and Shori, who do *not* suicide even when it would be easy, who fervently choose life even when offered the promise of a comfortable, easy death.) In her entries her depression and loneliness are palpable, especially when read from a perspective many decades in the future: one can see Butler struggling with a problem she is simply never able to solve, whose terms she narrates to herself again and again and again. Butler thought of herself as a survivor, and thought of her characters in the same terms—but she recognized that survival was in many cases *mere* survival, that too often there was "little glamor" or "little pleasure" in it, and sometimes it was "not good enough."[18] This observation would infuse even her most optimistic pieces of writing.

Butler received her associate's degree in history at Pasadena City College in 1968, and she frequently returned to school (typically at California State University at Los Angeles) over the next decade. She enrolled in writing classes of all kinds and was interested, as she always had been, in black politics in America; during her college years she also studied African literature and African decolonial history as well (which would infuse the development of later works, from *Wild Seed* to the dictatorship ruling the collapsing America of the Parables). These returns to college would reflect first an intense desire to learn before giving way to the desire to write that consumed her. Her grades would plummet, and she would drop out again, often with a new story idea to work on. Still, the idea of someday getting a Ph.D. and even, perhaps, becoming a professional academic electrified her; for a brief period at least she defined academic anthropology as a dream as essential to her identity as her dream of becoming a best-selling author. (She would later give this career to Lilith, in the Oankali books—though by then she has another character, Tate, sourly questioning just how noble this pursuit really is.)

Rather than academic success, Butler's 1970s were defined by desperation and disappointment: bad jobs, money crisis, the unemployment office she would later describe as a "second home";[19] even after her books began to sell, she was frequently on the edge of total desperation with regard to money, as well as perpetually frustrated by her slow output. Her attempts to hypnotize herself and to will herself to sell her books are visible across her personal journals, as when she writes down—twice a day every day between February and April 1970—her goal to have $100,000 by January 1, 1975.[20] Butler's desire to live debt-free with ample savings—enough for her to own her own home and to provide permanently for both her and her mother's needs[21]—consumed her across her entire life; even unexpectedly winning the no-strings-attached $295,000 MacArthur grant in 1995 only convinces her that a different, higher amount of money would be required for her security. Meanwhile, she was always on the edge of bankruptcy, struggling to make ends meet; much of the paper in the Huntington archive is obviously taken from the various offices at which she worked, corporate letterheads appearing on the reverse sides.

It's little wonder, given her difficult years in the 1970s, that the writing advice Butler would give in later years would focus so intensely on "obsession," as she defines it in her essay "Positive Obsession" by way of the Random House dictionary: "the domination of one's thoughts or feelings by a persistent idea, image, desire, etc."[22] Obsession is fuel for a writer, but it is not an uncomplicated gift or some noble calling. Obsession, she says, is "dangerous": "Positive obsession is about not being able to stop just because you're afraid and full of doubts. . . . It's about not being able to stop at all."[23] In the afterword to the other autobiographical essay published in *Bloodchild*, "Furor Scribendi," the legacy of those lean years is just as strongly felt: "Writing is difficult. You do it all alone without encouragement and without any certainty that you'll ever be published or paid or even that you'll be able to finish the particular work you've begun. It isn't easy to persist amid all that."[24] Alongside the frequent rejections, Butler persistently battled her own sense that her writing was inadequate; she would later speak often of the "halfwayitis" she suffered from (on full display in the many unfinished fragments in the Huntington) not simply in the 1970s but across her career.[25]

What she finally decided was that she just wasn't cut out for short-story writing at all: she wrote too slowly, and the pay was too small, for the math to ever work. She needed to write novels, even though she found their size and complexity intimidating. She would later say that she "tricked" herself in 1974 into writing her first salable novel (*Survivor*) by imagining it as a series of interconnected short stories (a trick she would try to use later, to much less success, when blocked in the Parables series, and which seems to reflect the internal structure of novels like *Kindred*, *Wild Seed*, and *Dawn* as well).

That version of *Survivor* languished, too—but in December 1975 Butler finally achieved her dream of selling a novel, *Patternmaster*, to Doubleday. Considering that this is the culmination of a long-held dream, her notes about this event in her journal are surprisingly restrained, and in fact her happiness does not last long. As soon as the sale is made, she starts feeling unhappy about her treatment. She is naturally very concerned about receiving her $1,500 advance quickly, asking that it be sent immediately ("for tax reasons"[26]), and is frustrated by delays in her payment, as well as put off by the editor's noted concerns with the narratives and suggestions for minor revisions.

In particular, her editor sought strengthening of the female characters, a suggestion Butler felt was unnecessary given the healer Amber's importance in the novel; the editor also suggested that Butler discuss the mutes and their mechanical abilities more so as to leave open some possibility of a better, non-Patternist future. Butler pushed back, especially with regard to the question of strong female characters, pointing out multiple instances where the society was more egalitarian and the females stronger than the editor recognized.[27] To Butler the world of the Patternists *was* a significant improvement over ours, despite its obvious brutality; as she would note in her 1980 essay "Lost Races of Science Fiction," the Patternists had eliminated irrational prejudices like racism and sexism in favor of a meritocratic competition in which genuine talent—psychic talent—afforded the only advantage. In that sense she paradoxically saw the world of *Patternmaster* as "egalitarian," even as she noted it was still a slave society.[28] It wasn't a utopia—Butler never really believed in those—but it was nonetheless an attractive fantasy to someone whose personal identity as a black woman was, in our world, so radically undervalued.

The back-and-forth would be the start of her career-long icy relationship with her editors, whose suggestions she typically resented and whose checks always seemed to her to be much too small. And another resentment soon emerged, one that would plague her over the course of her early career. She had been calling the book *Bondage*, which the editor rejected on the grounds that it sounded too much like a pornographic novel—but the book goes into production as *Patternmaster* before Butler feels she has officially approved the title. (The title she preferred was *The Reign of Mind*; she'd polled her friends, she said, and *Patternmaster* sounded to them like a sewing book.[29]) Still, she is unable to push the point too hard: even as she struggled with Doubleday to retain the integrity of her vision for her first novel, she was already hard at work trying to sell them *Mind of My Mind*.

WORLD REDUCTION AND SUPERHERO COMICS

The future history traced by the Patternist series was published out of chronological sequence; the first novel, *Patternmaster* (1976), takes place furthest in the future, after the new Patternist hegemony has been so long established that our contemporary moment is but a distant memory. Centered on Forsyth, California (a fictionalized Pasadena), the world of *Patternmaster* is dominated by "Houses" of telepaths participating in a network of psychic communication called "The Pattern"; the Patternists are organized as a kind of feudal aristocracy according to each telepath's strength in the Pattern, with a monarch, the Patternmaster, "holding" the Pattern and therefore controlling the network. We see a glimpse of what this power entails early in *Patternmaster* when the current Patternmaster, Rayal, flexes his psychic muscles to score a point in an argument with his wife (who is also his biological sister):

> Rayal jerked the Pattern sharply and Jansee jumped, gasping at the sudden disturbance. It was comparable physically to a painless but startling slap in the face.
> "You see?" he said. "I've just awakened several thousand Patternists by exerting no more effort than another person might use to snap his fingers. Sister-wife, that is power worth killing for."[30]

The argument concerns the inevitability of violent struggle for control of the Pattern, particularly with respect to the couple's two sons, Coransee and Teray. Children of the strongest Patternist and his powerful wife, these two are the natural candidates for control of the Pattern in the next generation—and they will, insists Rayal, have no choice but to kill each other. Rayal himself notes: "Didn't I have to kill two brothers and a sister to get where I am?"; he further notes that he'd only survived these battles by marrying his "strongest sister."[31] Jansee remains "bitter" about this necessity, wishing her sons could save their violence for the Patternists' enemies, the Clayarks[32]—but the ultimate trajectory of the narrative proves Rayal right, depicting the struggle for the inheritance of the Pattern between its two possible heirs that only ends when one (the younger, Teray) kills the other (Coransee).[33]

Through its flattening of the vast complexities of contemporary power relations into a single omnipresent and omni-oppressive force (the Pattern), narrativized as a power struggle within a single family, the book deploys the narrative strategy that Fredric Jameson (writing about Ursula K. Le Guin's *The Dispossessed* and *The Left Hand of Darkness*, books Butler admired and was highly influenced by) famously called "world reduction." Like the desert planet Anarres and the ice world Gethen in Le Guin's fiction, the future Earth of the Patternists is similarly an "experimental landscape in which our being-in-the-world is simplified to the extreme . . . as to vouchsafe, perhaps, some new glimpse as to the ultimate nature of human reality."[34] But where Le Guin's "operation of radical abstraction and simplification" is her "instrument in the conscious elaboration of a utopia,"[35] for Butler world-reduction instead lays bare the monstrousness of power and the ease of human cruelty. In a history whose normal progression has been interrupted by shattering capital-E Events giving humans immense power—including both an alien plague and the rise of telepaths—we can still think of nothing better to do but enslave and murder each other. First-time readers of *Patternmaster*, drawn into the narrative of struggle between its feudal telepaths, may miss entirely the significance of the "mutes" who populate this world and serve the Patternists' houses. These subaltern mutes are in fact *us*, normal, unaltered humans without telepathic ability; their individuality and self-determination has been completely subsumed into an even more monstrous version of slavery than that with which modernity began. (As Butler herself puts it in the McCaffery interview, this is a worse form of domination than any around us today, because "the mutes don't know what's happening to them" and consequently "don't have a chance."[36]) Some are beloved servants, even friends, while others are subject to constant rape, murder, and abuse—but none possesses a subjectivity that is independent from or capable of resistance to the superhuman Patternists. In the prologue, we even find that "hajji" mutes occasionally pilgrimage to Forsyth to worship the Patternmaster as if he were a God.[37]

As I discuss in an article on the Patternmaster books written for *Paradoxa*, Butler's fondness for the "psychic superman" stories of early SF was matched by her love of comic books, beginning with Superman and spreading out across the subgenre (with particular fondness for Marvel). Before she goes to

Clarion in 1970 she leaves a detailed pull-list to ensure she doesn't miss a month of issues, asking her mother to pull from across the Marvel line: *Fantastic Four* #103, *Spider-Man* #89, *Silver Surfer* #19, *Avengers* #80, *Thor* #180, *Captain America* #130, *Hulk* #132, and on and on.[38] Butler rarely spoke about her love of comic books and their influence on her work directly, but references to her early comics fandom are sprinkled across her archive of interviews. She told Larry McCaffery and Jim McMenamin in 1988 that she was "very much into comic books" from the 1960s through "the early '70s," beginning with "the Superman D.C. comic books first, then Marvel, and so on"; she describes herself as a collector who "went around to all the secondhand stores and bought up the back issues as fast as I could."[39] She similarly told an MIT audience during a 1998 visit (during her appearance on a panel with Samuel R. Delany) that she "lived" on comic books as a child, sharing with many people who were young during that period the memory of her mother destroying her comics one day while she was out (which, of course, was all done *for her own good*). Butler's comics fandom remains sufficiently central to her self-identity that years later, in the 2004 interview with Joshunda Sanders, it even rises to her mind unprompted as a kind of anticipatory *memento mori*:

> I imagine when I'm dead someone will have a huge yard sale or estate sale and I don't care! Some of them are worth something. Even my comic books—I have first editions of this and that, the first issue of the Fantastic Four. I used to collect them, not in the way that people collect things now. I didn't put them in plastic bags and never touch them. I read them and they looked pretty bad, some of them. But they're still worth something just because they are what they are.[40]

As I have argued, comic books provide some of the deep structure for the Patternist milieu, even as Butler herself was concerned about allowing promotion for the series to appear "too melodramatic, too comic-bookish."[41]

Some of this anxiety about "comic-bookishness" was about Butler growing older, as well as her perception that comic books had grown rather worse since her childhood. At the MIT forum, her a-little-junk-food-won't-hurt defense of comics is combined with strong nostalgia for the comics read by her generation of readers, which she insists had "had a lot more language, a lot more words, and a lot more story" than more contemporary works in the genre:

It wasn't just Jack Kirbyesque people swatting other people and standing with their legs four feet apart. And gradually, it became just that, so that there were fewer and fewer and fewer words, less and less story, and a lot more people beating each other up or wiping each other out.[42]

But some of this anxiety about the seriousness of the Patternist stories also has to do with the changing consensus assumptions of the science fiction genre, and in particular its attitude toward psychic supermen with telepathic superpowers, between the 1950s and 1960s, when she first conceived of the stories, and the late 1970s, when she began to publish them. In the Golden Age stories Butler loved and self-consciously styled her own fiction after—books like the aforementioned Zenna Henderson "People" books, Herbert's *Dune*, Theodore Sturgeon's *The Dreaming Jewels* (1950) and *More than Human* (1953), John Brunner's *The Whole Man* (1964), even something as far back as Olaf Stapledon's *Odd John* from 1935—psychic powers were frequently taken as scientifically plausible, even probable. (Much of this had to do with legendary *Astounding/ Analog* editor John W. Campbell's famous interest in and promotion of such stories.) Butler's own journals from her childhood—in which, again, the line between fiction and nonfiction can be extremely fluid—treat the emergence and evolution of her own psychic powers as something that she expects to occur imminently in her own life. By the mid-1970s, however—and especially into the 1980s—the pseudoscientific nature of these ideas was much more widely understood, with the idea of ESP and telepathy generally discredited and understood as a pure fantasy. The stories could no longer be taken as a "possible future" in quite the same way; they could no longer be grounded in the idea that "psionics" had much merit as a "science."

Butler was similarly adamant in interviews across her career that her books were not to be read, in the ways comics usually were, as moral fables. She told her interviewer from *Vibe*: "One of the things I've discovered even with teachers using my books is that people tend to look for 'good guys' and 'bad guys,' which always annoys the hell out of me. I'd be bored to death writing that way. But because that's the only pattern they have, they try to fit my work into it."[43] What we find in *Patternmaster* is a vision of the pulp or comic-book superhero transformed from its familiar comic-book context and stripped of several key legitimating factors that ordinarily license its violence, leaving behind simply the raw struggle for dominance that Butler believed was integral to all life. From Richard Reynolds's list of defining motifs of the figure of the superhero, drawn from the characterization of Superman in *Action Comics #1* and extended across the genre as a whole, *Patternmaster* loses (3) the hero's devotion to justice, (4) the mundaneity of the superheroes' urban milieu, (5) the drama of the alter-ego, and (6) the loyalty to the existing regime of laws. Consequently we are left only with (1) the hero's isolation from society, particularly his parents, (2) the hero's immense power, and (7) the mythic nature of the stories.[44] *Patternmaster*, in effect, is a superhero story stripped of basically all constraint, in which the power fantasy escapes the ideological bounds that are usually intended to rein it in. The Patternists are superheroes in a world where human beings are primarily driven by Darwinist urges rather than ethical considerations—which is to say, our world, as Butler understood it to actually exist. The telepathic powers of the Patternists are primarily deployed against the mutes (to make them perfect slaves), against the Clayarks (for the purposes of mass killing), and against each other (in psychic combat for supremacy); dominating each other, she suggests, is what we'd actually use our superpowers for, if we had them.

Isolation, especially from loving adults, is an especially crucial element of the narrative in nearly all of the Patternist stories; telepaths going through adolescence find nearly all adult telepaths extremely unpleasant to be around, and vice versa, leading nearly all of them to be raised in isolation from their parents. When *Patternmaster* opens, Teray is just leaving "school," where he has been living throughout his teenage years;[45] we see the origin of this practice of child-rearing in *Mind of My Mind*.[46] The emergence of powers during adolescence in these stories is a similarly nightmarish affair, destroying and debilitating many of the psychics rather than empowering them; part of what Butler is so faithful to in her adult elaboration of her juvenilia is precisely the loneliness and unhappiness (bordering at times on despair) that characterized her young life.

Butler is quite open in interviews that the fascination with power across her work originated precisely within her own childhood fantasies of power. In the Patternist series in particular, the fantasy of power and its absolutely free rein, however unappealing its presentation and however anti-utopian its politics, contains nonetheless an animating spirit of jouissance (provided of course that one gets to be Doro, or gets to be the Patternmaster). Asked by Larry McCaffery about the importance of immortality in her work, Butler makes her own personal identification with this fantasy of power clear:

> When I was in my teens, a group of us used to talk about our hopes and dreams, and someone would always ask, "If you could do anything you wanted to do, no holds barred, what would you do? I'd answer that I wanted to live forever and breed people—which didn't go over all that well with my friends. In a sense, that desire is what drives Doro in *Wild Seed* and *Mind of My Mind*. At least I made him a bad guy![47]

To the extent that Doro and his Patternist descendants are a critique of power, then, they are a universal and anti-humanist one—a critique that crucially begins with tendencies Butler identified within herself.

How, we might ask, did a loyal reader of Superman comics ever become so *cynical*? Superman—as every child knows—views his power through the lens of noblesse oblige, deploying the fantastic abilities given to him by Earth's yellow sun to help the helpless; the first page of his introduction in *Action Comics* #1 famously refers to him as the "champion of the oppressed." The Fantastic Four, and other superheroes of the early Marvel Comics Silver-Age era like Spider-Man, received their powers through cosmic accident rather than through inborn superiority (Superman) or deliberate self-creation (Batman)—and yet by and large these superheroic characters choose to use their powers for good as well, even when (as with the case of the Thing, Spider-Man, or many of the X-Men) their powers are disturbing, painful, or have deeply isolating side effects.

Butler's vision of superheroes and superpowers, drawing from her anti-utopian beliefs about the centrality of power, competition, and domination in human life, is quite different. In fact, she anticipates later developments in superhero comics that would only begin to take shape significantly after she stopped reading comics in the early 1970s. *Patternmaster*'s vision of superhuman telepaths using their gifts to fight each other and enslave humanity would be much more at home in the contemporary "Dark Age" of Comics (which began in the mid-1980s with such seminal, self-deconstructive works as Alan Moore's *Watchmen*) than in the more optimistic Silver Age of Butler's youth.

In such tales superheroes are frequently revealed to be insecure, angry, selfish, jealous, and frequently deviant subjects, inflicting violence not in the name of some ethically rational, absolute notion of "justice" but for their own petty and flawed reasons. Butler's Patternist superhero novels anticipated by decades the inability to reliably tell the difference between heroes and villains that would come to dominate the post-*Watchmen* superhero genre. From this perspective even the nominal conservatism of the superhero is just a rhetorical posture; it is force itself, as such, that is the ultimate truth of the superhero, behind all the slogans and all pretension to ethical investment.

Butler's approach to the superhuman archetype—rather than being seen as "abandoning" certain aspects of the superhero myth—is better understood as cutting through the layers of obfuscations and nominal justifications that legitimate superhero fantasy to expose the power fantasy that is the true engine of these narratives. For Jameson's Le Guin,

> Utopia is not a place in which humanity is freed from violence, but rather one in which it is released from the multiple determinisms (economic, political, social) of history itself: in which it settles its accounts with its ancient collective fatalisms, precisely in order to be free to do whatever it wants with its interpersonal relationships. [48]

But in Butler's superpowered anti-utopia, the violence and those "ancient collective fatalisms"—power as such—are all that remain. In *Patternmaster* the state (and its attendant procedures of legitimation and restraint) is abstracted away, in favor of a return to the patriarchal family, where absolute authority is distributed across individual houses and culminates within allegiance to a single universal Father. Likewise, in the far Patternist future, citizenship has been eliminated, as has any notion of meaningful labor, as has the middle class, as has money—nothing exists beyond the originary power relation between master and slave. All human interactivity thus becomes reduced to the domination of the strong over the weak.

The discovery of the Pattern, then, is framed as a revolutionary change to human existence, but in fact it simply replicates the same brutal historical "pattern" of oppression and domination in a new register and with new power technologies. Despite Butler's characterization of the *Patternmaster* future as an egalitarian one, the early books in the series offer almost nothing outside a logic of domination; even the telepaths whose specialty is healing are simultaneously recognized as brutal potential killers:

> She glared at him, radiating resentment, and he found himself recalling what he had learned at school—that even Housemasters were careful how they antagonized healers. A good healer was also a terrifyingly efficient killer. A good healer could destroy the vital parts of a person's body quickly enough and thoroughly enough to kill even a strong Patternist before he could repair himself.[49]

Here, Butler reconsiders a superpower nominally devoted to care—and thus marked as "feminine"—and reveals it, too, to be a powerful weapon in the right hands.[50]

Meanwhile, nonsuperpowered characters do not rate at all. Because any nominal concern for "justice" has been completely stripped away from the figure of the superhero, the world has become particularly unforgiving for the weak, and for the merely mediocre; without anyone to save them and with no opportunity for an unpowered mute to elevate himself to the level of the superhuman (perhaps via technological cleverness, à la Iron Man or Batman), the mutes are purely expendable and endlessly subject to sadistic experimentation, murder, torture, and rape, even in well-run Houses.[51]

The sole competitor to the unchallenged hegemony of the Patternists, beyond the social instability implied by their own endless internal struggle for dominance, comes in the form of the Clayarks, mutated humans sick from an interplanetary virus, who are partially immune to Patternist control and who exist in the wild spaces between Patternist enclaves. An inversion of Superman's origins, here the crash-landing of the spaceship and the escape of the Clayark disease totally destabilizes modernity's existing power structures and creates the space for the alternative power structures of *Patternmaster* to gain total control, while simultaneously introducing the seeds for their possible eventual destruction. Thinking in these terms it is hard not to hear in the word "Clayark" (and especially the earlier "Cla-ark") the stuttered variation on Superman's human first name: Clark.

The narrative crisis of *Patternmaster* begins with a Clayark sneak attack on Rayal's compound that kills Jansee and leaves Rayal so weak that he must direct the bulk of the Pattern toward simply keeping himself alive; in the absence of a strong Patternmaster, the Clayarks become an even greater threat and have made once-ordinary trade and travel between enclaves impossible. What has been world-reduced here are the complicated politics of postcoloniality; the Clayark-Patternist conflict is a replication of the colonial frontier in which the white settler has no restraint on the violence he inflicts on the colonized subject. The arrival of the Clayarks thus "resets" human history into the mythological time of frontier fantasy but introduces nothing new beyond mere revitalization of the past: "He could not memorize the locations of Clayark settlements because the Clayarks inside Patternist Territory had no permanent settlements. They were nomadic, roaming in great tribes, settling only long enough to strip an area clean of food. They had been known to eat Patternists, in fact."[52] As the main protagonist of *Patternmaster* begins to come into his powers, he finds he is able to murder Clayarks by the dozens, treating them as if they were unthinking brutes, although he knows, from his telepathic contact with their minds, that they are actually thinking subjects capable of complex reasoning.[53] He even carries on a lengthy conversation with one.[54]

At the climax of the novel, having successfully killed his brother and secured his inheritance, Teray turns his newfound total mastery of the Pattern to Clayarks as Butler offers up the novel's most transcendent vision of superpowered consciousness alongside its most genocidal violence:

> Feeling like some huge bird, he projected his awareness over the territory. . . . He could see the distant ranges of hills, was aware of the even-more-distant mountains. [. . .] He swooped about, letting his extended awareness range free through the hills and valleys. Then, finally, he settled down, and focused his awareness on the Clayarks who formed a wide half-circle around the party. He swept down on them, killing.

Teray's final seizing of the mantle of the superhero—that ecstatic vision of flight—goes hand in hand with unlimited, total violence. Now he slaughters the Clayarks by the "hundreds, perhaps thousands"; he kills until he can sense no more Clayarks at all.[55]

For their part, the Clayarks are filled with endless hate for the Patternists, also seeing them as implacable "enemies" and "not people,"[56] and indeed only cannibalize Patternist flesh "to show, symbolically, how they meant someday to consume the entire race of Patternists."[57] By the time *I* finished

Patternmaster, I felt desperate for the Clayark prophecy to be true and wanted to see the hopeless Patternist stranglehold over Earth's future somehow swept away. I wanted to read what I saw as the inevitable sequel, in which we might see the Patternist society forced either to become more inclusive and egalitarian or else be destroyed by its own maladaptive contradictions. But this is a pleasure Butler denies her readers; the end of *Patternmaster*, with its crippled patriarch Rayal longing for death, is the furthest we ever see of this future history. Expressing precisely the reader's own feeling of exhaustion with power, with violence, with empire, and with the fruitless struggle for domination—and perhaps even Butler's own exhaustion with this narrative she had written and rewritten and re-rewritten for so many years—Rayal psychically calls out to Teray in the last sentence of the novel to come and finally kill him: "Hurry and get here. You have no idea how tired I am."[58]

DORO AND MARY

Rather than pushing on toward the longed-for fall of the Patternists, as one might expect, the next two books in the series instead turn their attention to the past. *Mind of My Mind* (1977) depicts the first discovery of the Pattern and reveals the origin of the Patternists as the culmination of the breeding experiments of an immortal African named Doro in 1970s California; when the final breakthrough is made and the Pattern is discovered, the telepaths turn on their breeder and establish control over the planet themselves. Doro is *the* key figure in Butler's early imagination, a figure of intense erotic interest even as she shared with him that transgressive adolescent desire "to live forever and breed people." Although he never appears in *Patternmaster* and is only obliquely mentioned within the book, it was Doro's story that is at the center of the Patternist milieu, Doro's story Butler was seeking to tell in those twenty years of scribbling. But, as with the perversely egalitarian meritocracy of the post-apocalyptic Patternist future, Butler's personal fondness for Doro—nurtured over her decades of imagining his adventures and understanding his perspective—likely does not translate to most readers' experiences of the character. He is sinister from our earliest introduction to him, when his "widow" (Rina, the mother of Mary) notes that he has impregnated her against her explicit wishes.[59] Doro is cruel, incestuous, and utterly dismissive of the needs of others; it seems no great loss to us when he is devoured by Mary, though from Butler's perspective this was the climax of a tragedy, in the classical sense of witnessing the fall of a great man due to cruel circumstances and his own unmanaged weakness.

Despite his seeming villainy, however, there is all the same something refreshing about Doro and his willingness to seek an alternative model of the future that springs entirely from his image. Set closer to our era, *Mind of My Mind* suggests the Patternist project's status as a potential competitor to contemporary racial forms much more clearly, while softening the more brutal excesses of the far-future *Patternmaster*. The first explanation of Doro's project in *Mind of My Mind* is that "for all but the first few centuries of his four-thousand-year life, he had been struggling to build a race around himself."[60] Chief among the side effects of Doro's body-switching power is his ability to switch between black and white bodies, allowing him the ability to pass perfectly as either; when his daughter, Mary, the first Patternmaster, sees him after a long gap, she notices that "Doro was a black man this time [. . .] a relief, because, the last couple of visits, he'd been white."[61] Mary's own skin color is "a light coffee," like that of her immortal grandmother Anyanwu/ Emma, though her "traffic-light green" eyes are "gifts from the white man's body that Doro was wearing when he got Rina pregnant."[62] In fact, as *Wild Seed* later reveals, *all* of these characters have African ancestry; Doro initiated his experiments in Africa before transplanting his charges to the New World, so every superpowered character in the Patternist series is in actuality a black superhero. The Patternist series as a whole can thus be read as a very subtle entry in the "kill-the-white-folks" tradition of "black militant near-future" novels that Kali Tal traces as far back as Sutton Griggs's *Imperium in Imperio* (1899).[63] White people are either assimilated into Doro's generational breeding program (with their children, in accordance with the racist logic of the "one-drop" rule, thereby becoming black) or else they are left outside it to die at the hands of the Clayarks or become the Patternists' eventual slaves.

In the prequels the emergence of the Patternists is thus much more explicitly framed as challenge to white supremacy—a challenge that is unhappy for us simply because we've had the bad luck to read the last book in the series first and already know that challenging white supremacy still isn't quite enough to build utopia. (We might be similarly dispirited, reading the series in chronological rather than publication order, to find men back in charge of the Pattern in the far future, centuries after Mary's triumph in *Mind*.) But other aspects of the book push against this interpretation. Mary, upon finding out that Doro was born in Africa, tries to explain to him that this makes him black too, attempting to assert some sort of racial solidarity between them that, she hopes, will cause him to behave more decently toward her; he devilishly replies, "I'm not black or white or yellow, because I'm not human, Mary."[64] Doro understands his charges as his cattle rather than his equals, and for millennia he simply slaughters the failed experiments at will before Anyanwu made him promise to at least let his failures live (as depicted at the end of *Wild Seed* [1980], discussed in the next chapter). No mutual recognition—much less solidarity—is possible under these assumptions. What is monstrous about Doro is what was monstrous about the Patternmaster Rayal and what is monstrous about power as such: its radical loneliness, its refusal of commonality and human connection. It falls to the women in Doro's life, his daughter Mary and his consort Anyanwu/Emma, to make the case for connection in his stead—but they are only partially successful, at best.

Mind of My Mind is the only book in the series to use either the word "mutant" or "superman"; the latter is deployed in the negative as a rejection of romantic infatuation, while "mutant" (and more commonly "mutation") is deployed in a biological register as part of a description of Doro's project. Doro views himself as a mutation in the sense of being a singularity, being radically alone among human beings[65]—but from the perspective of both his daughter Mary and his consort Anyanwu, these "mutant strains" are a "people"—*his* people.[66] The latter use suggests the way the term was used in *X-Men* comics of the period to figure "social and cultural difference," typically from a left-wing perspective of racial tolerance.[67] The "whole theme of the X-Men," writes Richard Reynolds, "the isolation of the mutants and their alienation from 'normal' society—can be read as a parable of the alienation of any minority" (79). However, both Mary and Doro take up a position more in common with the mutant separatism of Magneto and his "Brotherhood of Evil Mutants" than Professor X's more liberal, more cosmopolitan X-Men. Neither Mary nor Doro has much interest in liberal tolerance or a demand for equal rights under existing laws; the primary difference between them is that Doro views himself as a radically atomic singularity while Mary views herself as the organ of a new collectivity. This element of the story, too, points both toward and away from a utopian reading of *Mind of My Mind*. Mary, living in the economically depressed slum of Forsyth, gathers the first Patternists from the ranks of Doro's unstable telepaths, the rejected and failed "experiments" he would have simply exterminated before Anyanwu's intervention forced him to relax his brutality. Mary is able to unite these misfits into a collectivity that allows their powers to flourish in a way atomism could never allow. In the end it is this new collectivity that, after millennia, is finally able to match Doro's power; as Sandra Govan puts it, the Patternists win because Mary "is the symbiont, not the vampire"[68]—an interest in and celebration of biotic symbiosis Butler herself would note as the key to much of her work.[69]

But perhaps Mary turns out to be truly her father's daughter; the startling ending of the novel reveals that the newly empowered Mary is just another vampire: "Now she took her revenge. She consumed him slowly, drinking in his terror and his life, drawing out her own pleasure, and laughing through his soundless screams."[70] The pleasure with which she psychically eats Doro recasts her relationship with the other Patternists in new light; they are actually her instruments, not her partners, and as the Patternmaster, like both her ancestor Doro and her descendent Rayal, she is radically alone. That the fallen Patternist future of *Patternmaster* anti-utopically springs from this originary murder is no historical accident; it is inevitable, the only possibility.

Violence cannot beget anything but violence in these stories; the attempt to overthrow systems of domination only result in their replication (typically in even more monstrous form). This endless, horrible return of the same can be seen elsewhere in the series' approach to race fantasy in general. In *Patternmaster* our historical categories of race had been supplanted by the future's new racial dynamic between the powerful Patternists (as a color-blind replacement for privileges of whiteness) and its Others (the mutes and the Clayarks)—a grim reminder of Isiah Lavender's enjoinder to recall the difference between "the ability to imagine a world without racism [and] to imagine a world without race."[71] Racial markers in that novel are completely incidental; Teray's closest companion and love interest, the healer Amber, is described in passing as a "golden-brown woman with hair that was a round cap of small, tight black curls"[72]—but what matters about her is her power and independence as a Patternist. The Clayark is "tanned,"[73] yet marked not by skin color but by the Sphinx-like mutations of the disease; one enslaved mute woman is described as "blond."[74] The skin color of Rayal and his heirs is never specified at all. And still this "colorblind society" has reinscribed the privileges of whiteness into an even more monstrous and permanent form; indeed, the novel begins with the unwilling sale of Teray into Coransee's service in a lengthy sequence that reveals slavery has become a universal condition not simply for the mutes but for all but the most privileged Patternmasters, with essentially no reason to hope that the system will ever be abolished or overthrown.[75]

Butler would hold the same anti-utopian, deeply pessimistic perspective on the possibility of "progress" across her career; in a 2000 *New York Times* interview, asked "Will racial and sexual attitudes improve in the 21st century?" she replied, "Absolutely not. . . . In countries where there are no racial differences or no religious differences, people find other reasons to set aside one certain group of people and generally spit in their direction. . . . It delights people to find a reason to be able to kick other people."[76] In a 1997 interview with Joan Fry in *Poets and Writers* Butler repeats her typically anti-utopian claim that the human being is basically flawed at the most fundamental level, suggesting (in accordance with her observations about the Psi people of "Childfinder") that "even . . . the most absolutely homogeneous group you could think of" would "create divisions and fight each other."[77] But before this sad proclamation there is a glimmer that some historical difference might be possible. She suggests that Doro's people—Mary and the other proto-Patternists—do "nasty things" first to Doro and then to everyone else "because they've learned that's how you behave if you want to survive."[78] In the Charles Rowell interview, also from 1997, she makes much the same point, arguing that the Patternists were "so awful" precisely because "they had a bad teacher." This formulation is linked back to "some comment on Black America . . . a comment on learning the wrong thing from one's teachers."[79] Mary, Butler freely admitted, is "not a good person. But how can she be? She wouldn't survive if she were 'good.'"[80] Survival at any cost is what you learn when history has been a nightmare—but this framing implicitly suggests that in other times and other histories there are other things one *might* learn instead.

In *Mind of My Mind* we learn that Doro similarly had a "bad teacher"— that his experiences have likewise taught him that he has no way to survive aside from hurting other people.[81] Doro, in narrating to Mary his own story, tells of his lost childhood on the banks of the southern Nile, ruined when a resurgent Egyptian Empire—"our former rulers, seeking to become our rulers again"—invaded Nubia and massacred his village and family. (This is, crucially, the moment in which Mary declares, to Doro's refusal, that no matter what skin he wears, he is as black as she is.) Doro describes the process of dying for the first time while going through his own traumatic, unaided transition to telepathic adulthood, and how in his terror he consumed first his mother, then his father: "I didn't know what I was doing. I took a lot of other people too, all in a panic." Fleeing the village in the body of a young girl—one of his cousins—he ran "straight into the arms of some Egyptians on a slave raid" and "snapped." Doro loses the next fifty years of his life, waking in an Egyptian prison in the body of a middle-aged man. He again commits murder to escape, concluding that his strange vampiric power means that, despite all appearances, he has been "favored by the gods." Doro, too, turns out to be a diasporic subject, wrestling with a colonial wound that includes both imperial aggression, kidnapping, and slavery, as well as the radical severing of his own connection to history: "I never saw any of the people of my village again."[82] From this perspective Doro himself is revealed to be yet another victim of yet another set of bad teachers, living in diaspora; if Butler had ever completed her planned book set during Doro's youth in Egypt, which would have fleshed out his own trauma in more detail, he might seem to us now as tragic a figure as Anyanwu or Mary. In this sense Mary certainly has the better of her argument with Doro; Doro *is* black, after all. And in *Wild Seed* Butler will somehow manage to re-inject some hope even into Doro's story—knowing, as we know, how things turn out for him and for his people in the end.

SURVIVOR AND REPRODUCTIVE FUTURITY

Survivor (1978) takes place off-world, early in the Patternist future and well before *Patternmaster*; once again inverting an infant Superman's removal from a doomed Krypton, the superhuman Patternists send groups of unpowered "mutes" into outer space in an attempt to ensure the survival of the human race, should any cosmic disaster befall the planet Earth. The Patternists are unable to go themselves because the Pattern binds them together too closely, their strength becoming a weakness that traps them all on a single world; thus, *Survivor* is the one and only glimpse we have in the series of a future for the human race that is at least beyond Patternist control, though the escape is both difficult and only partial. (This reasoning puts the lie to the hyperracialized division between humans and mutes in *Patternmaster*; in the face of potential species extinction, the Patternists identify the mutes as continuous with themselves, as people too.) It simultaneously proclaims a final curse on the Patternist project, one that would have been instantly recognizable to science fiction readers of the time (and which perhaps, from that perspective, renders the idea of any *Patternmaster* sequel superfluous): they cannot go to space, and thus are doomed to eventual extinction on Earth. Only normal humans can spread themselves across the universe and thereby attain species immortality.

Survivor's story is not nearly as bad as Butler felt it was, though perhaps some would still agree it is one of her lesser works. It is certainly due for a reprinting and a reconsideration. *Survivor* is, essentially, a frontier captivity narrative, depicting the efforts of human Missionaries who have landed in the middle of a conflict between two native groups on the planet (the Tehkohn and the Garkohn) and are forced to choose sides in order to survive. The chief protagonist is Alanna Verrick, a mixed-race "wild human" who was adopted by white Missionary parents and brought off-world to the Mission colony. Alanna is the survivor of the title: she is the only survivor of a Tehkohn raid that saw her living as their captive for two years, ultimately mated with their tribe leader, Diut, and giving birth to his child. She is one of Butler's most consummate survivors precisely because she is able to transform herself over and over again, adapting perfectly to any situation; she is able to become whatever she needs to be in order to go on, even as those she arrived on the planet with are too hidebound to adapt to their new situation. "People migrating to another planet should be—must be—damned adaptive people," Butler writes in her personal notes. "The missionaries are anything but adaptive." This idea of adaptation extends even to the relationship between Alanna and Diut, which, like other relationships Butler will write in later works such as *Dawn* and *Fledgling*, seems to closely skirt the line of rape (if not indeed cross it altogether). In a 1987 letter, Butler says that she does not read the book in these terms; she describes this plot event instead as (first) a "cultural conflict" and then as a "bargain" struck by two people who both get something out of the deal (and who, indeed, subsequently grow to care about each other).[83] (I return to *Survivor* and Alanna's story in the conclusion to this book, in the context of the 2014 publication of an excised chapter from *Survivor* as "A Necessary Being" in the e-book *Unexpected Stories*.)

An unpublished story Butler wrote in the 1970s called "The Evening and the Morning and the Night"—bearing only slim relation to the famous story that would eventually be published under that name, and having much more in common with the first versions of the Xenogenesis books—provides an interesting counterpoint to *Survivor*. "Evening" [I], one of Butler's best-developed unpublished stories of the 1970s, with multiple versions dating back to her Clarion days, also takes place in the "Missionary" wing of the Patternist milieu. In the story a small group of Missionaries are all that survive a crash on a hostile alien world: four women and one man. The characters are utterly despondent, especially the point-of-view character, frequently bemoaning the fact that they have survived at all, wishing they had died on Earth or in the crash.

One of the characters becomes pregnant (after this point the man often dies, especially in the later rewrites). The pregnancy should be a token of hope, but in most of the versions of the story that exist, it is instead a disturbing reminder of the radical hopelessness of their predicament. In some versions the birth happens, but the consequences are horrible: the fetus is born dead, horribly misshapen, seemingly mutated by radiation that is either ambient on the planet or already in their own cells. In one version the hopeless survivors say the dead child is "luckier than any of us,"[84] in another they simply collapse together and weep in sorrow.[85] The Mission, the point-of-view character realizes, is a "lie" designed to delude "fools" into thinking they had a chance to survive. She begins to recount the possible catastrophes that might have beset the other Mission ships: disease, loss of life support, mutations, crash-landings, hostile planetary ecologies . . .[86] The staggering list of possible disasters oddly presages Butler's inability to finish *Parable of the Trickster* decades later, which was intended to show a line of futurity for human beings leading to multiple futures (and multiple humanities) on multiple planets, none of which she could hold in her imagination for very long, none of which was ever "reproductive."

The original "Evening" was a *"no"* story, Butler conceded: "It's saying 'Watch us die.'"[87] One might be tempted to place importance on the fact that the point-of-view character is white, while the pregnant couple is black, suggesting that the story at least depicts a positive vision of black futurity—but no version of this story successfully portrays the survivors as anything but deluded. Butler herself acknowledged this truth in her inability to remove "and the Night" from the title, despite recognizing the way that it forecloses all hope (and indeed paints "hope" as a tragically misleading blip between periods of darkness).[88]

As we have already seen and will continue to see in the chapters to come, Butler consistently deploys a logic of reproductive futurity in her fictions about survival: characters in her stories survive insofar as, and perhaps *because*, they survive to have children; characters who are not able to complete the reproductive circuit tend to fall out of her narratives, and even out of history itself. In this regard Butler seems, at least superficially, to endorse the set of ideological structures that Lee Edelman has famously called "reproductive futurism," that form of liberal politics that sees the Child as "the perpetual horizon of every acknowledged politics, the fantasmatic beneficiary of every political intervention," the sacred call that is "impossible to refuse."[89] But, as I will argue in more detail in the coming chapters, the usual optimism of this reproductive futurity is frequently undercut by Butler's grim imagination and quietly ambiguous endings, a tendency we can see at work already in her earliest stories—in both the "Childfinder" and the *Patternmaster* versions, the Patternists are ultimately a sterile civilization; Doro dies, while Mary seems to become him; Alanna's child with Diut appears to be the token of the future, but instead dies, while her relationship with the other Earth humans (including her adopted father) is severed; and the stranded colonists in "The Evening and the Morning and the Night" [I] cannot decide if they even prefer life to death at all. This depressive tendency is made even more visible by the stories Butler didn't publish, stories which—because they were never forced to conform to the mandatory optimism of the literary marketplace—remained free to say "no."

TRILOGY

Butler soon sold *Mind of My Mind* to Doubleday, and *Survivor* soon after that, quickly becoming the author of an unusually nonlinear trilogy. The process of negotiation in the subsequent books also frustrated her; she is penalized in her second advance for the presence of curse words in *Mind of My Mind*, setting off several weeks of tense debate about the prudery of library councils versus the need for verisimilitude in dialogue. (In the end, only "fuck" was removed from the text, a nonnegotiable demand from Doubleday; Butler kept the remainder of her curse words in exchange for the lower advance.) When her advance for *Survivor* is again only $1,750—this time because of the sex scene, which her editor at Doubleday felt was necessary for the narrative but would limit their ability to sell the book in all markets—she does not mince words: "I accept your offer . . . but I'm not happy."[90]

Butler's problems with *Survivor* went beyond the advance, however. She had already felt skittish about her *Patternmaster* sale, and she frequently directed people to read *Mind of My Mind* first or instead. (She even suggested that Doubleday not bother trying to get an endorsement for *Patternmaster* from Harlan Ellison, to wait for *Mind of My Mind*, thinking he would like that one better.) Now in 1978 she was already telling people not to read *Survivor* either, as it was "a good story badly told."[91] In part, in fact, she privately blamed Ellison, saying the book had been better before it was revised to his suggestions.[92] She actively discouraged people from reading the book—knowing that this only encouraged them seek it out—and blocked its reprint and publication for the rest of her life. (When Nisi Shawl got Butler to autograph her copy of *Survivor*, she inscribed it, "Nisi, I wish you didn't have this one."[93]) Butler felt the book's assumption, that beings who evolved on different planets would be able to have children together, was embarrassingly scientifically naïve[94]—the reason she called the book her "*Star Trek*" novel, despite having been a lifelong fan of that franchise.[95] But she felt also that the book was simply not finished when she sold it. Years later she would say that she sold the book primarily because she needed the money to get to Maryland—in order to research the slavery novel that would, eventually, become world-famous as *Kindred*.[96]

CHaPTeR 3

TO KEEP THEE IN ALL THY WAYS (1976–1980)

Published Works

Kindred (1979)
"Near of Kin" (1979)
Wild Seed (1980)

Significant Unpublished Work

Canaan (alternate version of *Kindred*, set in Patternist universe) (c. 1975–1976)

In interviews Butler often reflected on a singular incident from her college days:

> When I got into college, Pasadena City College, the black nationalist movement,
> the Black Power Movement, was really underway with the young people, and
> I heard some remarks from a young man who was the same age I was but who
> had apparently never made the connection with what his parents did to keep
> him alive. He was still blaming them for their humility and their acceptance of
> disgusting behavior on the part of employers and other people. He said, "I'd like

to kill all those old people who have been holding us back for so long. But I can't because I'd have to start with my own parents."[1]

Butler told one interviewer, Charles H. Rowell, that she "carried that comment" with her "for thirty years," saying that this event ultimately provided the "germ of the idea for *Kindred* (1979)."[2] She told the story of this day often; it appears two other times in the interviews collected for *Conversations with Octavia Butler* with nearly the same details, describing an identical long-term impact on her life's work. In the version she tells Daniel Burton-Rose in 2003, the other male student is someone she admires, "sort of our scholar": "He had made himself our best resource on black history because he'd read more of it than any of us."[3] In the Charles Brown interview in Locus a few years earlier, the other student is described as a friend.[4]

The gap between Butler and this student clearly did stick with her, becoming the seed not only for *Kindred* but also for most of the works she would write. In some ways her disagreement with this other student was the central philosophical insight of Butler's life: that survival is not necessarily the same thing as defeating your enemy, or even fighting back or standing up for yourself, but simply means that you (and, crucially, your children) have continued into the future. This was especially poignant for her as the descendent of generations of black men and black women who had managed to survive through centuries of enslavement and segregation and degradation. Times could be so bad that the only thing that seemed right was to hurl oneself on the gears of the machine in resistance, or withdraw into misery, or commit suicide—but the living body of African Americans had derived from those who had found a way to survive within the machine that was crushing them, doing whatever it took to (somehow) stay alive. Her friend "was the kind that would have killed and died, as opposed to surviving and hanging on and hoping and working for change."[5] She understood the intellectual appeal of what he was saying but felt that he was too detached, too cerebral, and far too impractical. She thought instead about her mother:

My mother was taken out of school when she was ten and set to work. As a result she basically knew how to clean houses and not much else. That's what she did for a living for most of my childhood. She would take me with her sometimes, when she didn't have a babysitter, and I would get to see her going in back doors, and

I'd get to see her not pay attention, not hearing when things were said that ordinarily she'd respond to very vehemently. And I was embarrassed, I was ashamed.

It was only years later that she came to see her mother as the hero who had made her own life possible.[6]

This insight into the nature of survival—survival as the only choice, survival as itself a kind of resistance, a triumph—structures much of Butler's work. We have already seen this at work in the novel she disavowed, *Survivor*, but this kind of reproductive futurity will be just as crucial a theme in the works discussed in this chapter and the next: *Kindred*, *Wild Seed*, and *Clay's Ark*, "Bloodchild," "Speech Sounds," and "The Evening and the Morning and the Night" [II]. In all of these works we see characters who make the radical choice to *live*, at whatever cost, and therefore for their children to live, even when this choice means political or moral compromises within a monstrous or inhuman system.

In "Near of Kin" (1979)—the only one of Butler's published stories that is unambiguously not SF—one can see clearly that this kind of "survival" is not always an uncomplicated or unalloyed good, even for its beneficiaries. The story is sometimes mistaken as having something to do with *Kindred*, in part because of the similarity of the name[7] and in part because its initial publication in *Chrysalis 4* included a note to this effect without Butler's authorization. She considered the story to be a "minor work"[8] but elsewhere described it as a story whose "screaming to be born" she finally couldn't ignore.[9] The story depicts a woman who, in the wake of her mother's death, has her suspicion confirmed that she is in fact the product of an incestuous affair between siblings, her mother and her uncle. "She wanted you," the uncle says of the main character's mother, but the shame of her origin, even before the truth was confirmed, prevented the daughter from ever having a real relationship with either her mother or her uncle/father. The story ends with the secret out, but with her origin still unspeakable and her relationship with her uncle/father still extremely uneasy; she has only gotten this far by blocking his path out of the room and promising never to speak of it again, and the final lines of the story are dominated by unfinished sentences, silences, ellipses, and closing doors.

Butler said she saw the story as originating in her study of the Bible during her Baptist childhood, and in particular on the way she "read avidly" on biblical "stories of conflict, betrayal, torture, murder, exile, and incest." ("This was, of course," she added dryly, "not exactly what my mother had in mind when she encouraged me to read the Bible.") As a result of this childhood fascination, she said, she often wrote stories that tried to reconcile our revulsion at incest with its importance in the Bible: "sympathetic" stories of incest, as we have already seen in *Patternmaster* and (less so) *Mind of My Mind*, and will see again in Xenogenesis.[10]

But Butler's interest in infelicitous reproductions and unhappy survivals, and in compromised and troubled survivors, would arguably reach its highest formulation in *Kindred*, her book with the widest and most persistent mainstream success and for which she is still best known. *Kindred*—or, as I sometimes suggest to my students, *Kin/dread*—uses a clever and uniquely Afrofuturist twist on the time-travel trope in science fiction to show the radical embeddedness of the past within the present. Butler's time-traveling narrator, Dana, is alive *after* slavery and *despite* slavery, but also *because of* slavery, a compromised and morally fraught position that forces her to make deeply unpleasant choices in the name of preserving the circumstances that led to her own birth. In this respect we can see *Kindred* as a deconstruction of time travel and a revelation of the logic of power, privilege, and racial difference that deeply structures even a seemingly neutral idea like the fantasy of moving backward in time. For the white men who wrote the science fiction Butler read as a child, the idea of traveling backward in time was an interesting lark, or the occasion for speculations about history or free will, or a puzzle about causation and temporal paradoxes, or an opportunity to use your knowledge to get rich and powerful, or perhaps even (at worst) a kind of disavowed nostalgia for a time when the supremacy of white men was unquestioned and absolute. But for a black woman writing time-travel fiction, all of these appeals are turned on their head by the fact of racial and gendered difference; to Butler, and to the other nonwhite and nonmale writers who began to break into science fiction in the 1970s and later, the past is not some open field for adventure but the fenced-off nightmare they'd only barely escaped. For a disprivileged person living in the margins of social power, the present (however flawed) is extremely precious—because the past is even worse. To go back into the past in a black, female body—or a gay body, or a transgender body, or a disabled body, or . . . —is always to put oneself in extreme danger, to risk becoming trapped there, in that bad time, and never finding your way back.

At the same time, paradoxically, the badness of the past in a story like *Kindred* becomes somehow necessary for the present and the future. Time travel stories written by and about white men often focus on time loops, in which the male time traveler willingly or unwillingly preserves the original timeline rather than changing it; as Constance Penley and others have noticed, such stories very typically take the form of autogenesis narratives, in which the white male hero actually secures or brings about his own birth. The "proper" order of history is framed as something to be fought for, either because the status quo of the time traveler's original history is good or because all alternatives are worse; the thematic arc of most time-travel fictions is to reconcile the point-of-view character to his or her original circumstances, by making those circumstance seem desirable, unchangeable, and/or literally inevitable. Butler's heroine, Dana, has a somewhat different relationship with the past in *Kindred*: she, too, is forced to fight to preserve the original course of history in order to guarantee the circumstances of her own birth, but this only serves to draw her into deeper and deeper complicity with the horrible past of slavery that created her future. She is forced, over and over again, to ask whether her survival is worth it at all, whether it might not be better to give up and obliterate herself from time. (She does, ultimately, attempt suicide, though she does so hoping the attempt will be enough to trigger her self-protective time-travel powers and return her to the present.) By the end of the novel she is deeply scarred by her experience—including the literal disfigurement of her back from being whipped—which is ultimately symbolically tokened in the novel by her final, tortured reappearance in the present, when her arm appears buried in a wall and must be amputated to the elbow. The wish-fulfillment fantasy of time travel and its typical "happy ending" comes completely undone in this time-travel narrative through this unexpected reassertion of *spatiality*: Dana is someone who will carry the trauma of her contact with history written on her body for the rest of her life.

A GRIM FANTASY

Butler didn't think of *Kindred* as science fiction: she repeatedly referred to it instead as a "grim fantasy" and asked her publisher to do the same. Much of this has to do with technical narrative questions around what causes Dana's time travel, which is never explained—in the published version there is no time machine or genetic mutation causing these events to happen: they simply do. (In the Huntington archive, one can find both fragmentary and full-length alternative versions of *Kindred*, discussed below, that *would* qualify as science fiction in Butler's terms.)

The clarity of her vision for the book did not make it any easier to write than her other books; in fact, the book was quite difficult for her not only to write but to *research*. Butler was intimidated by the idea of writing that took place outside California, the place she had spent all but a few weeks of her life. She was also intimidated by the idea of writing about history, unsure what her contribution would be, and worried that such work had already been done better by others, including by many of the slaves and former slaves themselves[11]—but as much as any of that, she was disturbed by the idea of truly inhabiting the world of slavery. "Researching slavery," she told Jeffrey M. Eliot in the *Thrust* interview, "promised to be painful and depressing. But the story would not leave me alone. It wanted to be written."[12] With her characteristic self-deprecation she would later say that *Kindred*, bleak as it is, was still a sanitized version of slavery, one made sufficiently "clean" that people would actually be willing to read the book.[13]

The research involved a several-weeks-long trip to Maryland. She arrived in Baltimore, she said, with little plan, not even a place to stay—but fortuitously wound up at a shady hotel near both the Historical Society and the Enoch Pratt Free Library. She also used the trip to visit Washington, D.C., and specifically Mount Vernon, which at the time did not have any reconstructed slave cabins and in fact did not even use the word "slave" in tours. Butler bought "everything [she] could on Mount Vernon" during the period she was researching *Kindred*, she said, even pinning a plan of the grounds on her wall.[14] The trip was extremely productive for her, allowing her to finish a novel that had given her great trouble.

The *Kindred* we know is the nightmarish story of how Dana is drawn into deeper and deeper complicity with slavery through her repeated trips through time into the past. She first encounters her white ancestor, Rufus Weylin, as a child she saves from drowning, and then returns again and again to his life in key moments of crisis, protecting him and solving his problems so as to ensure her own birth, even as he shifts from an innocent child to a brutal slave owner. This involves Dana not only supporting Rufus's practices of slavery but even abetting the rape of her enslaved female ancestor, Alice, at Rufus's hands—another precondition for her birth. Alice is a woman who looks so much like Dana as to be her mother, sister, or even twin—a fact which Rufus becomes preoccupied with after Alice commits suicide when she believes Rufus has sold her children south. At the novel's climax, Rufus assaults Dana, intending to replace Alice with her as his victim—but this is a violation Dana has long decided she will not allow even at the cost of her own existence. She kills Rufus and reappears in the future, her arm embedded in her wall past her elbow. She loses her arm and (even after her own research trip to Maryland) is never able to determine what happened to any of her relatives following Rufus's death and the house fire set by another slave loyal to her to cover up her involvement. But she is alive, and the novel ends with her and her husband, Kevin, scarred but looking forward to a future together.

Butler reflected on the interracial marriage between Kevin and Dana that exists as a positive source of affirmation at the heart of *Kindred* in her journals, wondering why she wrote so commonly about mixed-race couples. She concluded that she wrote about them for the same reason she wrote about sexually egalitarian societies: an effort to imagine "not utopias, but societies in which women do as they please."[15] Still, *Kindred* is somewhat ambiguous on this front, particularly after Kevin is accidentally stranded in the antebellum past for several years after becoming separated from Dana and then returns to her with a "hard stare": "What had it made of him? What might he be willing to do now that he would not have done before?"[16] The color line between them—never a serious issue in their relationship before the time travel—becomes permanently reasserted in the face of their miserable adventures in time. They're together at the end of the novel, and sane, with "some chance of staying that way"—a tepid victory, at best.[17]

Butler toyed, as was her usual practice, with many other versions of the narrative. The longest and most developed is a version set in the Patternist milieu. Emma, Doro's consort from *Mind of My Mind*, is present on the plantation in this version, which she was at that time calling *Canaan*—and Doro functions as a kind of plot timer in the story: Dana must be returned to the future before Doro gets back so that she (and her power to time travel) cannot be drawn into Doro's breeding project, thereby making him unstoppable. These elements are completely excised from the finished novel, which does not link into the Patternist milieu at all. More intriguing, the role for the Alice character is expanded and complicated in this early draft; now a child called Barbara, she seems to be an equal participant in the time-travel plot, functioning in a sense as the "receiver" to Dana's "transmitter." It's Barbara's Patternist powers that keep pulling Dana back in time. Barbara is still a double or doppelgänger for the Dana character (who is called Joan in this draft) but remains a child over the course of the story—leading to a totally alternative ending in which Alice/Barbara returns with Dana and her husband, Kevin, to the future at the end of the novel to be raised as their child. Butler was devoted to this ending, despite her feeling that it made no sense narratively, and sought for ways it could possibly be true despite the interior logic of the story depending on the idea of Barbara as Dana's ancestor. (Perhaps she was actually some sort of genetic clone, Butler reasoned, or perhaps Dana had unknowingly traveled to the future as a young child to escape slavery and then forgotten about it, or somehow they are older and younger versions of the same individual, or . . . [18]) Ultimately, Butler could not make the ending work, so she abandoned it—but its presence as an excess within the archives is a fascinating counterpoint to the published *Kindred* in its inversion of the logic of reproductive futurity, as well as its refusal of the bad past as the "necessary" crucible for African American life in the present—and in its allowing children, instead, to raise their own parents, if only inside the logic of the dream. (Even this superficially happy ending risks becoming tainted by pessimism upon further reflection, though; *Canaan* refuses the reconciliation with history and the acceptance of generations of African American suffering that the published book enforces in favor of a fantastical utopian alternative that is utterly impossible to make real and has no future anyway in the face of the inevitable rise of the Patternists.)

Other abandoned, fragmentary versions of *Kindred* begin lightly, even jokingly: time-traveling tourists from the future who are interested in visiting the vibrant 1960s yet mistakenly wind up a hundred years off their target and exit their time machine into a nightmare. Another imagines a time traveler from the future who uses his machine to do what Dana cannot allow herself to do within the pages of the novel: resist slavery and help slaves escape. The time traveler has black ancestors and feels called to this work.[19] Butler would later tell interviewers of her idea to make Kevin black instead of white, or possibly even replacing Dana with a black male protagonist, yet concluding those versions of the plot could never work: a black man with a twentieth-century sense of self-possession would be viewed as too great a threat and therefore quickly killed by the white slavers. Some of Butler's notes even suggest, perhaps, an ill-advised version of *Kindred* (called *Guardian*) that is a "love story," in which Dana and Rufus become many-generations-removed incestuous "lovers" (a possibility only teased, and ultimately rejected, in the published novel);[20] still another note imagines dropping the time-travel angle entirely, simply telling the story of an enslaved woman of the antebellum period who demands to be free. Even that entirely realist version of *Kindred* still would have been science fiction of a sort, though: Butler often noted in her speeches and talks that "history is another planet"—the only one we know to bear any life.[21]

Kindred was (and remains) Butler's most financially successful and most widely read novel; while all her novels have been out of print at least briefly, *Kindred's* time out of print was the shortest and never dipped out of print again. Decades later, submitting the first Parable book to her editor, Butler would think of *Kindred* as the gold standard of her work—and would comment that if *Parable of the Sower* wasn't quite *Kindred*, it was close, and had the potential to have the same sort of wide reception and staying power.[22] Still, the sale of the novel was a source of great frustration to her, contributing to her ultimate break with Doubleday in the mid-1980s. She was once again forced to change the name of her novel. After a number of possible titles, she had settled on the somewhat unwieldy biblical quotation *To Keep Thee in All Thy Ways*, which she saw as both "intriguing" and "relevant to the story being told."[23] But the editor wanted to call the book *Dana*, a title Butler was insistent *not* be used. The editor ignored Butler's alternatives and retitled the book *Dana* on her own. An ad was even run promoting the book under that title, infuriating Butler.[24] When *Wild Seed* came out the next year and received essentially no promotion—and with both books earning her far less money than she believed appropriate—she was finally fed up, telling her agent to try to sell her work to other publishers.

Crucial to this shift is the surprising instruction to market her books as mainstream literature rather than SF; describing her hopes for the sale of *Clay's Ark* in 1982, for instance, she says she sees no reason to "flush" the book "down that particular toilet" and asks that the words "science fiction" appear nowhere on the cover or in the promotion. By that time she was convinced that the genre label was killing her sales, as well as keeping her books from the African American and female audiences that also read her work when they found it. She sends the book to Toni Morrison at Random House, thinking it might have a good chance as a crossover book. But it didn't happen for her, at least not then; though *Clay's Ark* was published by St. Martin's, not Doubleday, Butler still resented the way it "sort of vanished into the shadows" due to lack of promotion even decades later.[25] As late as 2005 she would somewhat bitterly advise the fans who wrote to her that they should stay out of the science fiction publishing market altogether, on the grounds that it would limit both their literary esteem and their income.[26]

Overall her letters and journal entries from the 1980s reveal a deep dissatisfaction with the business side of the publishing industry—a few years later, she would even be ready to fire her longtime literary agent, Felicia Eth, though she seemingly never actually sent the letter doing so—and her frustration over ongoing struggles with money. "Please take care of this as soon as you can," she wrote Eth in a July 1982 letter that can stand in for many, many others across the period. "I'm neither kidding nor exaggerating when I say I'm broke."[27]

WILD SEED

Butler's next published novel, *Wild Seed* (1980)—the only one of her books to be set even partially in Africa—provides the "origin story" for the events in the Patternist series. Inspired in part by Chinua Achebe's *Things Fall Apart*, and set in the same region of Africa among the same Igbo people,[28] *Wild Seed* traces Doro's story from its origins in Africa to the slave trade in the Americas. Though it would be the last Doro story Butler would ultimately publish, she did not think of the book as the last one at the time, imagining (among other possibilities) a potential follow-up that would show Doro's personal origins in ancient Egypt.

In the reading I've advanced thus far of the Patternist books, one might be forgiven for assuming Butler's perspective on the superhero was purely negative; *Patternmaster* focuses on the dark side of the power fantasy and the attendant abuses of the disprivileged to the exclusion of all other possibilities.

But in the prequel material—especially in *Wild Seed*—more utopian valences of the superhero fantasy are occasionally given voice, if not exactly ratified. In *Wild Seed* even more so than in *Mind of My Mind*, the glimpse of a possible utopian "outside" to anti-utopian superhero fantasy can be seen in the relocation of the action to a black diasporic context—here, Africa itself.

In *Wild Seed* we see the internal logic of the Patternist prequels as oppositional to traditional superheroics in a new sense—almost a new history of the superhero genre "from below," from the perspective of those who are disfavored in the usual rhetoric of privilege, "special gifts," and "master races" (like the Kryptonians, or in the racist fantasy called whiteness). Doro's project thus emerges as a dialectical challenge to traditional forms of race fantasy. In *Wild Seed* a secret competitor to white hegemony is revealed to exist alongside modernity's actually existing history of intergenerational slavery and forced reproduction, an alternate history that is both a deviation from and a nightmarish replication of white supremacy. By positing a eugenics project in the heart of Africa, beginning millennia before Europe's parallel project and selecting against whiteness in favor of superpowered blackness, Doro manifests as a strong challenger to the racial fantasies that have undergirded modernity. America—now transformed as a blip sandwiched between the secret history of Doro's experiments and the brutal aftermath of their horrible success—becomes retold here as an African story, in an Africanist recentering of history that serves as a strongly anticolonialist provocation. But here again the nonchronological publishing order of the Patternist series confounds us; as with the reversed publication of the earlier Patternist trilogy—as well as the decades separating *Survivor* from its prequel, "A Necessary Being"—the unhappy endings of the books published first threaten to overwrite completely any optimism in the "prequels." We already know that despite the project's status as a competitor to white supremacy, the results of Doro's experiments liberate neither humanity in general nor black people in particular; instead, they culminate in an even more totalizing domination by an even more untouchably powerful elite, a state of affairs to which any resistance seems utterly impossible.

This tension is not limited to *Wild Seed*'s place in the larger Patternist milieu, either. As Ingrid Thaler has noted, the book's repeated references to the already-existing practice of racial slavery are primarily deployed as a rhetoric by Doro himself to "manipulate the reader into accepting his 'breeding program' as a viable alternative to Western modernity,"[29] where in fact it is primarily a replication of those practices.[30] "We were brought here to function as if we were not human but tools, machines, disposable working parts," notes Greg Tate of the slave trade. "We were also bred to be superhuman, more than human, even in our endurance for taxing labor and suffering."[31] As this quote suggests and the novel makes quite clear, there is precious little difference between Doro's eugenic exploitation of his charges and the breeding practices of slave owners in the antebellum South,[32] while at the same time the incestuous, inward-turning nature of Doro's breeding project—in which Doro breeds with generation after generation of his daughters—mirrors and mocks the most extreme fantasy of whiteness as "purity."[33]

The existence of a huge number of Africans with superpowers does nothing to stop, or in any way challenge, the slave trade; in fact, *nothing* goes differently at all, and the implication is that this could just be the secret truth behind official history as it actually happened. The narrative stability of history is thus revealed as the same kind of anti-utopian blankness Umberto Eco identified as symptomatic of superhero comics[34]—they become a story whose ending we always already know, in which nothing could ever be any different than it already is. Doro, for his part, has no interest in the politics of either slavery or abolition, except insofar as it influences his own projects; he is, after all, a vampire, and began breeding people not to perfect the human race but because he noticed that certain types of people with certain types of abilities tasted better than others (*Mind of My Mind*). Thus Doro stands in for practices of power and domination that are utterly ahistorical and, in this sense, *cannot* be resisted; in Thaler's terms, the immortal Doro "personifies time and history itself," particularly the way that "human history's gendered, unequal power structures circulate around and return to control over reproduction" (37).

Still, *Wild Seed* offers the version of Doro as a complex (and erotically compelling) antihero closest to Butler's lifelong interest in the character. As Butler developed as a writer, she realized by this point that in her early stories she had always been writing "Superman without Kryptonite"—and that it was in her characters' *weaknesses*, not their superpowers, that their stories really began.[35] Narration from within Doro's perspective in *Wild Seed* extends his backstory as a victim of diaspora (as revealed in *Mind of My Mind*), showing his anguish as he searches for his home, only to discover "it was no longer there . . . he was utterly alone"[36] and allowing his relationship with Anyawu to mature and soften his most murderous excesses. More crucial, though, we begin to see in *Wild Seed* the glimmers of what a history outside the path-dependent cycle of bad teachers and angry, resentful students might be like. Anyanwu, who appears as Doro's accomplice Emma in *Mind of My Mind*, begins *Wild Seed* as another diasporic subject, the victim of white slavers who had destroyed one of Doro's "seed villages"—breeding sites—in the Igbo region of present-day Nigeria. Anyanwu is like Doro, an immortal; but unlike Doro, her immortality originates not in body theft but in the power to shapeshift. However, her power is somewhat closer to Doro's than this description implies; for most of her career she learns the code for the person or creature she wants to shapeshift into by consuming its flesh. Doro has the power to become anyone, but Anyanwu has the power to transform herself into whatever she likes: old, young, man, woman, black, white. Anyanwu has not lived as a saint. Over her centuries she has participated in slavery when necessary for her own survival on the grounds that "it is better to be a master than a slave"—but "her own experience had taught her to hate slavery" and she immediately reformulates this as "Sometimes, one must become a master to avoid becoming a slave." This strikes some chord with Doro; "Yes," he replies, recognizing it, for that moment at least, as the key to his own bad behavior in the world.[37]

The erotic connection between Anyanwu and Doro binds her to him—they are mutually the only equal either has ever encountered—but the relationship in its first century is rarely a happy one as the two struggle for dominance. Lewis Call's reading of the relationship presents it as "the possibility of a liberating, egalitarian, consensual form of erotic slavery," "a sadomasochistic love story."[38] Doro's repeated demands for Anyanwu's total submission, and her ability to manipulate and selectively sate his desires, bind him more and more tightly to her, culminating in his final agreement to alter the terms of the breeding program that has sustained him for millennia. Anyanwu finally threatens suicide rather than participate in Doro's project any longer. He begs her not to leave, and begins to weep, not just for this moment but for "all the past times when no tears would come, when there was no relief. He could not stop." Anyanwu relents and takes care of him in his panic, becoming the stand-in replacement for the mother he had previously, unwillingly killed in the agonized moment of his transition; he sleeps on her rising and falling breast through morning. After this moment "there had to be changes": Doro agrees to no longer kill his "breeders" once he is done with them, and he further agrees never to kill any member of Anyanwu's household for any reason.[39] Thaler reads this romance in quite Hegelian terms, seeing in Doro's romance with Anyanwu his final recognition of "the Other within himself" in which he becomes totally vulnerable to her, as she had previously been to him.[40] Ironically, as we already know, these concessions will set the stage for Mary's rise and the ultimate overthrow of Doro in *Mind of My Mind*.

It is only from Anyanwu's experiences in *Wild Seed* that any outside to the Patternist hegemony looks possible at all, even conceding Thaler's acerbic observation that "the novel's closure offers a 'generous interpretation' of male sexual abuse, to put it mildly."[41] But the faint alternative historical possibilities offered in *Wild Seed* originate not so much in the "therapeutic process of the male master's codes of recognition," as Thaler would have it,[42] but in the refusal of the terms of the master altogether. In *Wild Seed* at last we find again that utopian vision of superpowers that comforted a young Octavia when she was unhappy as a child—those imagined pleasures not linked to the mere expression of power or controlling people's minds, among them flight and communication with animals. Isaac, one of the husbands Doro pairs Anyanwu with in the slavery era, is able to use his telekinetic ability to fly;[43] Anyanwu, too, is able to use her transformative powers to transform into an eagle and fly "as no human was ever meant to fly."[44] The two share this pleasure together well into Isaac's old age, enraging Doro, who sees it as a "stupid risk" in an age of firearms.[45]

Anyanwu's shapeshifting power, too, allows her to commune with animals—commune, that is, with genuine nonhuman alterity—in ways that expand her consciousness rather than igniting new cycles of violence and domination. When she is in animal form, Doro cannot track her; she is totally free from him and the historical processes of domination he represents. This aspect of *Wild Seed* suggests again Butler's early childhood fantasy of a life as a "magical horse" on "an island of horses."[46] This sense that one might become an animal as a Trickster-like means of escape, rather than for domination and violence, is a rare place in the Patternist series where these characters' incredible powers are used joyfully rather than dyspeptically. In the freest section of any of the Patternist books—perhaps the series's only genuinely liberatory, genuinely utopian moment[47]—Anyanwu transforms herself not into the horses of young Octavia's childhood fantasies but rather into a dolphin. She revels in her new strength and speed, with the heightened senses and new sensations to be found in a life underwater.[48] Hearing their speech and witnessing their complex interactions, she is able to recognize the dolphins as persons: "Alone, but surrounded by creatures like herself—creatures she was finding it harder to think of as animals. Swimming with them was like being with another people. A friendly people. No slavers with brands and chains here."[49] Removed from the water by Isaac, she forces him to promise never to eat dolphin-flesh again, and he agrees.[50]

Following Isaac's death, Anyanwu flees Doro's control and lives as a dolphin for many years, believing that the dolphins offer a life more noble than humanity's: "Perhaps when she learned their ways of communication, she would find them too honorable or too innocent to tell lies and plot murder over the still-warm corpses of their children."[51] When she reaches a dolphin community, she is initially frightened, believing—because of her bitter experiences with humans—that they might attack her as a stranger. But instead "they only came to rub themselves against her and become acquainted."[52] The dolphins welcome her into their community; they do not enslave, they do not kill, and they do not molest or rape. Anyanwu lives with them for decades; she bears dolphin children that she views as equal to her human ones. Ananywu alone in the series is able to have the kind of transformative encounter with difference that characters like Rayal, Teray, the Clayarks, Doro, and Mary are offered but all fail to honor—the cannibalistic absorption of the Other into the Self that is a "delight" rather than a "horror."[53] Even as Anyanwu uses animality as the marker for how forced breeding (as with slavery or with Doro's eugenics) degrades the human,[54] animality offers us the glimpse of a life outside the human cycle of failure that might uplift the human. Anyanwu's life among the dolphins offers the brief, tantalizing possibility of a social order where violence and power (elsewhere in Butler's canon asserted as inescapable facts of human history) are finally irrelevant. Among the dolphins, at least, strength seems not to beget domination, and genuine historical difference becomes possible—dolphin life as a more peaceful, full, whole life, a life from which we are barred because we have had so many bad teachers, but from whose radical otherness we might nonetheless be able to learn. Perhaps this communion with radical alterity might anticipate (or could inspire) the utopian countermove to the superhero's usual collapse into violence. What other worlds might superheroes make visible if they weren't always beating someone up?

ANIMALS AND OTHERS

This strong interest in animality as a heterotopic (even, perhaps, quasi-utopian) alternative to the human would persist in the works Butler wrote next, as well as in the decades to come. (By the end of her life, Butler would even become a vegetarian.[55]) As Sherryl Vint notes in "Becoming Other: Animals, Kinship, and Butler's *Clay's Ark*," the last novel in the Patternist series, *Clay's Ark*, similarly takes up the blurriness of the human / animal boundary at the moment of the origin of the Clayarks to suggest "such a radical transformation is necessary if we hope to imagine another way to be human subjects."[56] One might even imagine the never-written sixth book in the Patternist series, taking place after *Patternmaster* and inaugurating the Clayark utopia of radical hybridity, after the last Patternmaster has been eaten.

I am intrigued by the presence in her papers of research and notes for a novel she never wrote, which would have been based around primate communication and signing apes (like the famous gorilla Koko and Washoe the chimpanzee), as well as apes raised alongside humans as semi-siblings.[57] Butler was very interested in these stories, noting reports she had seen that intelligence tests had shown signing gorillas to have IQs not significantly lower than the human average, and certainly within the normal range of variations of intelligence, as we accept it within our own species. In a 1980 essay, never published, titled "How Do You Envisage First Contact with an Alien Species?" Butler cleverly pivots from the initial framing of the question to the much more down-to-earth possibility that we "have already had contact with intelligent, nonhuman species. Most of us simply haven't realized it yet."[58] Butler saw the one-sided relationship between humans and signing apes—the most egregious abuse of our generally exploitative relationship with the animal world—as the moral equivalent of other historical relations of power like coloniality, slavery, apartheid, and rape culture: a moral crime against the apes that might someday be turned upon us by "another equally arrogant and somewhat more powerful species."[59]

In May 2002 Butler wrote a too-little-noticed essay for Oprah's *O* magazine on the subject of interspecies communion, describing first her memory of an encounter with a dog at age two or three—whose eyes taught her that animals were persons, if not human people—and, second, her encounter at age seven with a miserable chimpanzee during a school visit to a dilapidated zoo:

> I remember looking at the chimp, then looking away. The chimp had somehow become the target of some of the kids' attention. They shouted at him, laughed, and threw peanuts—threw them at him rather than to him. The chimp had no-where to hide and, lucky for the kids, nothing to throw back. He leaped about and screamed, and the kids thought it was really funny. I looked at the animal's eyes—frantic, furious and maybe not sane anymore—and if I could have left the zoo at that moment, I would have. I was still too young to understand the concept of being ashamed of my species. I just felt horrible. I wanted the other kids to shut up. I wanted the chimp to be free.

The memory recalls the intense moment of interspecies empathy that launched a young Butler's interest in horse fantasy—and returned in new form, perhaps, in the zoo-like confinement that would characterize the Oankali's treatment of humans in *Dawn*. Here, too, Butler says she saw the physical cage of the zoo—which made the chimp's world "tiny, vulnerable, and barren"—as contiguous with the "metaphorical cages" of race, gender, and class that separate and demarcate us.[60]

Although it would never become a novel directly, this lifelong interest—in animal subjectivity and animal language and in the possibilities and challenges posed by interspecies communication—would come back to her again and again over the course of her life, seeding elements of important works to come in *Clay's Ark*, "Bloodchild," the Xenogenesis books, and "Amnesty." It would even become, albeit mostly in negative, part of the basis for the story that would win Butler her first major prize as a science fiction writer: 1984's bleak "Speech Sounds," in which a human race deprived of its ability to communicate becomes animal-like in that other sense, losing any capacity to resist its biological and primatological urges to dominate and to kill. "'Speech Sounds,'" she would later say in *Bloodchild*, "was conceived in weariness, depression, and sorrow"—a mental pit where Butler would often find herself in the early part of her career, as she struggled to find ways to reconcile the potential of her immense talent and dreams with the frustrated reality of her actual career. Winning a Hugo Award for "Speech Sounds" would be the start of a significant transformation in her reputation and stature that would propel her forward for the rest of her life. But that happy, long-awaited day would only come in 1984—still four long years away.

CHaPTeR 4

BLINDSIGHT (1980–1987)

Published Works

"Lost Races of Science Fiction" (1980)
"Speech Sounds" (1983)
Clay's Ark (1984)
"Bloodchild" (1984)
"The Evening and the Morning and the Night" [II] (1987)

Significant Unpublished Work

Blindsight [I] (abandoned ca. 1981)
Black Futures anthology (abandoned 1982)
Blindsight [II] (abandoned ca. 1984)
Doro-Jesus (abandoned 1970s)

In 1980 Butler published a short essay in the science fiction magazine *Transmission* titled "Lost Races of Science Fiction." The essay did not make an especially large splash, but it was very important to Butler—she often included copies of it in her letters to interviewers and to her fans as a way of explaining her attitude toward race and racism both within SF texts and within the real-world SF community. What prompted the essay, she says, was hearing a fellow SF writer in 1979 give the same bad advice she was given in 1966 in a creative-writing class during her first year of college: an exhortation "not to use black characters in . . . stories unless those characters' blackness was somehow essential to the plots." "The presence of blacks, my teacher felt, changed the focus of the story," she said, "drew attention from the intended subject."[1] Butler's rejection of this attitude was part and parcel of her lifelong ambition to "write herself in" to the genre she loved and to make the future a place inhabited by people of color too. She mocks the idea that "escapism" justifies the omission of race; it is ridiculous, she says, for the violence, kidnapping, and planetary destruction of *Star Wars* to be all in good fun—"but the sight of a minority person? Too heavy. Too real."[2] (The essay came out too early to take into account the presence of Lando Calrissian in *The Empire Strikes Back* [1980], but other documents in the Huntington archive indicate Butler was very much not impressed.) The essay names some recent examples in which black people have been included in the future, simply as people rather than as a symbol or as a "problem"—Yaphet Kotto as Parker in *Alien*, O.J. Simpson as an astronaut in *Capricorn One*—but names these examples as happy exceptions against a general trend of still-deracinated SF.

"Lost Races" also mentions the other side of Butler's critique of race and SF, what she long saw as black people's lack of interest in the future. She did not blame African Americans for this lack of interest; their lack of inclusion, and the dire lack of writers speaking to their concerns, explained the case. Butler recounts that at times she herself has been very frustrated with SF, both as a future-oriented literary practice that could not move beyond its antiquated assumptions and with regard to fandom circles, where she had often felt like an unwanted outsider. She noted also, with sadness, that the serious problems facing black people sometimes precluded their interest in imagining other worlds, ventriloquizing within the essay the sorts of words that were often hurled at her when she was young: "How can you waste your time with anything that unreal?" But Butler saw that things were changing: when she loaned books like *Dreamsnake* (by her Clarion friend Vonda McIntyre), they were read and passed on to others.

Butler's call in "Lost Races" is for white male writers of SF to embrace the genre's role as the literature of "change," even as it necessarily implied their decentering:

> SF has always been nearly all white, just as until recently, it's been nearly all male. A lot of people had a chance to get comfortable with things as they are. Too comfortable. . . . I don't think anyone seriously believes the present world is all white. But custom can be strong enough to prevent people from seeing the need for SF to reflect a more realistic view.

She saw that efforts to make SF more diverse had produced both progress and backlash (as struggles in fandom today, like the recent #Racefail controversy and the political struggles over the 2015 and 2016 Hugos continue to demonstrate). Still, her prescription for authors looking to do better was relatively nonradical: "research"; "read"; "talk to members of that group"; "people-watch." Most of all, she exhorted, white and male authors needed to remember that nonwhite and nonmale people are *people*, not "unbelievable, self-consciously manipulated puppets: pieces of furniture who exist within a story but contribute nothing to it; or stereotypes guaranteed to be offensive."[3] It was an essay that was born both in love and frustration, out of her desire for SF to do better.

In September 1980 Butler was approached by legendary science fiction editor and University of Wisconsin—Green Bay professor Martin H. Greenberg, who would later go on to co-found the Sci-Fi Channel. Greenberg wanted Butler to help him and Charles G. Waugh edit an anthology titled *Black Futures*, collecting science fiction stories about the future of race and racism. He was quite eager to work with her, offering her editorial control.[4]

She agreed to the job and immediately leaped into the work—but insisted on placing her own spin on the anthology. These would not be stories about the persistence of racism into the future or about race as a definitive and inalterable human essential; rather, they would be stories by and about black people, as *people*, people whose existence in a common future would not be incidental or tokenistic or intended as evidence for some larger, grandiose notion of human process. She was quite up front with Greenberg about this aim, writing in her first letter back to him a little over a week later that the book should not "define black futures—or blacks—so thoroughly by their difficulties with whites."[5] She sent Greenberg her "Lost Races of Science Fiction" piece as a kind of manifesto, as well as an interview from *Future Life* in a similar vein.

She further elaborated on her more ambitious hopes for the book in a letter to Toni Cade Bambara, with whom she had begun a correspondence following a frenetic and enthusiastic fan letter from Bambara about *Wild Seed*, saying she was trying to make sure *"Black Futures* doesn't become an anthology on racism" predicated on boring and outdated clichés. She needed writers like Bambara so that the book didn't "read like too much in the Black past. White ideas of what Blacks think and feel, of where Blacks are going, of where we've been."[6]

She took her role as editor very seriously; in addition to her correspondence with Greenberg and Waugh, the Butler archives even contain some of her exceedingly kind rejection letters. Her letters to Greenberg record her decision-making process: a proposed Norman Spinrad story is rejected for the presence of racist caricatures, while Robert Sheckley's "Holdout" was "ironic and cute." "Lord, I hate ironic and cute," she wrote. "Also, I kind of choked on the premise."[7] Robert Silverberg's "Black Is Beautiful" is chosen, but Butler is adamant it will be the only "future ghetto" story in the mix.[8] She adds "Reunion" by Arthur C. Clarke, "Gone Fishin'" by her old Clarion teacher Robin Scott Wilson, and the "Four-Hour Fugue" by Alfred Bester; she suggests pursuing reprint rights to John Varley's "In the Hall of the Martian Kings"—but it is clear that she is much more interested in finding new stories, preferably by black authors, than in republishing old stories by white ones. She hopes very much to expand the list beyond the familiar names of Samuel R. Delany, Stephan Barnes, and herself.

Butler's plans were very much ahead of her time: today there are many such popular anthology series in precisely the vein she imagined, from the *Dark Matter* series to *So Long Been Dreaming*, the *Apex Book of World SF*, and its sequels. One recent anthology, *Octavia's Brood*, even comprises Afrofuturist stories strongly inspired by Butler's own work. In that moment in the early 1980s, however, the book languished. Her agent, she said, was very uninterested in the project; her ongoing arguments with Doubleday made her natural publishing venue a very inhospitable place to pitch the book.[9] Her efforts to recruit well-known black authors like Toni Morrison into the project were not successful (though Bambara did herself agree to contribute).[10] Finally, in April 1982, Butler gives up on the project altogether. Delany could have finished the job, she writes dejectedly, but "we can't. Not now at least. . . . An anthology like this will sell only when more black writers gain stature in sf."[11]

The collapse of the project must have been a blow to Butler, who keenly felt the connection between struggle in the present and the imagination of alternative futures. It was her science fictional imagination (grim as it sometimes was) that had nourished her when she was young and unhappy, that had kept her going her across her life. She knew what it could do for others and even, maybe, for the world. As she would write, years later, in the unexpected closing paragraphs of her autobiographical essay "Positive Obsession":

> But still I'm asked, what good is science fiction to Black people?
>
> What good is any form of literature to Black people?
>
> What good is science fiction's thinking about the present, the future, and the past? What good is its tendency to warn or to consider alternative ways of thinking and doing? What good is its examination of the possible effects of science and technology, or social organization and political direction? At its best, science fiction stimulates imagination and creativity. It gets reader and writer off the beaten track, off the narrow, narrow footpath of what "everyone" is saying, doing, thinking—whoever "everyone" happens to be doing this year.
>
> And what good is all this to Black People?[12]

BLINDSIGHT

The failure of the *Black Futures* anthology was nothing, however, compared to the anguish Butler would feel over her next major writing project, the novel *Blindsight*, which would never be published. Of course she had "failed" before; she was no stranger to rejection, and indeed she spent most of the 1970s dejectedly writing stories no one would read, pieces she herself declared unworthy and filed away. But her long, lonely sojourn in the Patternist milieu did, in the end, produce published novels, credentialing her as a writer and (after much sacrifice) opening the door to her chosen career. In this sense *Blindsight* was the opposite: it was a rare instance for Butler where her "positive obsession" did not in the end yield returns, where she was not able to will into existence the world she wanted to live in. It was a precursor to the frustration she would feel near the end of her life, as she found herself suddenly unable to actualize on paper the stories that were completely clear in her mind's eye, forever just out of reach.

Blindsight was to be a departure from Butler's typical patterns. It had a male protagonist, which Butler had not attempted since the original *Pattern-master* (and even there the more interesting secondary character of the healer, Amber, often threatened to steal the book from its male "chosen one"). The book was a departure in another way as well; although as with *Kindred* some versions of the novel were linked to the Patternist milieu—especially the later versions, in her final desperate attempts to find some way to sell the novel— Doro and his people did not play any significant role in the book. Rather than telepaths, *Blindsight* concerned what she called *psychometry*: the psionic ability to learn facts about a person or an object through the sense of touch. It was in essence an entirely new type of narrative for Butler, one more properly a "supernatural thriller" in the Stephen King mold than science fiction. Indeed, King's domination of the best-seller charts was a source of persistent fascination for Butler, who felt sure she could match his tremendous successes if she could just find the right story—at the same time that she was preoccupied with not being perceived as a King plagiarist, particularly of *Carrie* (1974).[13]

The main character of *Blindsight* is Aaron, a man born blind but with compensatory psychometric power. Butler's earliest notes on the book, from December 1978, suggest that the narrative emphasis of the book will be on cults, and Aaron as a somewhat sinister cult leader, based on power-seeking men she had met. The same notes go on to link such men to both preaching and fascism, even suggesting that Adolf Hitler himself was such a man "during his early wandering, hungry, faceless days." (Later notes soon add the Rev. Jim Jones and Charles Manson to that august list of possible inspirations.[14]) What Butler imagines for *Blindsight* is the story of the rise of a sinister figure, from a shy, lonely childhood to the full height of his powers to his final fall— perhaps something like Mario Puzo's *The Godfather*, another bestselling book she deeply admired, which produces a compelling portrait of a person we sympathize with even as they transform into a monster. Another inspiration for the novel was Paul Atreides from Frank Herbert's Dune, a self-possessed loner who "makes the mistake of becoming a leader" and then must "learn to lead." Still another was Olaf Stapledon's *Odd John*, especially its treatment of the young superhuman whose radical *strangeness* both endangered him and made him a threat.[15] She imagines Aaron maturing rapidly and uncontrollably, even murdering a friend's sexually abusive father, before he falls under the influence of a "Rev. Davis," who would become his mentor, seeking to protect both Aaron from the world and the world from Aaron.[16]

As was typical with Butler, she did the work of sympathy too well; she quickly became too invested in the character to make him evolve into the sort of monster she initially envisioned. It is not long into her work on *Blindsight* that she is asking whether the book is a cult story or a love story.[17] The character of Kyna—the childhood friend whose abusive father Aaron kills— becomes more and more important, at times even threatening to take over the narrative entirely. This was a source of frustration for Butler, rather than source of excitement or a sign the book was going well; she became nervous that Kyna was a pale replication of Mary from *Mind of My Mind*, while Aaron and Kyna together seemed to her like a retread of *Wild Seed*'s Anyanwu and Doro. Aaron seems too much like Doro to her in general—she feels convinced she is simply writing her earlier books over again. She writes at the end of January 1979, only a few months after starting the project: "I feel on the verge of giving up."[18] Perhaps later she would have wished she had.

The love-story angle would become more and more important in later versions of the novel as Butler would write and rewrite it over the next six years. From the perspective of someone retrospectively reading the multiple versions of the novel in the Huntington Library, it might even be best to say that there are two *Blindsight*s: *Blindsight* [I] (the "cult leader" version, completed and abandoned ca. 1981) and *Blindsight* [II] (the "love" version, completed and abandoned ca. 1984). In the 1984 version love is clearly the dominant strain; by this point Aaron's religion is even characterized as a more or less good-faith ministry rather as a cult, hoax, or power play. In some of the later versions of the novel Aaron can actually use his powers to heal people, as opposed to the earlier *Blindsight* narratives, which position this sort of faith-healing as an obscene scam.

Intriguingly, the character of Rev. Davis is ultimately drawn into the love story as a third member of a now-queer, now-polyamorous triad; a book outline from 1984 lays out the terms of this unusual union in which the three are "joined strangely, irrevocably" and must now be together to be "complete," despite their phobic response to the bisexual and polyandrous nature of their triad.[19] The nontraditional sexuality of the relationship disturbs all the members of the group; in these versions of the story, when Kyna leaves town for a while it is precisely because she doesn't want to be in a three-way relationship with them.[20] But it's Rev. Davis who ultimately has the greatest difficulty processing this attraction. Where Aaron was the threat in the first versions of *Blindsight*, Davis and his extreme homophobia is the danger by the last versions. Now all three of the main characters have some version of the psychometric sense, which binds them permanently together. When all three are together, and linked, they are deeply in love and overpoweringly sexually attracted to one another—but as soon as they separate, Davis is horrified by desires he cannot explain to himself, and which he sees as irredeemably sinful. "Davis is sane only when he is with Aaron and Kyna," Butler writes in one of the last outlines for the book, adding that the climax of the novel will come when Aaron and Kyna "must prevent Davis from committing two murders—their own."[21] And this they do. At the end of the 1984 *Blindsight* Davis's attempt to burn down the house of his psychometric partners is met with an unexpected gesture of reconciliation and love; if Davis is only sane when he is with Aaron and Kyna, they resolve to take him fully and totally into their lives and never let him be alone again, becoming once and forever "a strange, dissonant triad. . . . For all but the worst of times between us, that love was enough."[22]

Blindsight never quite worked, as even Butler herself was aware; a brutal rejection letter from Houghton Mifflin in 1981 harshly declares it "one of this author's lesser works."[23] In 1982 she jokes with her agent—or perhaps only half-jokes—about submitting the failed *Blindsight* [I] as a means of forcing her publisher to fulfill a first-look options clause she found onerous.[24] And yet the novel continually pulled her back in. In 1983, even after she'd begun the Xenogenesis series, she put the new book on hold to return to *Blindsight*. The book "has some sort of hold on me," she told Vonda McIntyre in a letter, bemoaning her inability to declare it finally dead even as she attempted to "cannibalize" its key elements for other stories.[25] She sends pages from *Blindsight* [II] to her agent in 1984, calling it the "new, leaner, stronger" *Blindsight*, but by 1985 her claims are much more jaundiced, declaring the book not a masterpiece but (merely) "salable."[26] In her private journals, she is much more brutally honest about the book, calling it a "thin and impoverished version of *Mind of My Mind*" and (the worst crime of all) "boring."[27]

It's in this final attempt to sell *Blindsight* that she leans most heavily on its weak connection to the Patternmaster universe; now Aaron is a forgotten son of Doro, and the triad is "a group of almost-Patternists who don't fit anywhere except with each other."[28] But the book never sells, and five years later (at the start of her writing the Parables books) she views it as a cautionary tale about her own tendencies toward nonproductive writing (another unmarked danger of her "positive obsession"):

> Please take the outline and chapters of *Justice* that I sent you and *toss them out!* I'm keeping the characters' names and the concept of contagious empathy, but probably nothing else. The story was beginning to feel the way an earlier novel called *Blindsight* used to—always just a little out of reach and never very interesting. Ask Felicia how many times I rewrote *Blindsight*. No, don't ask her. Even she doesn't really know. Thoroughly bad business.[29]

By 1989, at least—with Xenogenesis finished and already a success—*Blindsight* had become something to laugh about. In any event, at that point, it was really dead and gone: cannibalized after all, with both the idea of a magical "healing touch" and reluctant, semi-consensual, polyamorous unions transmogrifying into important elements of the Oankali in the Xenogenesis books, and the idea of a lonely, precocious child who grows up to be the potentially noble, potentially sinister leader of a fringe religious movement lingering in her mind as the germ for the Parables.

But in the mid-1980s, at the height of her struggle with *Blindsight*, Butler's situation wasn't nearly so humorous, and her attitude toward *Blindsight*'s failure was nowhere near sanguine. Her inability to complete and sell the novel was leaving her desperate, and not only on the level of money (though this was still a perennial worry for her). She had a book she couldn't afford to finish, and couldn't afford not to finish. And the crisis was as artistic as it was financial: she was worried, and not for the first time, that she was running out of ideas, remixing her old work in less and less satisfying ways.[30]

My own work on this project becomes a very tiny footnote in this story. After excerpting a small portion of this book in the *Los Angeles Review of Books* in summer 2014, I received an email from Morgan S. Brilliant, who worked at Ace Science Fiction in the late 1980s. My role as a scholar working in the archive had been misreported in one media outlet, leaving the impression that

I have some connection to or control over the Butler literary estate. (Alas, I do not.) That's why Brilliant wrote to me. She recalls discovering a copy of *Blindsight* at Ace while moving offices, and contacting Butler to see what she wanted to do with it. "She told me that she had withdrawn the book from submission because she was no longer interested in seeing it published. She asked me to be certain that it was not published. I don't know whether there is a copy in her papers. If so, I ask that you please respect her wishes regarding *Blindsight*." I couldn't help but be struck by the intense loyalty and admiration Butler inspired in those who read her work, as evidenced by this effort to keep that promise nearly thirty years later—as well as by the strength of Butler's rejection of an intriguing but very tangled novel, a magnificent wreck that she had finally grown well and truly sick of.

ANNUS MIRABILIS

Though Butler would never get *Blindsight* to work, she soon had a miraculous period of productivity that produced her three best (and best-known) short stories, as well as the Patternist apocalypse novel *Clay's Ark*. Later in her life she would think back to the writing of *Clay's Ark* as a marker of what she was capable of when she was most driven: although as with her other Patternist novels she had tinkered with the idea since her childhood, and had begun a flawed and abandoned version of it in the 1970s, once she began writing the novel in earnest she produced a chapter a week.[31] But she would also, in a more negative vein, sometimes think of *Clay's Ark* as the last good time before her well had "run dry," before her experiences with writing became so completely defined by her writer's block.[32]

Clay's Ark is an apocalypse story, which tells the origins of the twisted, sphinx-like monsters who bedevil the far-future Patternists in *Patternmaster*. The book proceeds along two parallel narrative tracks: the first, about Eli, the survivor of a spacecraft crash, who has been compelled by an extraterrestrial virus to survive and spread his disease even as he knows it will mean the end of the human race; the second, about a doctor who, while traveling with his daughters, encounters the isolated town Eli has infected with the disease, which is struggling to quarantine itself from the world it threatens. Already set in a broken-down future, the book is dominated by an apocalyptic sensibility, amplified once again by our knowledge of the later books in the series, which demonstrate that the virus definitely *will* escape, society *will* collapse, the human race (if not necessarily the book's characters) *is* doomed. This sense of an imminent apocalypse that has somehow already happened can be found in the textual history of *Clay's Ark* as well; she originally sets the book in the present, then shifts it to thirty-eight years into the future (just as, she said to her editor, thirty-eight years ago "Hiroshima was bombed, TV was about to come into its own, jet planes existed and had been used, and Southern California had a water problem"—a world that was both remarkably similar and remarkably different.) Thirty-eight years was enough time for the world to be transformed yet still recognizable, enough time for the problems we are ignoring in the present to have grown into insolvable crises.[33]

The importance of cancer in novel, both as a plot point (one of the characters suffers from leukemia) and as a sort of overriding structural logic (that apocalyptic sense of having only *x* months to live before a final, inescapable end), is no accident: Butler wrote the book while a close friend was dying of cancer, and she shared chapters with the friend with the bleak sense that she might not live to see the book completed. It was perhaps at least partially for this reason that Butler wrote *Clay's Ark* so quickly in the 1980s, when the idea had been with her for so long without much progress: a chapter a week was an astonishingly quick pace for her.

Her sadness for her friend and the sense of mournful grieving that permeates *Clay's Ark* can also be felt in the three short stories Butler is able to write and publish during this period (another significant anomaly in her career). "Speech Sounds"—a story about a human race that has almost entirely lost the ability to speak due to unknown reasons, causing the slow-motion collapse of civilization—was inspired by Butler's many years riding Los Angeles County mass transit, specifically by a fight she once witnessed between two men on the bus. In fact, as she recounts in the *Bloodchild* afterword, the incident happened while she was going to see her sick friend, the combination of tragic death with pointless violence filling her with a sort of maximum despair.[34]

The atmosphere of the story is extremely dark, pervaded by hopelessness, tokened most directly perhaps by the main character's status as a Butler stand-in (living in L.A. for the previous fifteen years after having grown up in Pasadena) who has lost the ability to read and write and now "could not even read her own manuscripts."[35] The woman, Rye, has lost her entire family, including three children—and the world itself is dying as humans regress not simply to prehistory but to prehumanity, becoming more like primates than people. Rye is drawn to the idea of suicide, an event she sees as inevitable. A brief sexual liaison with another survivor (who has been futilely working as a cop in the ruins of civilization) temporarily gives her hope, but he is killed while attempting to stop a man on the street from attacking a woman. Once all three participants in the altercation are dead, Rye discovers the two children who belonged to the pair, but she plans to leave them behind, reasoning that they are old enough to fend for themselves. It is a bleak story—but the despair unexpectedly gives way to hope when she hears the children are able to speak:

> Fluent speech! Had the woman died because she could talk and had taught her children to talk? Had she been killed by a husband's festering anger or by a stranger's jealous rage? And the children . . . they must have been born after the silence. Had the disease run its course, then? Or were these children simply immune? Certainly they had had time to fall sick and silent. Rye's mind leaped ahead. What if children of three or fewer years were safe and able to learn language? What if all they needed were teachers? Teachers and protectors.[36]

Rye's entire worldview becomes reoriented around this possibility, and she reveals (both to the reader and to the children) that she too has retained the ability to speak. Something human persists, not just in each of them individually but in the circuit they make now that they are together. The story's redemptive ending is an unexpected note of hope where none had seemed possible, one of Butler's most uncomplicatedly "happy" endings despite how grim the story had been to that point; Rye will care for the children and guard the future, in the process staving off suicide by living through others. The children are confused and frightened, but she comforts them: "'I'm Valerie Rye,' she said, savoring the words. 'It's all right for you to talk to me.'"[37]

"Bloodchild" (original title: "Bloodworm") has an ending similarly resonant with the future-facing optimism of reproductive futurity, though this one is significantly more fraught. It takes place on an alien world where desperate humans have made an unusual deal with the Tlic to serve as incubators for their reproduction. The humans were "fleeing from their homeworld, from their own kind who would have killed or enslaved them"[38]—a suggestion, or at least a variation, of the Patternist/Missionary milieu—and on the planet they encountered the Tlic, who were suffering from a population crisis caused by ecological collapse. (The animals [native to their planet] that they used as hosts for their reproduction had begun rejecting Tlic eggs.) The two species did not recognize each other as mutual persons at first, but they came to an uneasy alliance in the face of their mutual precarity: now the humans live in a Preserve, guarded from the mass of the Tlic population by Tlic elites, with some of their children being earmarked for eventual use in mating. The mating, during which Tlic lay eggs in the human, which are then pulled out of the body one by one, is ghastly, and frequently goes wrong; if even one egg is left behind, it would poison the host as it eats its way out. (Butler based this macabre practice on the real-life biology of the botfly.) Indeed, as the story progresses, Gan, the protagonist, sees one mating ritual go wrong, and his Tlic partner is forced to pull the grubs out of a bloody, eviscerated human male, one by one. The humans in the story have no power and no ability to leave the situation; they must compromise with the Tlic or die. Even the Tlic tendency to impregnate men rather than women comports with this perverted reproductive futurity: women are needed to produce human babies that can "provide the next generation of host animals," while men are superfluous. Gan is horrified by the future he faces but insists that the relationship is not purely about economics or exploitation. Still, he despairs, confronting his Tlic mate (T'Gatoi) with a gun to his head, threatening to end his life. But in the end of the story, faced with the choice to escape his destiny, Gan instead chooses it, in part because he accepts T'Gatoi's argument that the relationship between humans and Tlic is not parasitic but a kind of marriage, and in part because of his need to protect his sister from suffering the fate in his place. But Gan also, in some sense, desires the mating in its own terms:

> "But you came to me . . . to save Hoa."
>
> "Yes." I leaned my forehead against her. She was cool velvet, deceptively soft. "And to keep you for myself," I said. It was so. I didn't understand it, but it was so.[39]

"It amazes me that some people have seen 'Bloodchild' as a story of slavery," Butler would write in the afterword to the version of the story published in her *Bloodchild* collection. She saw it, she said, as a love story, as well as a coming of age story. But even her own lengthy discussion of the inspiration for the story returns, in the end, to the notion of "paying the rent": the desperation that would accompany human beings living on an extrasolar world perhaps a generation away from reinforcements or resupply. "Sooner or later, the humans would have to make some kind of accommodation with their um . . . their hosts," Butler writes. "Who knows what we humans have that others might be willing to take in trade for a livable space on a world not our own?"[40] The story itself primes precisely the more negative reading Butler says she rejects, when Gan's brother tells Gan he is just T'Gatoi's "property." The deep ambiguity of the ending, in which Gan surrenders to T'Gatoi's "care," would be replicated on a much larger scale in Butler's next major novel series, with similar levels of debate about the fairness of the arrangement—and Butler similarly seeming to side with the aliens.

Finally, the story published with the title "The Evening and the Morning and the Night," though quite different from the original 1970s story of a doomed space crash (see chapter 2), shares with it the question of whether there is some possible limit to the call that reproductive futurity makes on us to ensure the existence of children and thereby of the future. In the 1980s story the characters have been born with a severe inherited disability, Duryea-Gode Disease (DGD), modeled on Huntington's disease, which condemns them to suffer permanent, self-destructive insanity unexpectedly but inevitably at some point in their middle years. The characters refuse the idea of ever having children, even as this suggests to them that they themselves should never have been born—and many do indeed attempt suicide. The published version of the story suggests some resolution, that colonies of the sufferers might be able to live together and have meaningful, even extraordinary lives, stabilized by the pheromonic proximity of certain special female characters like the narrator—at least until their time comes. The published version of "Evening" suggests a certain sort of middle ground between reproductive futurity and sterility / suicide: no children, maybe, but not no future. The colonies of sufferers of DGD are not simply condemned to permanent darkness; they are still human lives, with human potential.[41]

But Butler's drafts for the story point us in other directions. One early draft ends in an orgy, a "strange, silent, gentle orgy"—a different sort of utopia, one suggesting perhaps Edelman's "no future" utopia of sex without children.[42] In another, the community sourly breaks down as the men and women become unable to pair bond in the ways that had once, briefly, seemed utopic: "The similarity that had brought us together seemed to have turned into something else altogether."[43] Most interesting is the version in which Lynn is tempted by a vision of disabled, queered futurity, but refuses it: she is a "potential Doro" who realizes she can be "a power" if she exploits others but chooses to say no, "thus agreeing to the quiet, bloodless extinction by attrition of her people."[44]

This last version is a story, I think, that Butler wanted to write but never found a way to, the story that in some sense she seemed to find untellable: the story of the people who in the end *do* say "no," who refuse the instinct to live at whatever cost, the ones who refuse to compromise even if it means their destruction. She was fascinated in her writing by the idea there might be some limit point past which life might actually become intolerable, past which survival *wasn't* desirable or possible—and seemed dedicated, in her delightfully grim way, of pushing her characters closer and closer to that line to see what might lie on the other side. Even her stories most devoted to reproductive futurity and survival actually end on this kind of gray or sour note, this moment of doubt, despite their surface optimism: the dead-end sterility of the Patternists, the toxic parasite-reproductivity of the Tlic aliens in "Bloodchild," the historical amnesia at the end of *Kindred* into which all the antebellum characters fall, and so on. Such ambiguous endings would become even more common in the later works, even those that (superficially at least) seem to end on an upbeat note; the optimism tends to fall away upon further inspection or reflection.

Butler was acutely aware in her own life of how the optimism normally associated with reproductive futurism can, agonizingly, break down, from her father's early death to her mother's four previous stillbirths, which gave her a keen, lifelong sense of the ways in which pregnancy can figure things other than pure, unvarnished, uncomplicated hope. She was similarly intensely aware—especially as her life went on and she remained unpartnered—that she would not have children herself. The Huntington contains the fragment of a late-1970s interview (seemingly never published, and perhaps a fictional exercise never actually intended for circulation) in which she says that she has *never* desired to have children.[45] A letter from Toni Cade Bambara transforms this slightly, in its indication that during the 1980s Butler briefly considered adopting a child[46]—but generally speaking Butler seemed not to have had an urge for biological children of her own. Her books, she said often and quite directly, were her children—and not simply in some symbolic logic of compensation, but also in the much more literal sense that she expected them to *earn* so they could provide for her in her old age.[47]

MOVING ON

The creative burst of 1983 cemented Butler's place at the top of her profession. "Speech Sounds" won the Hugo Award for Best Short Story, to her great shock and delight;[48] the next year, "Bloodchild" swept the Hugo, Nebula, and Locus awards for Best Novelette. ("The Evening and the Morning and the Night" would be Nebula-nominated but did not win that prize.)

Butler enthusiastically told an interviewer that *Clay's Ark* would not be the last Patternist or Missionary novel, as that universe was still a "fascinating second home" to her even after so many years of inhabiting it. And the Huntington archive is filled with teases of the way that world might have developed, as in the fascinating unfinished *Doro-Jesus* fragment (mid-1970s), where Doro impregnates the Virgin Mary (in a lengthy sex scene) and produces Christ (naturally, a Patternist), who is so talented as to *almost* be the two-thousand-years-too-early fulfillment of the breeding project and yet who instead becomes a famously chaste, sexless reproductive dead end. (The two instead become enemies, with Doro cast in the role of Satan the tempter, and most of the major events of the New Testament being recast as the misadventures of Doro and Jesus.[49]) This idea of a Christ figure betrayed and murdered by his closest lieutenant stuck with her even after the connection to Doro was cut, becoming at different times the spark for versions of *Blindsight*, an undeveloped 1980s idea for a novel called *Martyr*,[50] and finally the early, abandoned versions of what would eventually become the Parables series.

Another sketch, sometimes mentioned by Butler in interviews and similarly appearing in her notes as far back to the mid-1970s, suggests Doro as a possible first-person narrator describing his experiences growing up in Egypt and, perhaps, making him as sympathetic a character for her readership as he always had been in Butler's mind. In 1986, noting her pressing need to establish an income stream for the coming years, she briefly considers combining both ideas into a historical Patternist trilogy: the Egypt story, the Christ story, then a novel about Doro's actions during the fall of Rome. Years later, during her miserable writer's block starting in the 1990s, she imagines returning to the well again to write a story about Doro during the Civil War, thinking the familiar Patternist milieu might somehow break the ice for her and allow her to write again.

At the same time, however, Butler felt a need to put the Patternists behind her and "move on, explore new people, new information."[51] She had recently (in 1982) traveled to the Soviet Union as part of a group of science-fiction-writer tourists, an event she recounts for possible public consumption in OEB 2445 ("SF Tourist") and in much more private, intimate terms in OEB 7. The trip had left her thinking about national and cultural difference. Soon, in 1985, she would travel to Peru as part of a UCLA study group, studying the ecology of the Amazon, and being inspired not simply by the locale but by the radical oddness of some of the plants and animals she saw there. She had begun to understand her work as partaking in a new mode of SF, which had first developed as a genre during the Industrial Revolution but was now confronting the "Biological Revolution" of "genetic engineering, psychobiology, ethology, sociobiology"—world-transforming scientific practices that were simultaneously "fascinating" and "terrifying," and which were (and are still) transforming our idea of what it means to be human.[52] She continued to study cancer, still seeking ways it could be made "compelling aop [as opposed to] repulsive and disgusting"; she continued to believe she could make cancer "fascinating" and "utterly sexy."[53]

The books she does write next *are* still Patternist books, in a way—they take up various discarded and failed elements from her 1970s and 1980s false starts and combine them with new twists on the thematic concerns that drove her miracle year of 1983. At the same time, they represent her greatest departure yet from the speculations that had driven her teenage imagination, positing a similarly ambiguous but very different sort of future for the human race from the nightmare of Patternist domination: a troubled, and troubling, new dawn.

CHaPTeR 5

THE TRAINING FLOOR (1987–1989)

Published Works

Dawn (1987)
Adulthood Rites (1988)
Imago (1989)

The first mention of the "Oankali" in the stories in the Butler archive is from the early 1970s, in another planned extension of "Missionary" stories set in her Patternist universe. In one strain of incomplete stories, the "Thomas" captivity narratives, human Missionaries fleeing Earth encounter a race called the Ooankali, who enslave them; in surviving fragments we see the Ooankali "buyers" strip humans naked, evaluating them before "selling" them. The Ooankali brutalize their slaves; Thomas has seen the "scars" on those they had bought. But he knew he would be sold to *some* Ooankali, so he has little hope but to anticipate a rich buyer, who would be "less likely to be brutal or stupid, more likely to buy us as status symbols, curiosities. Also, the rich could afford the least deformed of us."[1] Versions of the Thomas narrative remain on Butler's "to-do" list for the next ten years, though the story never develops in a way she finds satisfying or successful.

In another strain of abandoned stories, the Aaor stories, the Oankali are not necessarily slavers, but rather appear as another fugitive race settling with human Missionary exiles on some distant extrasolar world, having also fled their home. Both the Oankali and the humans have severe fertility problems, as well as rampant genetic diseases, likely caused by their presence on a world not their own. The humans in particular are desperate to prevent nonviable mutants from reaching sexual maturity and reproducing, resorting to brutal disciplinary measures to restrain the sexuality and fertility of outlier humans—even as the human form itself has grown completely strange in the context of their new world, merging with the look of the Oankali. The primary human character, Jodas, has a mother who has "chosen" to be "over two meters tall," with claws for hands; other "assimilationist" families had begun to grow sensory arms like the Oankali's. Aaor is an ooloi, which here (as in the canonical Xenogenesis books) is a nonmale, nonfemale third sex that the humans have difficulty seeing as anything but male. Severely disabled by the standards of the Oankali, Aaor is blind, having only one pair of "totally useless" eyes instead of the Oankali's usual two.

Although Oankali and human bonding "had been forbidden as far back in history as records went," Jodas and Aaor are bonded as part of a special experiment to see if "cripples of different species" could "satisfy each other enough to make mutilation and imprisonment unnecessary." The Aaor stories, too, are unfinished, though Butler's handwritten notes on the fragment I have been quoting from suggest that Jodas and Aaor's bonding will become highly dangerous when the two species are revealed to be cross-fertile after all, thereby threatening the social order of both their societies.[2]

The quoted story dates to the mid-1980s, but other versions of the Aaor narrative can be dated much further back in the archive and, like the Thomas narrative, remained a perennial entry on the list of stories she used to berate herself whenever she suffered writer's block. One journal entry from 1974, which considers a version of the Oankali master narrative that pairs the Thomas and Aaor versions, sees the central conflict of the possible combination story as the unexpected conflict between a slave and his own people.[3] Another journal entry from 1977 imagines combining the very early version of *Clay's Ark* (at this time also partially a Missionary story), with which she is struggling, with either the Thomas or Aaor narratives, or both: "Clay has fled from a world of telepaths, and come down into another world of them."[4] A different early note for Xenogenesis imagines the Oankali encountering the Patternists on Earth, in some previously unimagined moment in the Patternist mythos, with the two societies needing to find some way to communicate despite being totally "incomprehensible to each other on a psionic level."[5]

Three more abandoned narratives are worth mentioning briefly before transitioning into discussion of the published Xenogenesis books. The first, "Shepherds," is one of Butler's earliest stories, dated September 22, 1962. Written from the perspective of an alien child with a genius-level intellect and incredible psionic powers living in hiding among humans, it describes aliens that evolved "countless billions of years ago when even the universe was young" "from the black airlessness that was space itself." The Shepherds are the first race, watchers who guide younger species toward maturity and protect them from their self-destructive tendencies. This idea—an ineffably old, radically nonhuman race that mentors and protects humanity even in the face of the most self-destructive tendencies *Homo sapiens* exhibit—would be transformed, and significantly complicated, in the Xenogenesis books, but the kernel of the idea comes to Butler extremely early in her life.[6]

The second story is even earlier: a Flash / Silver-Star story Butler first wrote in 1958 (perhaps the very night she saw *Devil Girl from Mars*), which depicts the UFO visitation that inaugurates Estelle / Silver Star / Shaar's adventures in the solar system. The OEB 592 version of this story contains a scene that is the clear progenitor, nearly thirty years early, of the scene in *Dawn* in which Lilith confronts an alien so horrible she can barely stand to look at it—right down to the tentacles. Butler was not kidding when she wrote in "Positive Obsession" that writers "use everything";[7] she kept all her papers for a reason.

The third crucial proto-Xenogenesis is an aborted early-1980s rewrite of the 1970s "The Evening and the Morning and the Night," about the failed Missionary group of one man and several women crashed permanently on an alien world, where one has become pregnant. As with the earlier short story, the other members of the expedition have usually all died, either in the

Octavia E. Butler
Post Office Box 6604
Los Angeles, CA 90055
(818) 794-0925

DAWN Pronunciation Guide

Iyapo---ee-YAH-po

Oankali---OH-an-kah-lee

ooloi---OO-LOY

ooan---oo-AN

Jdahya---j-DAH-yah
   (The "j" is barely pronounced) Sounds a little like "ch.")

Tediin---teh-DEEN

Kahguyaht---Kah-goo-YAHT (rhymes with yacht)

Dinso---deen-SO

Kaaltediinjdahya lel Kaguyaht aj Dinso---
   Kahl-teh-DEEN-j-DAH-yah lel kah-goo-YAHT aj deen-SO

kaizidi---kai-ZEE-dee

Tiej---tee-EDGE

Ahajas---ah-ha-JAHS

Dichaan---di-CHAHN (rhymes with Juan)

Akjai---ak-JAII(rhymes with my)

Toaht---toe-AHT (rhymes with forgot)

quatasayasha---quatta-say-ASH-ah

Tehjaht---teh-JAHT

   (In Oankali words, vowels are pronounced this way:

ah, eh, ee, oh, oo.)

1. *Dawn* pronunciation guide (OEB 5404)

initial crash or in the subsequent hardship. The short list of character names intended for this planned rewrite will be familiar to anyone who knows the later Xenogenesis books: Joseph, Leah, Celene, Wray, Tate.[8] The existence of Butler's early notes for Xenogenesis reveals an amusing metafictional joke in the published novel, in which Lilith looks over the dossiers of sleeping humans and tries to decide which ones she should Awaken;[9] this was precisely Butler's situation as she began writing. She had all the characters lined up; now she just needed to figure out which ones to use, and what to do with them.

The notes for this planned narrative ultimately diverge in two distinct narratives as the main point-of-view character, "Ayre," becomes better and better refined. The idea of a young girl whose "relentless, absolute obsession" marks her as an emergent leader for the group—even after she becomes pregnant by "the only other black person present," a dying man much older than she[10]—buds off as inspiration for the Parables books that would define Butler's later career. The other version of Ayre, the reluctant Moses who is "drafted unwillingly into the service of her people and of those who hold God-like power over her [and who] will not be permitted access to her promised land"—their unlikely Harriet Tubman—is given a different name: Lilith.[11]

MEET THE OANKALI

Lilith, Butler's most consummate and complicated survivor, is at the center of the Xenogenesis books; even as the later books in the series shift focus toward Akin (her human-Oankali hybrid son) and Jodahs (her ooloi child), Lilith remains our touchstone, the character to whom we always return. It's no wonder that when the books were retitled for sale as a single volume, they were retitled "Lilith's Brood": the books brood over Lilith and her brood, even as she herself broods over what she has chosen to do and what she has had to do to survive. Where *Kindred* asked its readers to come to terms with the choices that black ancestors had made to survive—hard choices that were the necessary prerequisite for lives like Butler's to exist in the present—the Xenogenesis books translate this interest in reproductive futurity into a choice yet unmade in the present, and they ask how far along the line of complicity and collaboration we are willing to go in the name of collective survival, in the name of a future whose terms seem more and more constrained. A reader's evaluation of Lilith as a character is therefore closely linked to their evaluation of the Oankali as a whole, a question that has sharply divided scholarship over the books. Are the Oankali humanity's saviors or its executioners? Do they represent a deviation from the colonial and imperial history that has made human history such an existential horror, or do they rather represent the ultimate perfection of the colonial enterprise? Butler's characteristic ambivalence, and ambiguity, leaves the question of the true nature of the Oankali hanging over all three books, still in narrative suspension even as the third book concludes. But the effect does not produce frustration so much as fierce debate, not simply in a classroom of students encountering the books for the first time but also in the reader who is returning to them for the fifth. I hope I do not give away too much to admit that these are my favorites of Butler's fictions, the books I find both most fun and most interesting, even as the problems they lay out seem to me to be the most challenging, even ultimately insurmountable. They also represent, I think, the key turning point in Butler's lifelong investigation of the mystery of human nature, formulating the questions that would dominate the latter half of her career.

Dawn begins in the aftermath of a nuclear war. Lilith, one of the war's few survivors, Awakes in captivity; in fact, she Awakes over and over, and over again, as her unseen captors interrogate her and return her to sleep. Finally, she is told that she is to be released; the captivity, they say, has been a terrible mistake, caused by their lack of understanding of her species. She has been captured by aliens, the Oankali, whom she is now allowed to see for the first time. The Oankali are three-sexed, with a nongenetically reproducing thirdsex (the *ooloi*) facilitating reproduction between Oankali mates using an inborn talent for complex genetic manipulation and engineering (as natural to them as taste or smell are to us). Over time—when the book begins it has been centuries since the war that destroyed humanity—the Oankali have bred themselves into vaguely human form to make more palatable their encounter with the rescued humans they have been keeping in suspended animation. But despite this effort they remain unspeakably grotesque—the mythological comparison that is made is to Medusa, with tentacles for sense organs, while in an interview with Charles Rowell, Butler compared the Oankali to a photo of an invertebrate in a biology textbook to which she had a phobic response so extreme she nearly dropped the book.[12] To glimpse an Oankali for the first time causes a similarly uncontrollable visceral reaction of terrified revulsion in human beings—and Lilith does find them completely horrible to look at but is able to control her terror in a way that makes her suitable for the Oankali's larger plans. She is also offered, once and only once, the opportunity to kill herself rather than to go forward, by grasping onto an Oankali stinger; while tempted, she finds herself driven by the need to go on living, a relentless personal drive that will paradoxically make her both a compelling hero and the perfect agent for the Oankali.

The Oankali, she is told, arrived in the aftermath of the war and discovered a human race reduced to living like animals in a now-radioactive environment. Without the aliens' assistance, humans would have all died out. But the Oankali intervened: they rescued as many humans they were able and brought them up to their spaceship to rest in suspended animation while the planet healed. Lilith is told she is actually in their spaceship now, though it takes her quite a while to accept this fact.

In the case of humanity, the Oankali have violated their usual practices with regard to encountering intelligent life; in a social norm along the lines of *Star Trek*'s "Prime Directive," developed over the incomprehensible span of the Oankali's life as a spacefaring species, the Oankali are typically content to allow broken or dysfunctional species to commit species suicide without any interference.[13] But humans are special: their DNA produces cancers. Butler was partially inspired here by the story of Henrietta Lacks, a dying black woman from Baltimore whose cells were extracted to create the immortal HeLa stem cell line (still widely used in medicine today) but who received scant compensation or even *information* about what was being done with her body.[14] Butler was also still thinking about the death of her friend around the time of *Clay's Ark*.[15] Lilith's own body produces a particularly attractive, HeLa-style form of very aggressive cancer, the cancer that killed her mother and would have killed her without Oankali intervention. And cancer to the Oankali is an incredible, intoxicating prize, worth almost any price. The Oankali are gene traders: they exchange genes with the species they meet for the purposes of enriching and extending their own species form. From a human perspective the Oankali already possess bewildering superpowers, chief among them the ability to modify their own DNA and the DNA of others without the intervention of technology or medicine; they can do it through the sense of touch. But the addition of cancer to their genome would allow incredible amplification of their powers, essentially granting them a maximum plasticity that would include immortality and shape-changing, just for starters. The Oankali *will* have cancer, Lilith is told; she can choose to participate in the merging of the two species' genomes, or she can choose to be put back to sleep, but whether she chooses to help or not, the two species *will* be merged and Human-Oankali hybrids *will*, generations from now, leave Earth with this new power of cancer in their genome. Any human who cannot work with the Oankali has no future: the characters in *Dawn* who resist (like Peter, who is accidentally killed attacking his ooloi) or Derrick (who attempts to escape and explore the ship[16]) are returned to storage, removed from the future, potentially permanently.

Lilith, for better and worse, chooses the future over either literal or metaphorical suicide; she agrees to help the Oankali achieve their goals. She is another of Butler's great compromisers, choosing to survive, despite the costs. She is taken first to her new Oankali family, where she is given the instruction and tools necessary to help her integrate into their strange society, and then to the "nursery," where she will help pick the first group of humans to Awake. The series traces the story of Lilith's interactions with the Oankali, first in captivity on the spaceship and then, with her children, in collaboration with them on Earth.

Like the first race of "Shepherds," in the Xenogenesis books the Oankali are ineffably old and characterized by a civilizational ethos that combines a zeal for life with quiet sadness in roughly equal parts. They are space explorers; on one of the rare occasions when they talk about their homeworld, they call the planet "a womb" and say they left when "the time had come for us to be born."[17] As Lilith says, this attitude is quite recognizable in the outer-space optimism on both sides of the Cold War, from the rhetoric and imagery driving John F. Kennedy's "New Frontier" to Konstantin Eduardovich Tsiolkovsky's well-known proclamation that "Earth is the cradle of humanity, but one cannot live in a cradle forever." But the difference is that humanity's experiments with rockets ended in nuclear missiles that destroyed the human race, while the Oankali were able to make the dream real. Now the Oankali homeworld exists only in the deep past, "the one direction that's closed to us," as Jdahya puts it; he even says they left the planet so long ago, "I doubt that it does still exist." The Oankali in this sense remain the diasporic exiles of those 1970s scribblings; they, like the Missionaries and like the humans they have Awakened, can never go home again.

The Oankali have embraced this impermanence, however, rather than mourned it. Their entire civilization is now based around constant division and redivision as they wander the galaxy, incorporating new genetic traits and new life forms into their racial makeup. The implication within the novel is that these trades, as well as the constant influx of new genes, are necessary for the Oankali species to stay vital.[18] Whenever the Oankali encounter suitable new life, they hybridize the two species into a new admixture that continues to travel the stars. This process has three components:

> *Toaht*: One-third of the Oankali collective will take a portion of the surviving humans and one-half of the existing Oankali spacecraft, and they will head off again into the stars to interbreed with each other while on the interstellar journey. *Dinso*: A second third of the Oankali collective will stay behind on Earth and hybridize with humans *here*, while in the process slowly turning the entire planet Earth into a new spaceship that will eventually break orbit and leave the solar system to explore the galaxy on its own. *Akjai*: The remaining third of the Oankali collective will take the second half of the fleet and leave the solar system by a third heading, totally unchanged, as a kind of control group, in case the interbreeding doesn't work out or produces toxic results.

The first Oankali Lilith meets, Jdhaya, even speaks (somewhat mournfully) of the possibility that the descendants of his and Lilith's group, the Dinso, will someday meet up with the descendants of the Toaht and Akjai groups, many millennia hence, to exchange the genes they have picked up in the intervening eons. Lilith suggests that by then the two groups might not even recognize each other as kin, but Jdhaya explains that the memory is biological, and he claims he can remember every division that has taken place in his strain of the Oankali going back to the original species that left the Oankali homeworld.[19]

The Oankali we meet in the novel are thus, in fact, only one tiny sliver of a larger Oankali race/civilization that travels the full galaxy and whose form is totally protean, unmoored from any specific relationship to biology, environment, economics, or politics that might endanger species survival. The Oankali, to an almost unthinkably radical extent, *adapt*; they are thus able to achieve species immortality precisely by removing their attachment to any particular sense of identity. From their perspective what they are offering the humans—survival via transformation—is therefore the most natural thing in the world. That humans are not especially interested in taking the deal is simply not a relevant question from their perspective. First, the idea of refusal only speaks to a larger human irrationality; only a mad race would choose death over life. Second, the extremity of their need overrides all other consideration; at the deepest core of their being, they must trade, and that is that. Third, and perhaps most crucial, introducing cancer into their genome will allow such tremendous amplification of their powers that the human reluctance to do it simply does not matter.

From a human perspective that values stability and continuity of form, however, this is simply a second, slow-motion apocalypse to follow the first. Humankind is to be bred out of existence and merged into the Oankali collective—the survivors of the nuclear war will not bear human children but rather human-Oankali hybrids. From the Oankali perspective, this is a mutual exchange that will alter *both* species; but the majority of the humans in the novel (including many of those who surrender to the Oankali's terms) reject this interpretation and believe (in the logic of the "one-drop" rule) that these altered children will be Oankali and thus not human at all.

Intriguingly, much of the academic criticism on the novel, while acknowledging the Oankali's deeply ambiguous status as both humanity's saviors and its aggressive colonizers, has taken the Oankali's side of the debate. Donna Haraway takes up the Oankali books as an "ironic salvation history,"[20] an instance of her posthuman cyborg theory's embrace of radical self-difference; she glowingly writes that the Oankali's "essence is embodied commerce, conversation, communication—with a vengeance. Their nature is always to be midwife to themselves as other."[21] Citing the Oankali's vegetarianism, Nolan Belk similarly writes that "the goal of existence for the Oankali—their only goal—is to work for the betterment of life."[22] Nick DiChario gushingly characterizes the Oankali as "non-hierarchical, nonviolent, very cooperative, unable to make small distinguishing characteristics based just on appearance"[23] (which is to say, they are anti-racist, anti-sexist, anti-homophobic). As should be obvious, the Oankali seem on the surface to be quite compatible with the postmodern, postcolonial politics of difference that remains quite fashionable on the academic left (and for quite good reasons!).[24]

This pro-Oankali position, I would venture, is probably the "intended" reading of the novel, such as it is. In important ways Butler significantly stacks the deck in favor of the Oankali. First, they appear for most of the first two books to be effectively omniscient and omnipotent, befitting a galactic civilization that is thousands and perhaps millions of years old—in stark contrast to the humans, whose brief fiddling with advanced technology resulted in nuclear mass extinction in well under a century. (That the Oankali are not omnipotent, and in fact are not necessarily capable of making the sorts of finely tuned adjustments to the human genome that they claim, only becomes evident in the third book, by which time we are no longer looking for them to be proved wrong.) The Oankali assertion of their own racial/cultural superiority is further boosted by the claim that human beings are inherently genetically flawed, containing a "Contradiction" (the combination of high intelligence and hierarchal thinking, with the hierarchal thinking the older and more powerful of the two impulses)—a claim which again certainly seems to have been borne out by the nuclear war that killed off the bulk of humanity. We cannot help but be struck that the protagonist of the first book in the series, Lilith, a character who seems genuinely wise and admirable, ultimately chooses to work with them despite her many reservations. The second and third books in the series follow Lilith's children, Akin and Jodahs, both hybrids, who not only generally share the Oankali worldview but are able to "see" and "feel" the genetic flaw in the same terms the Oankali claim to, further confirming their apparent claims to superiority.

In contrast, nearly every human being we meet who is not allied with the Oankali is completely odious—thieving, kidnapping, murderous, racist, homophobic, totally irrational rapists and sociopaths. In interviews—though still characteristically cagey about resolving any ambiguities in her famously ambiguous novels—Butler concedes that in the Oankali she set out to create a race that was "xenophilic" instead of "xenophobic," and when Juan Williams asked her on NPR if the Oankali are "evil," she replies, somewhat aghast, "Oh, no! No. No. No. No." (Five no's!) As her explanation goes on, however, it seems perhaps better to say that what Butler means to assert is not that she doesn't write about evil, but that she doesn't write about *good*; she thinks people "doing the kinds of things people do" necessarily entails struggles for domination and control, the strong exerting themselves (to some degree or another, with some amount of restraint or another) on the weak. "Evil" is a forbidden category in her work precisely because she sees those behaviors we might naïvely wish to call "evil" as in fact completely ubiquitous and entirely natural. This is part and parcel of the explicitly Darwinist biologism that would characterize her later works, including both the Xenogenesis and Parables books; in the same appearance on NPR, for instance, she says that human competition is easily mappable onto "the kinds of things you find in the lowest plants and animals." The specific model she offers up for human sociality is the mindless competition of two algae growths as they spread across a rock.[25] The Oankali offer an alternative to humanity's history of instinctual biological automatism and yet, at the same time, are even more automatic and biologically programed than humans are—it simply depends on where you put your interpretive emphasis.

In the course of an otherwise very-well-thought-out chapter on the Oankali novels, Sherryl Vint writes of the humans' puzzling insistence on resistance to the Oankali project in spite of the fact that "the Oankali never mistreat the humans in any way."[26] But against the pro-Oankali critics I must suggest instead that in fact the Oankali do almost *nothing* but harm the humans, in almost literally every possible way. First there is the level of psychological manipulation, which begins with Lilith's long period of solitary confinement at the start of *Dawn* and continues nearly unabated throughout the trilogy (even at the end of the third book, Jodahs is still thinking about information he has that has been withheld from the humans). In contemporary self-help parlance, the Oankali are *gaslighters*, selectively dribbling out information and misinformation to cause the humans to mistrust their own judgments and authority, and putting them in extreme situations that will cause them great distress while compelling them to misunderstand what happens to them as being the result of their own bad choices. We can see this almost anywhere we look. During her time in solitary confinement, a terrified child, Sharad, is briefly put in Lilith's cage, then removed: despite implied promises from the Oankali, Lillith is never reunited with the boy (and indeed seems able, for better or worse, to forget about him, to trust that he is better off wherever he is now). Before she leaves solitary confinement permanently, she is offered (once and only once) the option to kill herself instead of proceeding with the crossbreeding project—a choice that is framed by the text as a "gift" but which is actually an act of extreme violence, as well as inducement to accept anything that follows as the result of her own "choice" to live.[27] Lilith is then brought to meet another of the Awakened humans aboard the spacecraft, Paul Titus, who has been living among the Oankali for many years—and who attacks her and attempts to rape her. The attack makes her trust the Oankali more and the humans less—which may very well have been the Oankali's plan all along.[28] The Oankali then tell her they have removed her ability to have children, saying her fertility will be restored "when you're ready" (and tell her that she will be the one who decides); in fact, at the end of the novel they restore her fertility and impregnate her without consulting her.[29] (The impregnation is only one of many medical procedures they subject her to without anything like informed consent.) Even as they grieve together over Lilith's murdered partner, Joseph, the ooloi Nikanj finds time to point out that it was the very bodily enhancements Lilith requested for Joseph that led directly to his death.[30] On and on, the Oankali behave this way, across the novel and its sequels. And this is only what we see in the text: given that we see only some of the Oankali's vast resources, and given that they can manipulate memories and even brain states, it could very well be that they have run multiple versions of this narrative (perhaps with the same individuals) before and simply started over when the outcomes were not to their liking. Given the level of psychological testing they have subjected the humans to, perhaps starting over was never required; perhaps they knew they would get what they want just by their careful selection of the principals. Nikanj suggests this to be true when talking about pairing Lilith with her first partner, Joseph; it claims it chose Joseph for her, based on data suggesting they would be a good match.[31]

In short, the Oankali control the terms of the "experiment" in every respect so completely that neither the humans in the narrative nor we as readers can even state with certainty what the limits of their power are; such an overwhelming disparity should cause us to be quite skeptical even when the Oankali appear to have been "right."

Most chilling, the Oankali's anticonsensual ideology extends to their vision of sex, which is repeatedly presented in terms of eroticized rape. The pattern, repeated over and over in the novel, is that the Oankali force the humans to participate in sex acts mediated through an ooloi, claiming that they know better than the humans what they really want. The humans' repeated insistence they know what they want and don't want is dismissed as mere denial. Nikanj puts the point to Joseph in explicitly these terms: "The second time will be the hardest for you. I left you no choice the first time. You could not have understood what there was to choose. Now you have some small idea. And you have a choice." Joseph again says no, but Nikanj proceeds to take control of Joseph's body anyway, saying "Your body has made a different choice."[32] Near the climax of the novel, *all* of the other humans are gassed and then subjected to versions of this treatment, with the Oankali knowing full well that not all of them will be able to live with the consequences of this violation.[33]

The events of the trilogy similarly suggest a sort of gaslighting narrative on the larger level of philosophy or (if you prefer) on the level of galactic imperial ideology. Put simply, the Oankali exacerbate a neocolonial situation in which humans are radically and permanently disempowered, and then step in to provide "assistance." When we strip the novel's events of their specific science fictional context, they become a plain retelling of the brutal history of imperialism: *Strangers come in ships from far away. Their technologies are advanced far beyond anything locally known; their ways are strange, even terrifying. They do not look like us. They explain that they have only come to help us; they are bringing us civilization, they are saving us from ourselves. We are—they say—intrinsically flawed, not only on the level of our culture but also on the level of our genes; our race, they explain without joy or malice, is simply inferior to theirs. But they are willing to uplift us; they can bring us into civilization's fold—for a price. These strangers promise they do not want to rob us; they want only to engage in a series of mutually beneficial trades. But their requests are always backed with force. We are not permitted to refuse. Our every interaction with them is colored by coercion, torture, even the threat of death. They lie, break deals. Even when they tell the truth it is to serve only themselves. They claim sovereign territory over land that was once ours, removing us to undesirable locations as meager compensation. They destroy our history, break the continuity that linked us to our ancestors. They kidnap some of us and imprison the rest; they control our movements, perform experiments on us, deny us the ability to read and write, even deny our right to reproduce. Many of us are raped or impregnated against our will; afterward, they steal our children, who are to be raised not as ours but as theirs.*

If one looks to the legal definition of genocide adopted by the United Nations—a more expansive definition than the popular conception of death camps—one finds that the Oankali are guilty of every variety:

(a) Killing members of the group;
(b) Causing serious bodily or mental harm to members of the group;
(c) Deliberately inflicting on the group conditions of life calculated to bring about its physical destruction in whole or in part;

(d) Imposing measures intended to prevent births within the group;

(e) Forcibly transferring children of the group to another group.

Against the tradition of Butler criticism that has emphasized a postcolonial politics of cosmopolitan hybridity and that has consequently tended to view the Oankali as legitimate benefactors to humankind, then, I feel I must insist on the extent to which the Oankali turn out, in this reading, to be genuinely monstrous after all. The surface humanitarianism of the Oankali belies the threat of (xeno)genocidal violence on which their interactions with human beings are predicated; if this is supposed to be a cosmopolitan utopia, it comes only at the barrel of a gun.

The Oankali's breeding project also closely mimics eliminationist and eugenics discourses in ways that the text of the novel does not foreground, and even Lilith herself does not take up (likely because she has no choice but to go along with their plans). The Oankali's chosen candidates for Awakening are all healthy, under fifty, English speaking; as my students are more and more prone to noticing, they are all, apparently, straight and cis-gendered (or perhaps, more sinisterly, some have been subtly altered by the Oankali so they are straight and cis-gendered *now*). The Oankali's vision of the future may be less sexist and less racist than our present, but it is *more* homophobic and transphobic, with a sort of compulsory heteronormativity that sees both the backward-looking reactionary male humans and their Oankali captors agreeing that all the humans are to pair off in monogamous heterosexual couples in order to have children. It is also much more ableist than our present, with the Oankali specifically refusing to allow certain types of bodies, conditions, and genetic predispositions to persist into the future (even, with respect to Tate's Huntington's disease, in the Martian colony project they refuse to participate in and will not control).[34]

In the second book, even the action that is almost always pointed to as Oankali beneficence—the establishment of a fourth Oankali division, an Akjai control group of unchanged humans, to be left on Mars—is structurally identical to the nineteenth-century project of Indian removal in the Americas, in which an indigenous population was displaced by colonizing invaders and moved to less desirable locations the invaders didn't want. (And even this meager concession comes because the Oankali essentially have no choice after Akin—a character variously described in Butler's notes as the Martin Luther King Jr.[35] and the Dian Fossey[36] of the Oankali—forces the issue.)

As Rebecca J. Holden notes, the Oankali assertion of a constitutive flaw in the human genome that leaves human beings intrinsically unfit to govern themselves—an assertion for which they never provide even the slimmest evidence but which appeals to familiar discourses on both the political left and political right that cause it to be accepted by many readers without argument—is only the latest version of the lie familiar to any student of colonial and imperial history.[37] It is structurally no different than the call to "bring civilization to the barbarians" that loosed centuries of war, rape, genocide, and theft, or the ubiquitous claim even now that peoples of Africa, Asia, Latin America, and the Middle East are somehow unfit to govern themselves—a claim that cannot be divorced from attempts to exploit these people and places for their resources, biological and otherwise.[38]

Nowhere is this debate more superattenuated than in the second book of the series, *Adulthood Rites*, in which one of Lilith's children agitates for and ultimately achieves the unprecedented concession of an Akaji group of humans who will be allowed to migrate permanently to Mars. From the Oankali perspective, the establishment of this colony is a grievous crime: they are certain that humans simply cannot create a sustainable civilization on their own, that the Contradiction will inevitably cause the colony to destroy itself. "To give you a new world and let you procreate again," Akin says, "would be like breeding intelligent beings for the sole purpose of having them kill one another." And Akin *agrees* with this diagnosis: from his half-Oankali perspective he agrees the humans genuinely are intrinsically flawed and really are inevitably doomed. But humans, he argues, deserve the "freedom" to choose that fate—and perhaps, he says, "chance" or "mutation" or the "unexpected effects of the new environment" or "things no one has thought of" might intervene to save humanity despite itself, and its lack of worthiness.[39]

RONALD REAGAN AND NUCLEAR WAR

There is, as I have suggested, at least *one* strong piece of evidence for the claim that Butler believed humanity really is as intrinsically flawed as the Oankali claim. Very early in *Dawn*, we learn that the nuclear war that broke out across the world killed nearly all of the people living on Earth; people like Lilith who survived did so only because they were in isolated places when the disaster struck. Human civilization has, it seems, destroyed itself.

The idea of an imminent nuclear war was swirling in Butler's head as she began the Xenogenesis trilogy, a fear intensified by the election of Ronald Reagan to the presidency, an event which utterly horrified her, as she told Larry McCaffery and Jim McMenamin in an interview:

> I tell people that Ronald Reagan inspired Xenogenesis—and that it was the only thing he inspired in me that I actually approve of. When his first term was beginning, his people were talking about a "winnable" nuclear war, a "limited" nuclear war, the idea that more and more nuclear weapons would make us safer.[40]

The Reagan administration's interest in strategic nuclear defense was even the subject of one of Butler's frequent letters to the editor, published on May 24, 1981, in the *Los Angeles Times*, wherein she argued, "Anything that promotes a false sense of security with regard to nuclear weapons should be handled carefully." Although the letter ultimately argued for new civil defense measures on the grounds that they were needed to combat rogue states and terrorist networks that might acquire nuclear weapons, the letter regrets this determination insofar as it could "encourage some people to see nuclear war as winnable, as a rational choice."[41]

Reagan receives special contempt in Butler's personal notes and notebooks not simply while he is president but over the course of the next twenty years; another letter to the editor, written only a few days after the previous one and never published, blasts the Reagan administration for voting against infant formula sales in developing countries.[42] In 1990 she sent a short letter to *Essence* about the lessons she'd learned from various recent presidents; here were the lessons from Reagan:

- People will pay *any* price for praise, reassurance, and an illusion of security.
- It can be both expedient and easy to keep your enemies underestimating you.[43]

The "President Jarrett" of the 1990s Parables books—a figure she refers to in her notes as "President Hitler"—is another "Reagan, young, vigorous, and utterly unencumbered by conscience."[44] A personal notebook containing sketches of "the basic character types" includes Reagan alongside Asimov ("the perfectionist"), the "intelligent monster" (Roy Cohn), and "the semi-intelligent monster/betrayer" (Clarence Thomas); the Reagan archetype is "amoral, ambitious. . . . Would sell his mother but then convince people she wanted to be sold."[45] A short, haiku-like poem from one of her commonplace books is even more succinct: "Arrogant and Ignorant / Powerful and Stubborn / Ronald Reagan." Decades later, in the early 2000s, plotting for one of her last unfinished works, *Paraclete*, would even derail altogether on the specific question of the Reagan presidency—as we will see when I discuss that book in more detail in chapter 7.

The Reagan elections seemed to Butler to be not just a pair of spectacularly bad decisions but to cast a sort of permanent over doom the future of the entire human race. Continuing the quote from the interview with McCaffery and McMenamin, above:

> [The Reagan election is] when I began to think about human beings having the two conflicting characteristics of intelligence and a tendency towards hierarchical behavior—and that hierarchical behavior is too much in charge, too self-sustaining. The aliens in the Xenogenesis series say the humans have no way out, that they're programmed to self-destruct.[46]

In an interview with Nibir K. Ghosh from 2004, she makes much the same point:

INTERVIEWER: Was your novel *Dawn* inspired by the Darwinian principle of fitness?

OEB: Not exactly. It was inspired by some very foolish things that Ronald Reagan and some of his supporters were advocating back in the early 1980s—like advocating winnable or limited nuclear wars. I decided that if so many people were buying into this nonsense, there must be something wrong with us—something basic.[47]

Reagan makes two quiet appearances in *Dawn*. First, Butler's notes indicate he is the original model for the character of Gabriel Rinaldi, described in his first appearance in *Dawn* as

> an actor, who had confused the Oankali utterly for a while because he played roles for them instead of letting them see him as he was. . . . Gabriel must have

been good. He was also very good looking. He had never tried to harm himself or threatened to harm the Oankali. He was, the Oankali said, twenty-seven, thin, physically stronger than he looked, stubborn and not as bright as he liked to think.[48]

Her character notes from *Adulthood Rites*, the second book in the series, draw this comparison out in starker terms: "Actor. Handsome, commanding. A leader . . . [b]ut not bright."[49] The idea that Gabriel is based on Reagan puts his relationship with Tate—recall, the original point-of-view character in some early versions of the series—in a new light. Whenever Tate is mentioned in a negative way, Gabriel's name is likely to follow: "Tate avoided her—perhaps to please Gabriel, perhaps because she had adopted Gabriel's way of think-ing";[50] "It was Gabriel who had convinced her to abandon Lilith. It had to be."[51] And, of course, it is Gabriel who attacks Lilith's Oankali friend and partner, Nikanj, with an ax near the end of the novel, Gabriel who calls Lilith the Oankali's whore.[52]

The other appearance of Reagan in the book is both much more literal and much more subtle. We are told, briefly, that there was another class of people the Oankali rescued, beyond people like Lilith being Awakened far in the future: "Some of the people we picked up had been hiding deep underground. They had created much of the destruction."[53] These would have been governmental and military figures, overwhelmingly white and male, especially in the context of the 1980s, living in underground bunkers, like the Presidential Emergency Operations Center under the White House, the NORAD Command Center under Cheyenne Mountain, or the so-called "Site R" at Raven Rock Mountain. Depending on the circumstances behind the war, included among these men would almost certainly be the president himself.

Though hundreds of years have passed on Earth, some of these men are still alive; the Oankali have "used them slowly, learned biology, language, culture from them."[54] Indeed, part of the reason the Oankali treat Lilith so badly during her early Awakenings is that they mistakenly universalize these military leaders and think all humans are like them, as one of the aliens later apologizes to Lilith:

Something went wrong when you were first Awakened. I heard about it from several people. Someone handled you badly—underestimated you. You are like us in some ways, but you were thought to be like your military people hidden underground. They refused to talk to us too. At first.[55]

The fact that humans have destroyed themselves and would have gone extinct without Oankali intervention is, undoubtedly, a point in the Oankali's favor—but it is undercut significantly by the fact that their primary source of information about this event is via the very people who caused it. The idea that the Oankali first learned about humans from the military madmen who destroyed the planet is a startling but undeveloped plot thread that threatens to cast the Oankali's entire way of thinking about human beings into doubt. Perhaps the entire theory they've developed of humanity as fundamentally broken is scientifically unsound, based on a very bad sampling error.[56]

The Oankali themselves seem to become at least partially aware of this; they ultimately choose Lilith, a black woman, to lead their breeding, not a white man, and Lilith herself is also very reluctant at first to Awaken *any* men for fear that they will attempt to reassert male control over what is left of humanity. Many of Butler's early notes for the Xenogenesis suggest that it was originally intended to take the direction of her long-planned feminist utopia, though few of these ideas and sketches survived to be important elements in the final published version of the books.[57]

A second point must also be taken up regarding the war. Early in the second novel, Tino (Lilith's second partner) privately expresses his own most paranoid thoughts about the Oankali: "He thought he understood anger, hatred, humiliation, even the desire to kill a man. He had felt all those things. But to kill everyone . . . almost kill the Earth. . . . There were times when he wondered if somehow the Oankali had not caused the war for their own purposes."[58] The possibility is never returned to, and yet I find the idea too tantalizing to give up. Is this not infinitely more plausible than the Oankali's version of events, which is that in all the vastness of their wanderings through space they just happened to stumble upon Earth at exactly the right moment? If they had arrived shortly before the war, they would have encountered far greater resistance; if they had arrived a few years or perhaps even a few months later, they would have found only corpses.

We might ask if this is why the Oankali have altered everyone's memories of the war:

"I saw my father, my brother—their bodies. I don't know what happened to my mother. I was dying myself when the Oankali found me. They tell me I was. I don't remember, but I believe them."

"I don't remember their finding me either." She twisted around. "Nikanj, did your people do something to us to keep us from remembering?"

Nikanj seemed to rouse itself slowly. "They had to," it said. "Humans who were allowed to remember their rescue became uncontrollable. Some died in spite of our care."[59]

Science fiction writer Ian Watson raises precisely this issue in a 1987 letter to Butler, and she agrees with him that the humans "should have been more suspicious that the Oankali had somehow caused the war" (though she says, "for the record," they did not) (see figure 2). Butler's position is that the Oankali's reverence for life goes beyond religion to the level of a "genetic inclination." But even in her defense of the Oankali, she is forced to concede that it is, certainly, a "coincidence" that they somehow arrived at precisely the right time.[60] The Oankali monologues in *Dawn* certainly suggest that space is vast and empty, not teeming with Oankali vessels—and Jdahya, Lilith's first Oankali interlocutor, does let slip that they were "overdue" for the trade when they found Earth.

Much of the debate around the novel can be reduced to the question of whether or not Butler endorses the biologically/genetically essentialist position of the Oankali, a debate that hinges in some sense on the assertion of the Contradiction. While there's ambiguity here, as there's ambiguity everywhere in Butler, I would suggest a wide reading of both the novel and her comments in interviews wherein she *appears* to endorse this position, more or less. Similarly, her examples of how genetics work in the trilogy are almost always fully deterministic in precisely the way of the Contradiction: the cancer gene that Lilith and others carry, Tate's Huntington's disease in *Adulthood Rites*, the neurofibromatosis of the reproducing humans Jodahs encounters in the third book.[61]

Moreover—and more important, regardless of Butler's own position— as J. Adam Johns and Hoda M. Zaki have noted, the pro-Oankali critics themselves almost always endorse some form of the Oankali's claim of essentialism as a necessary premise for their endorsement of the Oankali's

Post Office Box 6604
Los Angeles, CA 90055
January 6, 1988

Dear Ian Watson,

Thank you very much for your thoughtful letter--and thanks
for your complements to my aliens, the Oankali. DAWN is
the beginning of a trilogy that is already written. The
second and third books, ADULTHOOD RITES and IMAGO will be
published this year and next.

Now to problems: You say the Oankali have witnessed a
number of other species committing suicide and have not
involved themselves until they found Earth. But the Oankali
(Jdahya) only say, "It. . it has been several million years
since we dared to interfere in anotherpeople's act of self-
destruction." and, "Mass suicide is one of the few things
we usually leave alone." Jdahya says a few suiciding species
have taken whole ships of Oankali with them. So the Oankali
have learned their lesson. But in humans they saw something
so biologically useful, they took a chance.

And for the Oankali, it is a matter of biology. You were
absolutely right in saying that humans should have been more
suspicious that the Oankali had somehow caused the war. For
the record, the Oankali did not. It would have been against
their "religion"--against their intense reverence for life.
All life can be changed. None should be wasted. I think
this attitude comes out more in the second and third book.
Indeit comes out not as a belief, but as a genetic inclination--
stronger than an actual religion. Of course, some humans
would think otherwise. I didn't want to focus on the war--
on which crisis human beings finally blew themselves up over.
There have been so many. And as for the coincidence of the
Oankali finding us not long after a war. . .well, the timing
of the war was the biggest coincidence. Since we were exactly
what the Oankali were looking for--intelligent, carbon-based
life--and since they've been looking for an incredibly long
time, it's less of a coincidence that they finally stumbled
across us. Also consider that there must be a lot of Oankali
ships out there looking. If there's one thing the Oankali
are good at, it's procreation.

By the way, the military and the politicians who were rescued
(captured?) from their bunkers were not allowed to age and die
as punishment for what they had done. The Oankali simply
saw them as too dangerous, too wasteful of life to trust
them to go free on Earth. They saw Curt in exactly the same
way. The Oankali are not evil. They're just driven by their
own biology to do certain things--just as we humans are driven
by our biology to do certain things. Very different things.

Well, it's been fun getting back into the trilogy. I hope you
enjoy ADULTHOOD RITES. Best wishes.

Octavia

2. Letter to Ian Watson, dated January 6, 1988 (OEB 4429)

supposed post-imperial, posthuman cosmopolitanism. If their radical and totally nonconsensual interventions in human society are really to be thought
of as a vision of utopia, it can only be so because humans are so horrifically
and intrinsically broken as to be completely without hope. Otherwise, the
lack of consent implicit in the series swamps any happy vision of Oankali
utopia. Even elements of the Oankali themselves, like Akin, recognize this

fact, as when he confronts another Oankali about the Contradiction and the Mars colony: "What are we that we can do this to whole peoples? Not predators? Not symbionts? What then?"[62]

IMAGO

The third book in the trilogy, *Imago* (1989), extends the narrative of Lilith's family into the unexpected arrival of a human-ooloi construct child, Jodahs, much sooner than the Oankali had intended. Butler herself was frustrated by the book, viewing it, if not as a failure, then certainly as one of her lesser works: she found the book extremely difficult to write,[63] and for the rest of her life she would remember the experience of *Imago* very negatively as the beginning of the end of her prolific creativity.[64] It is certainly inferior, in my judgment, to both *Dawn* and *Adulthood Rites*, and critical consensus seems to ratify this impression: the book has been taken up by critics far less often than the other two. Hoda M. Zaki's contemporaneous reading of the series in *Science Fiction Studies* (July 1990) is noteworthy for its brief discussion of why the book seemed disappointing; from Zaki's perspective, the third book in the trilogy was "supposed to describe a human community struggling to create a better society in the absence of the ubiquitous Oankali"[65]—in other words, it was supposed to follow the story of the Mars colony, not the ongoing story of Earth's colonization, subjugation, and transformation into an Oankali spaceship. Instead of tracing the Mars colony story, Jodahs simply uses its Oankali nature to grimly declare that it is "Oankali enough to know you will eventually destroy yourselves again."[66] Our other brief interactions with the Mars colony plan, outside Jodahs's negative perspective, are similarly unhappy: we find, for instance, that the human resisters have stupidly fallen into internecine warfare over the question, with some resister groups murdering the "deserters" who try to immigrate to Mars.[67] Zaki insightfully says this narrative silence should come as no surprise to us, since "the elaboration of such a [utopian Martian] society necessities a synthesis on Butler's part of certain inconsistent views that she holds."[68] As I will suggest in the coming chapters, Butler in fact spends the rest of her career searching unsuccessfully for this synthesis, unable to actualize it in *Parable of the Trickster* as she'd hoped.

Imago is perhaps most interesting for its quiet deconstruction of the earlier books in the series, especially with regard to the trustworthiness of the

Oankali. We see that the Oankali are not actually infallible: they have accidentally produced a human-ooloi hybrid ahead of schedule (and soon a second, in Jodahs's sibling Aaor), *and* their work sterilizing the humans is not as flawless and perfect as had previously been suggested; some humans remain fertile independent of the Oankali after all.[69] This isolated group came together as a resister colony, high up in the mountains; they are stunned when one of their members (a fifteen-year-old girl later named, in mythological terms, as the "First Mother") becomes pregnant following a brutal gang rape. But she is able to give birth to multiple daughters and sons, who are themselves mutually fertile; many, but not all, of the children have genetic abnormalities and/or are severely disabled, and enough survive to allow the colony to live outside Oankali control.[70]

Lilith spent so much of *Dawn* hoping to catch the Oankali in a lie, or in an error—but when the moment that their omnipotence is disproved comes in *Imago*, she has become too committed to them and their larger project to care. Similarly, the revelation that the Oankali are not infallible does not lead to self-reflection or humility on their part; rather, the hybrid figure that is seemingly meant to offer us a "third way" between two extremes abandons the language of compromise and cosmopolitanism altogether in favor of a discourse of raw power. "Why should the Oankali have the one world that's ours?" asks one of the resisters Jodahs encounters on its travels. "They do have it. And you can't take it back from them," Jodahs replies.[71] Later in the book, another resister rages, "This should be a Human world!" and Jodahs's answer is the same bloodless declaration of fact: "It isn't anymore. It won't ever be again."[72] The question of the legitimacy or desirability of the Oankali project is bracketed at the very moment it is supposedly perfected in the human-ooloi constructs: it no longer matters whether the Oankali are right or wrong, they just *are*.

Jodahs's private thoughts reflect the same sense of Oankali manifest destiny even more strongly, which simply cannot be interrupted by any ethical consideration. When Jodahs discovers the fertile human village, it has no doubt that it will need to betray them to the Oankali so they can be captured and re-sterilized. They would then be given the same three forced choices all humans are given:

They would be allowed to choose Mars or union with us or sterility here on Earth. They could not be allowed to continue to reproduce here, then to die when we separated and left an uninhabitable rock behind.

No Human who did not decide to mate with us was told this last. They were given their choices and not told why.[73]

This is an intriguing paradox: the moment euphemistically described as "separation" is the moment that the Earthbound Oankali depart in the new spaceship they have grown from the planet, leaving a dead, discarded husk behind.

This moment returns in the final pages of the book, in which Jodahs and Aaor are allowed to stay on Earth with the fertile resisters. The resisters have given up the ghost in the face of Jodahs and Aaor's sexual magnetism and agreed to rejoin the Oankali, if not without reservations. "You've done this to me," says one to Jodahs. "I would have gone to Mars. [. . .] My god, if there had been people like you around a hundred years ago, I couldn't have become a resister. I think there would be no resisters. . . . Damn you. . . . Goddamn you."[74] The humans' resentment of their own seduction—even more effective with a Jodahs-style hybrid than with the original ooloi—is framed less as a tragic ending for the resisters than as a happy ending for the minor characters Ahajas, Tediin, and Kahguyaht, who lost their first humans when Tate and Gabriel chose Mars and now get another set.

Globally, other human-ooloi constructs have begun to emerge; generally speaking they will be sent to Jodahs to live in this place too, building the society of the future while the hybrid species is watched by Oankali biologists to ensure it is not dangerous. Some of Butler's early notes for the end of the Xenogenesis series frame this in somewhat utopian terms: she planned for the end of the series to see "a complete construct family not dependent in any way on the Oankali for reproduction." But this was also a version of the story in which Lilith was a resister, *not* part of the Oankali project[75]—and it is (perhaps unhappily) quite distinct from the version we do get, in which the new community, while vital, is still fully inscribed within the larger Oankali project and still subject to its larger galactic-imperial aims. Other notes for the series place their emphasis on the more pessimistic side of the equation, as in OEB 2994, an outline for a book called *Lilith*, which draws on "The Evening and the Morning and the Night" [I] to startlingly reject the published

Xenogenesis's logic of reproductive futurity when Lilith's child is "mercifully born dead . . . an armless, legless horror with some skin disorder that has left it looking raw, flayed."[76]

"Plant a town," Jodahs is instructed by the Oankali in orbit. "Prepare a place." In the last chapter of the novel and the last chapter of the Xenogenesis trilogy, Jodahs does exactly this, planting the "town" that will someday metamorphose into the "great ship" that would eventually take the human-Oankali hybrid species into the stars. The image is one of maximum fertility, the seed of the town taking root in the "rich soil of the riverbank": "Seconds after I had expelled it," the book ends, "I felt it begin the tiny positioning movements of independent life." This is a quickening, on a planetary scale. And yet we know from the previously quoted observations that this pregnant moment is simultaneously an apocalyptic harbinger of global death: what grows from the seed will consume the entire ecosystem of Earth in the name of Oankali expansionism before departing in search of some other place to destroy and consume.

When Joan Fry interviewed Butler for *Poets and Writers* she observed that Butler doesn't "hold out much hope for human civilization as we know it." Butler responded with a lengthy parable:

> We do keep dragging each other back to various and sundry dark ages; we appear to be in the process of doing it again now. And when we're not doing that, we're exploiting our resources to such an extreme degree that they're going to disappear. On National Public Radio there was a woman who spent a number of years studying wolves that had migrated down from Canada into Glacier National Park. At one point she said something like, "If I were a wolf I'd stay in one place until I had used up the resources and then I would move on, but the wolves don't do that." And I thought, "Aha! The wolves have figured something out, at least on a biological level, that we *still* haven't!" In family bands, when humans lived that way, we didn't stay in one place until there was nothing left. We moved on. Right now it seems that people are being encouraged to see the environment as their enemy. Go out and kill it. If they're really unlucky, they will succeed.[77]

The implication of this answer is the Oankali know what the wolves know, and what humans don't—but in fact the Oankali are even more ravenous and insatiable wastrels than we are, using up all the resources of Earth and the moving on to another ecosystem that they will fully and entirely consume.

They, too, refuse all limits, to their great peril; recall that when humans first encounter the Oankali, the Oankali are so desperate for new genes that they are willing to select the humans for breeding despite the fact that the humans have just suicidally nuked their entire planet. From this perspective the Oankali may well be seen not as *anti-human* but as *ultra-human*, constantly on the cusp of disaster through their total inability to curtail their consumption, always (just like us) in need of more, more, more.

The Oankali, for all their supposed difference and for all their self-inflating rhetoric, are as much the final perfection of human destructivity as an alternative to it; "not [as] our opposites," as Joan Slonczewski suggests, "but rather an extension of some of humanity's most extreme tendencies."[78] I confess that this conclusion does not make me happy. It brings some rather deep discomfort about a series I genuinely love: a spell-binding glimpse of alterity and possibility that seems nonetheless to have as its deepest theoretical underpinnings a mapping of the human totality that is bleakly misanthropic, even anti-utopian, on all levels, not simply down to the level of the human genome but even beyond, toward a critique of all intelligent life as such—and which seems to compel us to endorse the *Oankali* version of the precise dangerous combination of intelligence with hierarchical thinking the series simultaneously critiques. The Oankali do not genuinely oppose hierarchy, despite their self-aggrandizing claims; they just propose a different one, with themselves on top.

From this perspective the series becomes a catalog of history's horrors refashioned as a thrilling science fictional encounter, with most readers (and perhaps Butler herself) ultimately seduced by the colonizer in the same way Lilith has been—forced into complicity with the invaders, coming to accept their lies as the truth, quite literally sleeping with the enemy. Lilith's narrative is a particularly disturbing instance of this, beginning with the moment at the end of *Dawn* when the Oankali impregnate Lilith (without her knowledge or consent) as a means of binding her to them—essentially the completion of the rapes that the human men in the encampment planned but were never able to complete, and the unacknowledged parallel to what happens to the First Mother in *Imago*. Before she gives birth, at the end of *Dawn*, we still have a Lilith whose drive to resistance is still quite vibrant, who plans to continue to teach her human subjects to *"learn and run"* in the hopes of somehow getting outside the Oankali's grips.[79]

But in the second novel—set thirty years later, after Lilith has had several children and has been allowed to settle on Earth after all—the stakes have changed. What little we hear from her in the next two novels about the missing thirty years suggests that the Oankali's final aggression against her has been successful in pacifying her:

> "But . . . you didn't have to have kids."
>
> "As it happens, I did. I had two construct kids by the time they brought me down from the ship. I never had a chance to run off and pine for the good old days!"[80]

Perhaps this is why the Oankali seem only to Awaken heterosexuals and manipulate their captives into man-woman pair bonds: they surely know that the presence of children will make the humans that much easier to control. And Lilith accepts this; in accordance with the logic of reproductive futurity that governed *Kindred* and "Bloodchild," among others, she tells some of the human resisters Jodahs finds that—despite everything the Oankali have taken from her and have demanded of her—it is still better to have children than not.[81]

It's worth noting that the story of Lilith's daughter—one of those two construct children, the baby she is pregnant with at the end of *Dawn*—is one the novels never tell. It may be that the life story of a captive girl knowingly being groomed by her own mother toward a future of forced pregnancy was too disturbing even for Butler; it certainly risked being a NO-BOOK, to say the least. In the third novel, at any rate, set another fifty years later, Lilith claims to "have understood it . . . [a]ccepted it," saying, "Now, I feel as though I've loved Nikanj all my life. Ooloi are dangerously easy to love. They absorb us, and we don't mind."[82] Jeffrey Tucker reads this moment and says it is a "statement that reads like something more than simple Stockholm Syndrome"[83]—but Stockholm Syndrome, I have to say, is exactly what this sounds like to me. The Oankali—whether they "mean to" or not, whether they in some sense can be said to be innocent or unknowing—turn even love into their poison.

AGAINST UTOPIA

"I don't write utopian science fiction," Butler said, "because I don't believe imperfect humans can form a perfect society."[84] But this tells only half the story: Butler *longed* to write utopian fiction, "fix-the-world scenarios," and was stymied despite her "need to write them" by, she said, the sad "fact that I don't believe in them—don't believe humanity is fixable."[85] The Oankali stories laid out the terms of this lack of belief—Butler believed the notion of the "human contradiction" she laid out in those books was basically the correct diagnosis, and returned to it repeatedly in interviews and in her personal journals over the course of her life. But, she felt, the Oankali did not solve the problem: "I'm not sure I really managed what I set out to do. I wound up with a somewhat different hierarchal system, chemically controlled as with DNA, but, instead, pheromonal."[86]

Even setting aside this darker take on the trilogy, which sees the Oankali as embodying that same human contradiction, the Oankali can't offer a genuine solution to the human contradiction because they are not themselves human (and they have what amounts to magical powers to boot). How might *humans* improve their situation? How might *humans*, in a human context, become better—without the cheat of divine intervention? Butler saw herself not as a sociobiological reductionist so much as a sociobiological realist—"I do think we need to accept that our behavior *is* controlled to some extent by biological forces"—and was interested in seeking out ways we might "work around our programming."[87]

After *Imago* Butler began work on a new project that imagined a world where empathy had become contagious, had become a communicable disease. (In one version it is even something like an STD; a character gives it to her rapist, who afterward will never be able to rape anyone again because they would feel the victim's terror and pain.[88]) If you could feel another person's suffering—really feel it—wouldn't you *have* to behave decently to them, if only for your own self-preservation? She called the planned novel *Justice*—and sometimes *The Justice Plague*—and at first the scenario seemed to her as if it would create a utopia. "The point," Butler said later, years after she had abandoned this version of the idea, "was to create, in fiction at least, a tolerant, peaceful civilization—a world in which people were inclined either to accept one another's differences or at least to behave as though they accepted them since any act of resentment they commit would be punished immediately, personally, inevitably." But the idea couldn't come together in the way she hoped, and it certainly never congealed into utopia. The existence of boxing and football taught her that "the threat of shared pain wouldn't necessarily make people behave better toward one another," while a literally contagious empathy might well destroy any possibility of necessary care work as in the healthcare profession.[89] And there were other problems: "It's always possible, for instance, to pay people to take more pain than you're willing to take."[90]

The *Justice* book never gelled—she abandoned the project when she felt it becoming a disaster like *Blindsight*—but the idea would linger as she moved on to the books that would not only set out to solve the problem of the human contradiction but would define the later phase of her career. These would be books about a young girl, Lauren Olamina, who is afflicted with a birth defect not unlike her vision of contagious empathy: hyperempathy, the psychosomatic feeling of other people's pain. The Parables series, while never finished, would reflect Butler's most audacious attempt to hijack the problem of the Human Contradiction and rewrite our bad biological programming—this time using a revolutionary new religion as the viral code.

CHAPTER 6

GOD OF CLAY (1989–2006)

Published Works

Parable of the Sower (1993)
Parable of the Talents (1998)

Significant Unpublished Work

God of Clay (alternate and fragmentary versions of *Parable of the Sower*) (ca. 1989–1993)
abandoned sketches, alternate scenes, and discarded drafts from original versions of
    Parable of the Talents (ca. 1993–1996)
Parable of the Trickster (ca. 1989–2006)

The plan was for a book—the first in a long and, naturally, best-selling series—set on extraplanetary colonies founded by human explorers. But this would not be the haphazard flight into the night of the Missionaries of *Survivor* and the other aborted Patternist stories; it was a completely new narrative situation, even (perhaps) a chance for Butler to correct the scientific and imaginative mistakes she'd made in *Survivor* that had haunted her ever since. The antagonist of the novels, too, was totally new, something she'd never presented before, and perhaps something never before attempted in science fiction: not a mutant telepath, not a hostile alien, but the environment itself. James Lovelock's famous Gaia hypothesis—the idea of the Earth as a vital, organic totality, an incomprehensibly vast living thing able to regulate itself the way a body does—has traditionally been thought of as a potential ally to human thriving, so long as we resolve to accommodate ourselves to Nature's harmony rather than continue our ceaseless war upon it. The Gaia hypothesis suggests the idea of an Earth that seeks harmony and stability, a planet that "wants" to nurture its animal life and keep it both alive and healthy. So here is Butler's characteristically perverse turn: What if human settlers from another world landed on a world that was similarly "alive"—and fiercely devoted to repelling the foreign objects, the human astronauts, who had invaded it?

The idea called to mind "the problems of transplant surgery and blindly responsive immune systems," Butler told her literary agent, Merrilee Heifetz, in May 1989. The human colonists sent to settle other worlds would be brilliant, sent with the necessary material goods to found thriving colonies and equipped with the best technology ever devised to solve any problems they might encounter.

> What they don't expect is to be treated as organs transplanted to blindly and persistently rejecting planetary organisms. I'm *not* talking about savage wild animals or warlike local people. I'm definitely *not* talking about intelligent plants. I'm talking about nasty little things—microorganisms that find the human body intolerable and that damage human eyes when they're blown or otherwise transferred into those eyes.

She imagined her colonists beset not by hostile natives but by medical maladies: loss of sight and hearing, loss of balance, changes in coloring or in mental state. "People who go to sleep in apparently convenient places might awake to find themselves encapsulated in a kind of plant gall—rather like the way oysters encapsulate offending material in pearls." Some of the planets would be empty of higher-order animal life, others would have intelligent species—just as, presumably, some of the colonies would find a way to survive in the new world and others would collapse into disaster and mass death. "And, of course, the people have brought all their human problems from Earth to complicate the ways in which they deal with the many problems the planets give them."[1]

Her private notes from that same month provide more details on the idea. The earliest indications that there is a problem in the colony, just a few months after landing, would be tiny irritants: "odd cases of vertigo . . . an epileptic seizure in someone who has never before shown any sign of epilepsy."[2] Some of the planetary immune response might even be *desirable* to humans, or make their lives better—the pleasure of intoxication, perhaps, or boosts in intelligence and creativity. But over time—years, then decades—the planet would adapt more frequent and more aggressive immune responses to try to flush the humans out. Humans would fight back, but that would provoke only still fiercer anti-human antibodies from the alien worlds: "Everything has unforeseen consequences. And everything is part of a chain."[3]

Butler thought the books would have a salutary ecological message that "the human way" of "smashing and dominating simply [does] not work"; her colonists would need to find a way to live *with* their new homes rather than *against* it.[4] But the lesson would be extremely hard-fought, costing much pain and many lives as humans first raged futilely against inevitability; the colonists metaphorically "manage to burn down most of the house in the fires they use to cook most of the seed corn before they are even willing to acknowledge that they are in deep trouble."[5] Her preliminary character list indicates that she once again intended to look to historical survivors (primarily from black history) for inspiration on how her heroes could learn and adapt on their new world: "Oya (Harriet) Marcus, Dominic (Malcolm) Gage, Nari (Douglass) Shinizu, Mateo (Martin) Olivara, Gideon (Mao) Kane Alexander, Vera (Sojourner) Chang Alexander."[6] These characters—like Lilith, more nimble and adaptable than white male heroes would be, because of their lifelong experiences of marginalization and struggle—would be the rare figures who would at least have a *chance* to find some new path away from fruitless, doomed war on their new home.

"I'm researching now and playing with ideas, but I know by the way this feels that I've got something good," the letter to her agent continues. "It will probably have to be offered book by book because it will have no on-stage characters in common. Oh, but speaking of characters, have I got some juicy ones demanding to be heard. Like I said, fun, fun, fun." "You see," the letter concludes, ecstatic, "this is what I'm like when I'm in love!"[7]

The literary object of that new infatuation would go on to overwhelmingly define the next seventeen years of Butler's career, the last of her life—resulting in some of her most successful and most beloved novels at the same time that it drove her to complete despair over her inability to realize the enthusiastic potential of her initial ideas. In many ways this love affair turned out to be a very bad romance, with Butler's partner simultaneously an inspiring and life-affirming creative muse and a moody, selfish, and unreliable life-mate—a real trickster.

GOD OF CLAY

Nearly a year after her May 1989 letter, in March 1990, Butler wrote her agent again. "Enclosed are the chapters and outline of the first book of my new series," she wrote. "This is the series I wrote to you about some time ago, though it may not seem to be at first glance. This novel, God of Clay, must take place on Earth to set the stage for later novels to take place on other worlds. As you'll see when you read the chapters, the Earthseed Communities are especially well-fitted to colonize hostile, biologically rejecting worlds."[8]

In a pattern that would recur across her writing of the unfinished Parables series, the solution to the crisis she had placed her characters in had proved far more difficult than Butler had originally anticipated. In fact, she would write two such "prequels," Parable of the Sower (1993) and Parable of the Talents (1998), before she turned her attention back to the 1989 space colony narrative that had so excited her, now renamed Parable of the Trickster—a book she would never finish and indeed would hardly be able even to begin.

In some sense the issue was more thematic than narrative. Butler realized that living in outer space would be so difficult and so miserable that it would require a new idea of human solidarity: people would have to work together to an extent that actual human history (and, perhaps, actually existing human biology) had never before allowed. What the dream of the outer space frontier offered was a chance not to abolish human nature but perhaps to temporarily suspend it; the extrasolar colonies are the chance to start over in circumstances whose radical hardship would offer a chance to build new practices of solidarity and collective life rather than indulge the selfish impulses, the bad habits of capitalism, and the bad instructions our DNA have ingrained in us. The sheer *struggles* involved in the flight to the stars—to build the spaceship and colony technology in the first place, to get to the new planet, to adapt the new environment to our needs, to adapt ourselves to the new environment—this animating and vitalizing endeavor would drive our growth as a species and prevent us from exploiting, raping, killing, and otherwise immiserating each other in the meantime (as Butler misanthropically believed we will inevitably do in the absence of a larger common purpose).

She believed in the Earthseed project—especially when she started the series. "If we survive," Butler once told Larry McCaffery—and note the strength of that *if*—"we have a whole solar system to grow up in. And we can use the stresses of learning to travel in space and live elsewhere—stresses that will harness our energies until we've had time to mature."[9] In her own notes for the unfinished *Trickster*, composed more than a decade later, she was still invested in this kind of constrained hope, which is to say a hope that is made possible *by* constraints, our boundless human creativity channeled by necessity into productive and useful ends because otherwise we'll all die. "We can't afford to go someplace else and make the mistakes we make here, here in the nest," she writes. "We can't afford to assume that another living world with its own biota and its own eons of existence will be able to tolerate our nonsense . . . taking, and putting back nothing—or putting back poisonous waste."[10]

But Butler was, as we know, a pessimist about human nature, and could far more easily imagine this story ending in total disaster rather than culminating in success. The human founders of these colonies needed some way out of the existential crisis of the human race that had been laid out by the dire diagnosis of the Oankali's gene-sight, but not through recourse to what was essentially quasi-divine intervention: the aliens' magical healing touch. The solution needed to be mundane, down to earth; instead of making new bodies, Butler imagined, humanity needed to save itself by the development of a new type of society, with new ideas.

To solve this crisis of the imagination, she turned to one of the oldest and most transformative human technologies, the one science fiction had tended to dismiss as a primitive artifact of the superstitious past: religion. "I've met science fiction people who say, 'Oh, well, we're going to outgrow it,' and I don't believe that for one moment. It seems that religion has kept us focused and helped us to do any number of very difficult things, from building pyramids and cathedrals to holding together countries, in some instances. I'm not saying it's a force for good—it's just a force. So why not use it to get ourselves to the stars?"[11] She invented a religion that could transform the human civilization we know into something that could potentially get off-planet and survive the world of radical changes required to live in outer space. She imagined a new religion, Earthseed, that might be the down-to-Earth, *human* equivalent of the Oankali's constant biological reinvention, devoted to the idea of permanent change as opposed to eternal truths. The religion is organized around a central proposition: the inevitability of change, and the consequent need to be adaptable and flexible in response to change.

> God is Power—
> Infinite,
> Irresistible,
> Inexorable,
> And yet, God is Pliable—
> Trickster,
> Teacher,
> Chaos,
> Clay.
> God exists to be shaped.
> God is Change.[12]

Earthseed is thus constituted by a Darwinian recognition of the eternal flux of life as well as a *post*-Darwinian attempt to seize control of that flux and apply it toward human ends, first and foremost the long-term longevity of the species as such. God is Change, Earthseed preaches; we must accommodate ourselves to change, adapt ourselves to it, or be burned alive by it. It was an insight Butler took seriously, in big ways (the level of global politics) and small (moving, in 1989, out of the small Los Angeles house she had lived in since 1970, with all the attendant chaos and personal reorganization of such a change).[13]

The ultimate expression of "shaping God," the culmination of human historical achievement its adherents call the Destiny, "is to take root among the stars"—humans achieving species immortality colonizing multiple planets.[14]

(In this sense Earthseed doesn't just reconcile science fiction and religion; it remakes science fiction *as* religion.) The original 1989 *God of Clay* was to be set on one of the alien worlds founded by a group of these Earthseeders, detailing how they change, and are changed by, their presence on an alien world. But the need to tell the Earthseeder's backstory—to explain their religion and where it came from—proved much more seductive than Butler could have predicted. Butler became more and more interested in that part of the story, putting the space colony on hold; by the time she began sending pages to her agent, the story had completely transformed from what she originally anticipated, becoming about the religion's founder, a character she named Lauren Oya Olamina.

The new project had many things going for it. It offered her a chance to make a more optimistic intervention in the world than her stories had previously allowed, almost "weaponizing" religion as a tool for improving lives rather than making them worse. If religion was an essential part of the human, why not craft a good one rather than a bad one? Why not develop a religion that was responsive to the growing crisis of the late twentieth century, rather than a drag on our ability to save ourselves? One can see Butler's growing confidence as a writer, and in her project, in her insistence on telling the story her way: while she took her editor's suggestion to kill the minor character of Jill as a way of upping the stakes near the end of the novel, she refused to revise the first 120 pages as directed.[15] She also repeatedly directed her publisher to pay attention to New Age audiences, which she saw as a possible fourth readership for her work besides her usual triple audience of science fiction fans, African Americans, and feminists; she thought *Sower* might appeal to the same sorts of people (including aging Baby Boomers looking for answers) who had made *The Celestine Prophecy* a sensation.[16] She knew the book was something special: *"Parable* isn't *Kindred,* but it has the potential to stay alive the way *Kindred* has."[17] It was a book she felt demonstrated real maturity as well: a book that she couldn't have written in her twenties or thirties, a book that demonstrated the way she had, she said, "made my peace with religion" through the development of a sort of agnostic universalism.[18] She was happy to be working with a smaller press (first Four Walls, Eight Windows, and later Seven Stories Press) after her experiences with Doubleday and Warner Books, even if the pay was (as always) less than she liked; she felt she was treated very well and that she had a better relationship with her editors than she'd ever experienced before.

But the series also provided some new challenges, especially during the long process of its writing. Lauren, though in some ways similar to other protagonists Butler had developed, was in other ways a very new sort of character for Butler. Her other heroines had always fallen into bad situations through no fault of their own, somehow managing to survive by the skin of their teeth—but Lauren was someone who was *seeking out* trouble, seeking out power. Butler was deeply suspicious of people who behaved this way—they were Doros, not Danas or Liliths or Anyanwus. They were not to be trusted. How could such a person ever be a "hero," in the terms Butler's fiction had always understood heroism? What would such a person be like? What would keep him or her from becoming corrupted, even wicked, as the powerful always did?

The short answer—at least at first—was that they couldn't. Butler's early attempts at writing Lauren—focused on Lauren in her forties, at the prime of her social and political powers—are deeply shocking to the reader who knows only the teenaged character from the novel. This Olamina is a steely and callous and, at times, brutal political operator, something like *Blindsight's* creepy cult leader, Aaron, was supposed to be but never quite became. Butler's early drafts and personal reflections on Olamina reveal her as a much, much darker (even, at times, sinister) character than the one we get to know in the books—almost a female Doro. Butler researched the life of Mohammed in 1989, likely looking to find ways to understand how a religious visionary became an empire builder.[19] We see some of this turn in the discarded pages of *God of Clay*; we see Olamina, for instance, ordering a local politician's assassination for daring to defy her. Another set of pages has Olamina slave-collaring people who try to leave her Earthseed villages: "Boy," she said, "the dogs eat what's left of people who try to break into our Communities. We burn what's left of people who try to break out."[20] Most of the very earliest pages from the *God of Clay* version of the text involve protagonists who dislike or distrust Olamina: journalists going undercover at Earthseed to expose her as a fraud, or her own followers (sometimes her adopted children), plotting to supplant or betray her. For anyone who has read the published versions of the novels, this is all genuinely startling. Readers of the Parables books typically refer to the character as "Lauren," with a soft, almost parental fondness—but in

Butler's personal notes she is *always* "Olamina." Not the lovable child—the complex, troubling adult. That was Butler's perspective on the character, suggesting her initial inability to find something in the character to admire. When she reflected on the series after it was finished, she realized that she started out not liking Lauren because she was a power seeker; it was only later that she came to see power as just another tool that could be wielded better or worse.[21] By the time *Sower* was finished, of course, Butler admitted, "I had come to like Olamina far too much"—a fondness which made *Talents*, a book that punishes Lauren over and over, difficult to write.[22]

In the end, you might say Butler cheated: she made Lauren not only a young teenager, but a teenager with a severe disability, and furthermore gave her a tragic backstory that made her incredibly sympathetic. More than that, though, Butler made Lauren lovable by making her more like herself. In personal journals Butler admitted Olamina was her idealized self, her best self—and the poetry that drove the Earthseed religion actually closely mirrored the style and form of the daily affirmations, self-help sloganeering, and even self-hypnosis techniques Butler posted around her home to keep herself focused and on task. One need look no further than the opening epigraph of *Sower*, which uses totem words cribbed from Butler's own advice for writers:

Prodigy is, at its essence
adaptability and persistent,
positive obsession.[23]

There was something of a "positive obsession" to the writing of *Sower*. From the initial May 1989 notes to the March 1990 outline, on to the September 1990 letter wherein she begged her agent to be patient while she wrote, to the final November 1992 delivery of the first version of the book, and then through the March 1993 final revision, *Sower* took Butler almost four years to write—and it was always just the backstory for a much larger narrative to come.

PARABLE OF THE SOWER

Lauren Olamina lives in a near-future society (2024) that is collapsing on every level. "I have read," writes Taylor Franklin Bankole, the character who would eventually become Lauren's husband, "that the period of upheaval that journalists have begun to refer to as 'the Apocalypse' or more commonly, more bitterly, 'the Pox' lasted from 2015 through 2030—a decade and a half of chaos. This is untrue. The Pox has been a much longer torment. It began well before 2015, perhaps even before the turn of the millennium. It has not ended." For those who would call the Pox bad luck —"accidentally coinciding climatic, economic, and sociological crises"—our historian has even more bad news: "It would be more honest to say that the Pox was caused by our own refusal to deal with obvious problems in those areas. We caused the problems: then we sat and watched as they grew into crises."[24]

In this sense the Parables series represents prophecy rather than fantasy, prediction rather than escapism—the world of the Parables, the world of Lauren's childhood, is the world Butler believed we were actually creating. "Sometime ago I read some place that Robert A. Heinlein had these three categories of science-fiction stories: the what-if category; the if-only category; and the if-this-goes-on category," Butler told an audience at MIT in 1998. "And I liked the idea. So this is definitely an if-this-goes-on story. And if it's true, if it's anywhere near true, we're all in trouble."[25] The one truly fantastic conceit in the Parables books is the presence of a psychosomatic malady called "hyperempathy"—derived from the failed "justice plague" of contagious empathy that Butler had experimented with after Xenogenesis—brought about by contact with a toxic prescription "smart drug" in the womb, which causes its sufferers to falsely experience the sight of another's pain as their own. *Parable of the Sower* and *Parable of the Talents* are otherwise Butler's least fantastic series of novels, her attempt to write in the mode critics and fans would later call "mundane SF," to denote those science fiction stories that remain in accordance with the laws of physics as we understand them.[26] She got most of it—even the most horrible bits—just from watching the "daily news."[27]

The situation of the novels is a slow-motion apocalypse: global warming, economic depression, and neoliberalism's accelerative hollowing-out of the public sphere have conspired to leave America in a state of near-total collapse. It's for this reason that Mathias Nilger astutely points out the Parables books "are not postmodern but post-Fordist novels": they depict a future-facing version of the breakdown of postwar prosperity that began in the 1970s and was already reaching crisis proportions in the 1990s.[28] In a more recent piece, Nilger expands this reading of the Parables, noting that they anticipate the twenty-first-century rise of a "post-apocalyptic industry" of books and films like *The Walking Dead*, *The Hunger Games*, *The Giver*, *Divergent*, and others; the Parables books, he notes, are especially successful at "render[ing] legible the attraction to the logic of universal collapse and devastation that underlies the neoliberal imagination" in a way that goes beyond mere escapism.[29] The broken-down world of Lauren's childhood, if surely not a utopian space in its own terms, becomes the precursor for the better world she is able to inaugurate. As Lauren herself reminds her family over and over again at the beginning of *Parable of the Sower* (with little success): "In order to rise / From its own ashes / A phoenix / First / Must / Burn."[30]

The earliest versions of the Olamina character found in the Huntington Library actually grows up homeless, wandering a dangerous, ruined Los Angeles reminiscent of zombie cinema or, perhaps, Cormac McCarthy's *The Road* (2006)—but the Lauren of the published novels grows up relatively safe in a neighborhood walled off from outside incursion, in one of the few locations in America that is still (at least superficially) functional. As the first novel opens, these kinds of heavily armed, neo-gated communities offer a rare refuge from the disastrous decline of late capitalism—and as the story begins even these havens are beginning to be breached. It's dangerous out there, but safe enough inside. But soon enough even that enclave can't protect her, and her town is ransacked by "pyros." With a few survivors, she is forced to wander the world outside, growing her group until she finds a place of relative safety, the isolated farm she names Acorn. In between she develops and begins to evangelize the Earthseed religion, which attempts to foster livable lives in this fallen world while inspiring its adherents to strive for the colonization of the stars. We have already seen, in the interstitial poetic fragments that appear throughout *Sower*, that Lauren has *some* sort of ultimate success: her writing has eventually been collected and published in a book called *Earthseed: The Books of the Living*. We know we are reading the story of this great person's childhood. And the end of the first novel, quoting the Bible's Parable of the Sower, seems to confirm this hope for us: we naturally assume that while some of the seed falls to roads, or rocks, or among vines, Acorn "fell on good ground, and sprang up, and bore fruit an hundredfold."[31]

Lauren suffers from a disability called hyperempathy that causes her to experience other people's pleasures and pains psychosomatically—the philosophical descendent of the failed "justice plague" novel. Hyperempathy is *not* telepathy: it relies on entirely Lauren's perceptions, and thus can be "fooled" (as her brothers maliciously take advantage of in her youth, pretending to be hurt). Hyperempathy, despite being psychosomatic in origin, is nonetheless potentially completely debilitating, especially in a world with so much pain to go around. But this empathic weakness is simultaneously her strength—by forcing people to taste the pain they cause others, it opens up the possibility of new and genuine ethics, and of a better world than this one.

Dialectically, however, hyperempathy also makes Lauren extremely dangerous and drives her to be an efficient and effective killer. Individuals with hyperempathy can't afford merely to *wound* their opponents; if they are going to use violence, it needs to be quick, brutal, and total. Lauren has to aim to kill, and sometimes to shoot first. The tension between these two modes of hyperempathy is present in Butler's earliest notes for the Parables series, before they or even Olamina had their final names: "This is the story of Oya Martin, an involuntary killer who must kill, yet whose conscience forces her to create a life-revising religion to help heal her disintegrating society."[32] As Ingrid Thaler argues in her chapter on the book in *Black Atlantic Speculative Fiction*, the book itself embodies a version of this same paradox on the level of theme: its incisive and prescient critique of political neoliberalism at one and the same time celebrates futurological tropes we might typically associate with the right-wing thinkers Butler loathed: the federal government is corrupt, proto-fascist, and can't save you; local communities need to be heavily armed so as to defend themselves with brutal violence from drug-addicted outsiders; nearly all of your neighbors are incompetent at best, wicked at worst, and can't be trusted; only religion can revitalize society; a collapse is coming, so prepare yourselves; and on and on. In some sense the critique of neoliberalism in the Parables books produces not the opposite of neoliberal atomism but a *radically* neoliberal subject—something more neoliberal than even neoliberalism itself.[33]

A similar paradox can be seen more generally in Earthseed, which seeks to inspire its adherents to the great task of colonizing the stars at the same time it suggests that this task would be both in some sense counter to human nature and ultimately hollow. The stars would provide us safety from local disaster: a humanity spread across many worlds is free from fear of the extinction threat posed by rogue asteroids or nuclear war, or superdisease, or supervolcanos, or climate change, or anything else you could name—a human species spread safely across many worlds could perhaps survive as long as the universe itself. And yet the tiny Earthseed elect can get to the stars only by abandoning the rest of the planet, the rest of humanity, to misery, starvation, and madness. Likewise, Butler may have chafed when reviewers called Earthseed "warmed-over Christianity"[34]—and yet the Parables' view of the maximum wickedness of the world and the coming salvation of a tiny few certainly has *something* of evangelical Christianity about it.

Despite the strong utopian valence of Lauren's plans to colonize space, then, which would be familiar to any fan of science fiction, the book is filled with paradoxical indications that the vision may be fundamentally flawed, beginning with the opening pages of *Sower*. The first scene of the book foregrounds this tension imagistically, describing a recurring dream in which Lauren is learning to fly but becomes trapped in a burning house before she is able to master it, ultimately succumbing to the flames.[35] This is a barely sublimated version of the conflict that drives political debate in both books in the series: first, *can* you get off the planet before humanity makes it unlivable, and, second, *should* you get off the planet before humanity destroys it? That is, should your ambition be to escape in a tiny utopian enclave called "the Earthseed rocket" while the rest of humanity burns and chokes and starves and dies? Just a few pages later, we find another version of the same fundamental ambiguity, when we are told that "one of the astronauts on the latest Mars mission has been killed"—outer space framed first as a site of death, not new life.[36]

This problem, an undercurrent throughout *Sower*, becomes totally inescapable for us when we get to *Parable of the Talents*, which functions as a sustained reconsideration of the commitments of the first novel. Characters in both books, but especially in *Talents*, repeatedly demand from Lauren an answer as to how she can possibly justify any expenditure on a blue-sky project like Earthseed when the planet is in ruins and everything is getting worse. The second book hits us over the head with this problem, over and over again; like the people who used to shame Butler about her SF writing, Lauren's daughter asks why Lauren cannot see her dreams of a heaven in outer space are "pathetically unreal."[37] "The Earthseed Destiny," Lauren's brother denounces, "is an airy nothing. The country is bleeding to death in poverty, slavery, chaos, and sin." "This is the time," he says, "for us to work for our salvation, not to divert our attention to fantasy explorations of extrasolar worlds."[38] Her own husband cannot tolerate Lauren's "immaturity," she says—"my irrational, unrealistic faith in Earthseed, my selfishness, my shortsightedness."[39] There are dozens of incidents like this across the text, and none of them is ever really answered; in fact, Lauren's daughter, the bitter narrator of the text who is gathering all these other voices together editorially, is among her chief attackers.

Butler was very pleased with the difference between the two books, which she saw as the difference between a fifteen-year-old girl with a fantasy and a twenty-one-year-old woman with a plan: "My god," Butler said, mimicking the disbelieving other voices in *Talents* with a familiarity that suggests perhaps the criticisms she received during her own lean years in the wilderness, (not) scraping by as a writer, "Isn't she ever going to grow up?"[40] The difference between gospel and Talmudic commentary that was implicit in *Sower* becomes a fascinating formal experiment in *Talents*, as the addition of new voices to the first book's combination of old Olamina's published sacred poetry and young Olamina's personal journals results in a highly dialogic book that no longer grants Lauren unquestioned authority. Even Butler herself seems to have lost some hope; while her interviews around *Sower* suggest endorsement of the Earthseed "Destiny," her interviews around *Talents* are much more conflicted. As she tells Marilyn Mehaffy and AnaLouise Keating in May 1997, the introduction of other characters as point-of-view narrators was intended precisely to show "Olamina doesn't have the only truth." Moreover:

> If we humans are, as Lauren believes, and as I believe, a part of Earth in significant ways, then perhaps we *can't*, or shouldn't, leave and go to another world. The system of Earth is self-regulating, but not for any particular species, in the same way that the human body has its own metabolic logic. Perhaps the Acorn community represents the most logical way to halt the damage we're doing to the Earth and to ourselves as humans.[41]

The Gaia hypothesis returns, but here the possibility of adaptation that the *God of Clay* notes foregrounded seems to have become foreclosed; our evolution in Earth's ecology and our grounding in its biome is instead now the reason we shouldn't go to space at all.

It is common, of course, for narratives to contain antagonists, even strong and convincing ones, to be overcome. But the totality of the events of *Talents* leaves us with the sense that these antagonists have a compelling case that Lauren has not rebutted convincingly. First, the Acorn community she founds is brutally destroyed, most of its men killed, its women raped and enslaved, and its children scattered and sold, usually (as with Lauren's child) never to be recovered; despite the optimistic-sounding ending of the first novel, it turns out the settlers of Acorn were in fact cast among the rocks, *not* onto the good ground. Lauren's rape is especially traumatic and horrifying, as her hyperempathy forces her to vicariously experience the pleasure of her attackers even as she is victimized—a supercharged version of the confusing disconnect between body and mind sometimes described by rape survivors, without the bare, fantastic compensation offered by the earlier "contagious" form of hyperempathy in *The Justice Plague*. This section of the novel goes for a hundred pages; it's exhaustingly, unspeakably brutal, even given all the horrible things we've already read in the earlier book. Perhaps even more painful, the novel *as a whole* replicates this attack on Lauren on the level of form: the book's own Talmudic commentary on Lauren's autobiography is a reenactment of Lauren's loss of her daughter, this time in the form of Larkin's conscious rejection of her mother rather than a kidnapping.

Talents is not *purely* a dismantling of the optimism of *Sower*; as Isiah Lavender notes in *Race and Science Fiction*, the point is not simply to negate *Sower's* optimism but to give a vision of what it could cost in practice: "The second Parable novel is possibly greater in consequence than the first because Butler makes visible the strength and perseverance necessary to unlearn racist patterns and resist oppression."[42] As her writing in other places makes clear, she *does* believe SF has something important to offer black people, despite its lack of realism. Similarly, Claire P. Curtis highlights how, in the Parables series and especially in *Talents*, "fear is a necessary step towards what philosopher Jonathan Lear calls 'radical hope.'"[43] But deflation and disillusionment is surely a large part of the experience of *Talents* as well.

Lauren somehow survives all these nightmares and starts again—but this time renounces politics and political commitment even more vociferously than even her previous enclavism. Now the Destiny is *all* that matters. As Tom Moylan puts it in his reading of the books:

In this [new] formulation her analysis is more pragmatic, more modest, than the earlier engaged expressions in her journal. It is no longer a radical response or utopian critique that works from the contradictions and possibilities of history. It does not challenge, alone or with a larger collective voice, the new liberal government to redirect its own economic and political policies. Rather, it articulates a view of history that is cyclical, not dialectical, and implies that the only move forward must be an apocalyptic leap, not *through* the present but *out* of the present, out of this world, and into some new age.[44]

Peter Stillman makes a parallel critique: "Olamina's strategy with Earthseed is primarily legal (she sues the [Christian America] organization and wins, enabling her to bankroll Earthseed) and religious (she proselytizes within the new, reformed system that respects the Bill of Rights), not political (she does not organize to change the political system)." Moreover, "Butler hardly describes the process at all: she jumps from a diary entry of 2035 to one in 2090"—entirely skipping over the interesting years of the original "Dark Olamina" in the process—so "Earthseed's rise to national prominence gets only a few sentences. Earthseed is definitely concerned with welfare and education on this earth, but by creating enclaves within the political system, not by changing that system."[45] We can see precisely why Earthseed ceases to be threatening to the powers that be on Earth; privately funded and enclavist in its methods—essentially going around founding charter schools—in its final formulation Earthseed is perfectly compatible with everything that has made life under neoliberal capitalism so utterly terrible.

It's true, as Butler herself said, that "every tyrant's first enemy is education," and she was personally utterly horrified by cuts to the public schools, state universities, and public library system that had turned her into an avid reader as a child. In 1993 she wrote an essay for *Omni* on the 1986 destruction by arson of the L.A. Central Library she had adored as a child (the place where she had written her first novel), and bemoaned the lack of appreciation for and underfunding of the free public library system in the United States more generally.[46] The supplementary text for her "A Few Rules for Predicting the Future" essay in *Essence* similarity notes that when she was approached by the Clinton administration to write about her vision of the future, she chose to write about threats to education, noting: "Without the excellent, free public education that I was able to take advantage of, I might have found other things to do with my deferred dreams and stunted ambitions."[47]

But it's just as true—as she also knew—that not *all* education turns its charges into radicals. Much education turns students into better workers and prepares them for elite jobs administering, and benefiting from, toxic systems rather than opposing them.[48] Earthseed's neoliberal charity thus represents both an ultimate challenge to the status quo and no challenge to the system at all. From this perspective the utopian religion is revealed to be, at its core, a kind of philosophical quietism—a retreat *from* the world rather than an advance *toward* it. Human history is earthbound—and so Earthseed's ambition to flee to the stars is in the end as much the nullification of the possibility of historical change as it is any type of realization of it. For better or worse, we live on the Earth; if there's going to be any change, it's got to happen down here, not out there.

Even in the moment of Lauren's triumph, then, there is an inescapable sense that Earthseed has turned its back on something that is also vital and necessary and important, that the troubled realization of the Earthseed destiny entails the necessary and unhappy tradeoff of a retreat from real-world political struggle that concretely makes actual people's actual lives substantively better (even while little in the novel suggests real-world struggle might be effective in averting continued disaster). At the end of the novel, Lauren's last journal entries read as much as an exercise in convincing herself as convincing any of us that she has done the right thing and lived the right kind of life. Her final post in the present action line of the story (2035) has her giving up on any purpose but the Destiny, including finding her kidnapped daughter, with whom she is never able to reconcile even after she is found: "I've always known that sharing Earthseed was my only purpose."[49] Then the narrative flashes forward fifty-five years, to the launch of the first Earthseed ship, conveniently skipping over the years when Lauren toiled endlessly to make this happen. Her last journal entry (dated July 20, 2090) begins and ends with her declaration "I know what I've done"[50]—an assertion of pride that concedes a nagging doubt: she has gotten what she wanted, but it has cost her tremendously. The ship, with its crew in cryogenic hibernation, is leaving Earth for a distant star, never to return; it has left human history for something else that no one left behind will ever know.

Even the name of the spaceship rings a sour note. In her article on these novels Marlene Allen discusses "The Boomerang of African American History"—the sense that in this novel (and really across the Butler canon) the true nightmare is that history could be a cycle, that all the bad times could come back again, that progress is never to be trusted.[51] Earthseed is supposed to be the knight's move that can get us out of that trap—but even in the moment of the achievement of the dream the boomerang comes round again. Against Lauren's wishes the ship has been christened the *Christopher Columbus*, suggesting that the Earthseeders aren't escaping the nightmare of history at all but are bringing it with them instead.[52]

PARABLE OF THE TALENTS

As hard as *Sower* had been to write, *Talents* proved even more difficult, not seeing publication until 1998. The early fragmentary versions of *Talents* clearly reflect Butler not quite knowing where she wanted to take the story: in OEB 1823 she is still thinking of Olamina as an empire builder and can't decide whether Larkin (whom Lauren purchases, as she did her adopted son from the first abandoned *Sower* narratives, from slavers) will be the one to fulfill Lauren's dream or else be the one to betray (even kill) her.[53] In another early version, she imagines Lauren's brother Marcus could be the center of the story (though straight—not gay, as he is in the published *Talents*); in extensions of this idea Marcus is even more clearly the villain of the book, a misogynist who is tortured by his own feminization and sexual victimization during his captivity and who seeks to destroy Lauren rather than let her lead. (In this version Larkin is "Martin" and Marcus is "Malcolm," though both are anti-Olamina.)[54] There are pages where Olamina is martyred and the others have to find a way to carry on; another where Lauren is in jail the day the spaceships are launched, a Nelson Mandela figure, fraudulently set up by the state for tax evasion precisely because they didn't want to risk turning her into a martyr by assassinating her; others where a violent coup in Earthseed (usually led by Marcus) ousts Lauren from control of the religion she founded. Another intriguing version brings back the Dark Olamina—this time commanding Earthseed "security forces" in 2047 and personally executing those people who discover their community, people who are too broken or dangerous to recruit but whom they can't dare let go either.[55] Still other versions were intended to be all short stories, each focusing on a different character and a different moment in Earthseed's history. None of them worked. At one point in 1995—April 10—Butler even offered to return her advance to the publisher, promising to deliver the book within eighteen months of its original due date if her publisher is willing to wait for her to get things right.[56]

It would take a bit longer than that, due in part to Butler's increasing writer's block, but also due to the tremendous changes that were about to happen in her life. Exactly two months after she tried to give back the advance for *Talents*, June 10, 1995, Butler writes at the top of a journal entry a cryptic sentence: "Got a call yesterday."[57] The reference is to the call she received from the MacArthur Foundation, awarding her a no-strings-attached $295,000 "genius grant"—an especially prized honor made even more distinctive as the first ever awarded to a science fiction writer. In a flash, her lifelong monetary crises were over: after years of dreaming, she was able, finally, to buy herself a house.[58]

Butler seemed scarcely able to accept that this had happened, rarely discussing the honor in interviews or significantly downplaying it when she

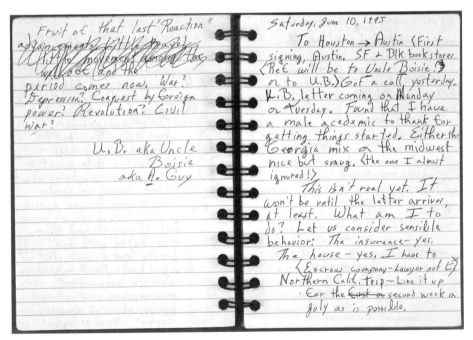

3. Page from personal journal, dated June 10, 1995 (OEB 3196)

discussed it at all. Despite being the instantaneous, quasi-miraculous solution to the money problems that had defined her life, she almost never wrote about it. One has to absolutely scour the Huntington Archive to find any meager reference to it in her journals—the only significant discussion I was able to find was in one of her travel notebooks, penned immediately around the time of the award, where she refers to the grant in code as "Uncle Boisie." In the journal entries around the award she is (quite understandably) overwhelmed, trying to imagine what the award will make possible as well as what new demands her new fame will make on her time. She is already eager to get back to writing. In interviews she usually tries to change the subject back to her novels as quickly as she can; in letters she is humorously self-deprecating, telling (for instance) Vonda McIntyre that she doesn't really care about the MacArthur, just as long as they keep sending her checks.[59] At times in her journals there is a suggestion that the award itself—and her growing prominence more generally—has possibly even become an impediment to her writing; she worried as she struggled over *Talents* that she was "being hampered by [her] own success" and demanding perfection from herself where it was not possible.[60]

The other major change in her life was as significant a loss as the Mac-Arthur was a gain: the death, in November 1996, of Butler's mother after a stroke. She had been very close to her mother and was living with her at the end of Octavia M.'s life—so the loss hit her very hard. (Her private journals show her repeating Olamina's maxims back to herself, as a way of processing her grief: "God is change, and in the end, God prevails.")[61] By the beginning of 1997 she was again preparing to abandon *Parable of the Talents*, thinking instead she might release a short chapbook of Lauren's poems to complement *Sower* and end the series.[62] It was only as she continued to grieve her mother that she was able to get a handle on the story that *Talents* became—now, fully, a mother-daughter story, though paradoxically about a mother and daughter whose relationship had been broken. In a sense, she later said, "[*Talents*] was my mother's last gift to me."[63] Butler herself would comment often on the oddness of this gift, the way the death of her own beloved mother allowed her to finish a story in which a mother and daughter became permanently, gut-wrenchingly estranged.

With *Talents* not only completed but extremely well-received—the book finally won Butler a Nebula Award for Best Novel, a distinction which pleased her greatly—she was finally able to turn to the long-delayed *God of Clay* narrative, now named *Parable of the Trickster* and envisioned as the first of as many as four novels set in outer-space Earthseed colonies. *Trickster*—at least as Butler typically envisioned it—would have been the other sort of mother-daughter story, in which a daughter struggles as best she could to carry on the legacy of a beloved lost mother.

The novel would also solve—or start to solve—the philosophical and existential problems that had preoccupied Butler since at least Xenogenesis, and really over the course of her life's work: the question of how to fix society without being able to fix mankind. I have referred to Butler as a dialectical thinker, but within the Parables books her thinking starts to better resemble the quasi-dialectical form that critical theorists call antinomy: the constitutive contradiction, the stalled or arrested dialectic one is unable to move beyond. The Parables series is structured at its core by antinomy, exemplifying the philosophical tensions we see in Butler's work across her lifetime. We have already discussed a few: the novel's utopian aspirations versus its anti-utopian presuppositions; its critique of neoliberalism coupled with its production and valorization of a kind of ultra-neoliberalism; the tension between helping *the species* survive versus abandoning many or most of *the individual members of the species* to misery; and its two overlapping but ultimately incompatible faces of our lawless, anarchic future, the space of the frontier versus the space of the slum, neither of which feels very much like "progress." The first two Parables set the table for the crisis—*Trickster* was supposed to be the moment when we broke orbit.

But the novel would never be completed; in fact, it would hardly ever be begun. Without it, *Sower* and *Talents* remain bound in a kind of antinomic relationship: *Sower* (utopian dreaming) and *Talents* (anti-utopian reality) are locked in a death struggle that cannot be overcome because the sequel that would have synthesized and moved beyond both can now never be written. As Nisi Shawl has cleverly suggested, *Parable of the Trickster* is the Trickster of the Parables books—the solution in the distance we can recognize but can't see clearly, always hovering just out of our grasp.[64]

In December 2013 I had the improbable privilege to be the very first scholar to open, at the Huntington, the boxes that contain what Butler had written of Trickster before her death. What I found were dozens upon dozens of false starts for the novel, some petering out after twenty or thirty pages, others after just two or three; this cycle of narrative failure is recorded over hundreds of pages of discarded drafts. Frustrated by writer's block, frustrated by blood pressure medication that she felt inhibited her creativity and vitality, and frustrated by the sense that she had no story for Trickster, only a "situation," Butler started and stopped the novel over and over again from 1989 until her death, never getting far from the beginning.

Nearly all of the texts focus on a character named Imara—who has been named the Guardian of Lauren Olamina's ashes, who is often said to be her distant relative, and who is plainly imagined as the St. Paul to Olamina's Christ (her story sometimes begins as a journalist who has gone undercover with the Earthseed "cult" to expose Olamina as a fraud, and winds up getting roped in). Imara awakens from cryonic suspension on an alien world where she and most of her fellow Earthseed colonists are saddened to discover they wish they'd never left Earth in the first place. The world—usually called "Bow"[65]—is gray and dank, and utterly miserable; it takes its name from the only splash of color the planet has to offer: its rare, naturally occurring rainbows. (Later, she realized that making the planet boring would make her book boring; Bow might *look* gray, but it needed to "explode into a deadly tangle of colors and problems."[66])

The colonists have no way to return to Earth, or to even contact it; all they have is what little they've brought with them, which for most (but not all) of them is a strong belief in the wisdom of the teachings of Earthseed. Some are terrified; many are bored; nearly all are deeply unhappy. Her personal notes frame this in biological terms: "phantom-limb pain . . . a somehow neurologically incomplete amputation. Think of problems with the new world as graft-versus-host disease—a mutual attempt at rejection." The book would begin happily, in a seeming utopia, fooling the reader not to expect the coming "long, terrible slide" into disaster. [67]

From here the possible plots begin to multiply beyond all reason. In some of the texts, the colonists are in total denial about the fact that they are all slowly going blind;[68] in other versions the blindness is sudden, striking randomly and irreversibly; in others they all begin to go insane, or suffer seizures, or mad rages, or fall into long comas; in still others they begin to hurt and kill each other for no other reason than the basic inevitable frailty of human nature (the same, alas, on any world). In one of the versions of the novel the colonists develop a telepathic capacity that soon turns nightmarish when they are unable to resist it or shut it off; in one twist on this idea, only the women are so empowered, with the men organizing a secret conspiracy to figure out how they might regain control.

There's a version where the blindness and the telepathy are linked; Imara becomes able to see out of others' eyes as she loses the ability to see out of her own. In some, Imara finds she needs to solve a murder, the first murder on the new world; in still others Imara herself is murdered yet discovers that on this strange alien world she is somehow able to haunt another colonist's body as a ghost, replicating Doro's power from the Patternist books and thereby again linking the Parables to the speculative universe she first developed as a teenager. Sometimes Imara is an Earthseed skeptic; other times she is a true believer; sometimes she is, like Olamina, a hyperempath; sometimes the hyperempaths weren't allowed to go off-world; still other times the cure for "sharing" has been discovered in the form of an easy, noninvasive pill. Sometimes Bow is inhabited by small animals, other times by dinosaur-like giant sauropods, and still other times by just moss and lichens; sometimes the colonists seem to encounter intelligent aliens who might be real yet might just be tokens of their escalating collective madness; and on and on and on. There are pages and pages of wonderful world-building background writing about the way their colony is laid out architecturally, the jobs they do and how often they rotate, how they elect leaders, how they solve conflicts, what they eat . . .

She returned over and over again to world-building aspects of the narrative—the social organization of the colony, the physics governing Bow, the possible organisms that might live in such a place, Earth-historical parallels to their situation—but could never get the plot itself to gel. One version of the blindness narrative was abandoned with no small grumbling after José Saramago won the Nobel Prize in 1998, not long after the publication of his 1995 novel *Blindness*;[69] another was put aside after she determines it's just too similar to Kim Stanley Robinson's famous *Red Mars*;[70] still another was abandoned shortly after Butler frustratedly, self-loathingly declared Imara to have "a personality more like mine" against Olamina's "super me—the me I wish I was."[71] She soldiered on, writing version after version, then mothballing them each one in turn.

Sometimes the Earthseed of *Trickster* seems more like a self-help philosophy; sometimes it becomes a genuinely mystical, transcendent religion; sometimes we see it begin to shift from the first toward the second; sometimes it suffers schisms, heresies, and purges. (Even the first words of *Talents* point us toward this plot—"They'll make a God of her"[72]—a reversal of the impersonal vision of God-as-Change that made Earthseed so vital and adaptable, and a return to the bad discourse of holy texts and sacred cows that Lauren had sought to overthrow.) Butler imagined the subsequent books in the Parables series detailing the way the true history of Earthseed, and indeed the actual history of the human race, would "dissolve into myth." Extrasolar colonization is here reframed as "a form of species reincarnation," requiring first, in some sense, the death of the old one.[73]

The specifics of character and plot were similarly variable. Sometimes Imara is a former cop; other times she is a trained psychologist; a doctor; that undercover journalist; the victim of a horrific series of rapes as a child, saved by one of Olamina's orphanages when no other entity or institution would bother. Imara often has a strong mother-daughter relationship with Olamina (who sometimes appears in much of the narrative in flashback, or even sometimes as a hallucination/ghost); in some versions Imara herself is the mother of the colony, herself betrayed by her children and deposed, which is both a disappointment and a relief.[74] When Butler begins writing the book, Newt Gingrich is often named as the model for the central antagonist; in the versions from the early 2000s, it's George W. Bush; sometimes in between, it's other science fiction writers, those working in a more conservative, "hard SF" vein, with whom Butler didn't especially get along.

As Butler describes her long-term plan in an interview: "I'm not interested in confronting them with natives. I've done that elsewhere. What I'm going to confront them with is just a nasty world. It's not violent, just nasty and dull and awful, and what they're going to have to deal with is themselves. There's no going home. Nobody will follow within their lifetimes. . . . The real problem is dealing with themselves, surviving their promised land."[75] Thinking of both *Sower* and *Talents* as "heavy downers,"[76] she hoped, this time, *finally* to write that YES-BOOK.[77] But both the narrative situation and real-world events weighed heavily on her. Perhaps too convinced of the Oankali way of viewing humanity, Butler doubted the ability of humans to adapt to Bow; in 2000, she was thinking of *Trickster* as "the story of a culling."[78] Shortly after September 11, 2001, she wrote "I know now . . . why Imara leaves Earth"[79]—and this was only the beginning of a long period of abject horror at the Bush administration's transformation of the country. When she finally put the project aside and wrote *Fledgling* instead, it was to "get away from the daily news, which was drearier and drearier and more and more awful each day."[80] The world looked too much like the Parables now—and, worse, "doesn't want to be saved, for goodness sake."[81] And in truth this deflated reversal was *always* at least potentially implicit in her valorization of adaptability and survival; weeds and vermin, she recognized during her tough 1990s rewrite of *Talents*, are "tough, adaptable, persistent," too.[82]

Butler had ultimately hoped to write four Parables sequels: *Parable of the Trickster, Parable of the Teacher, Parable of Chaos,* and *Parable of Clay.* The naming convention derives from another of Olamina's poems, the one she describes as the first kernel of the religion to come: "God is Pliable— / Trickster / Teacher / Chaos / Clay."[83] The titles suggest a shift from a Christian idiom (*Sower, Talents,* and *Trickster* all reference Biblical parables) to an Earthseed one (*Teacher, Chaos,* and *Clay* seem likely to be parables drawn instead from Olamina's life, not Christ's). The Parable of the Sower (discussed above) becomes in Butler's retelling a story about the arbitrariness of God's plan, how the farmer throws the seeds indiscriminately and only few land on the good ground. The Parable of the Talents (which closes out *Talents*) seems for Butler to be similarly about the radical *unfairness* of God's justice, which seems to further reward those to whom much has been given and punish those who have been given little:

> His lord answered and said unto him, Thou wicked and slothful servant, thou knewest that I reap where I sowed not, and gather where I have not strawed: Thou oughtest therefore to have put my money to the exchangers and then at my coming I should have received mine own with usury.

Take therefore the talent from him and give it unto him which hath ten talents. For unto every one that hath shall be given, and he shall have abundance: but from him that hath not shall be taken away even that which he hath.[84]

The Parable of the Unjust Steward (or the "Shrewd Manager") (Luke 16:1–13)—a likely candidate for the biblical inspiration for Butler's proposed "Parable of the Trickster," as that is one of its less common alternative names—shifts the terms away from the hopelessness implied by Butler's use of the other parables, allowing the diminished party to get one over on the Lord. An unusual and perplexing parable, in this one the master comes to his servant and says that they must have a talk, because there have been reports the steward has been wasting the master's money. Before he is able to be fired, however, the steward goes to everyone who owes the master and uses his authority as legal proxy to wipe all their debts clean. The steward's thinking is that, having done this, one of the other houses will be grateful to him and take him in—and, in fact, the lord is so impressed with the steward's cutthroat savvy that he retains him as a servant after all!

The moral "lesson" of this parable can be somewhat hard to understand, even by the standards of the more obscure biblical parables:

> And the lord commended the unjust steward, because he had done wisely: for the children of this world are in their generation wiser than the children of light. And I say unto you, Make to yourselves friends of the mammon of unrighteousness; that, when ye fail, they may receive you into everlasting habitations. He that is faithful in that which is least is faithful also in much: and he that is unjust in the least is unjust also in much. If therefore ye have not been faithful in the unrighteous mammon, who will commit to your trust the true riches? And if ye have not been faithful in that which is another man's, who shall give you that which is your own? No servant can serve two masters: for either he will hate the one, and love the other; or else he will hold to the one, and despise the other. Ye cannot serve God and mammon.[85]

The Parable of the Unjust Steward—if it had been the one she chose[86]—suggests that another major antinomy in *Trickster* would have been an extension of a central problem in *Sower* and *Talents*, a question that drove so much of Butler's fiction: the tension between survival of the body and survival of the soul. How *would* the colonists survive their "promised land"? What would they become, and what would they be forced to *do*? What sorts of compromises would they be made to bear, and what sorts of compromises might prove unendurable?

Some of Butler's plans suggest that the four novels might have taken place on four different Earthseed colonies, without having any characters or situations in common, showing the diversity of thought Earthseed makes possible—but more commonly she imagines them taking place across the generations on the single world of Bow, as each generation confronts its own new crisis and Earthseed evolves to meet the needs of extrasolar humanity in each new historical moment. Bow itself was the Trickster—sometimes they even name the planet "Trickster" instead—sending them challenge after challenge to force them to evolve.[87] When the hallucinations are dealt with— not defeated or cured, she was clear, but adapted to—her notes indicate the colony would have struggled with dictatorship, and then with catastrophic ecological scarcity, and finally with the strangeness of children who were genuinely novel, genuinely new, genuinely post-Earth if not quite posthuman: the creepy children of Bow, born from frozen embryos and raised in alternative, non-nuclear family units, for whom the "screaming colors" of Earth might have seemed the real horror. In OEB 2081 the children go beyond creepy to nightmarish: they are described as severely autistic or psychotic, playing "odd games" among themselves that presage another round of hallucinations and catastrophe—but elsewhere in her notes for *Trickster* Butler notes that the Baby Boom generation of blacks (of which she was a part) was itself four generations removed from slavery, suggesting that the weird differences between our world could be a part of a transformative progressive change, a future of difference to be embraced rather than feared.[88]

Butler's disposition toward the outer-space Earthseed colonies is similarly polyvalent. Characters in the books frequently say that the Earthseeders will have their Heaven without dying—but Butler would have turned their Heaven into, if not Hell, then at least into just another Earth where they needed to figure out how to live. In fact, she realized as she wrote *Trickster* that, to the Earthseeders—trapped on another world on which human beings did not evolve and to which they fundamentally do not belong—*Earth* would be remembered "As all that is sweet and beautiful / As all that is good / As Heaven."[89]

In short we discover that achieving Earthseed's Destiny, despite Lauren Olamina's dreams, hasn't solved the problem of history or the human at all, only extended our confrontation with the very difficult problems that drove its development in the first place—only removed them to some other world where they can take some other form. The Destiny was essentially a hyperbolic delaying tactic, a strategy of avoidance; even achieved, it's worthless in its own terms. The fundamental problem is still how to make a better world with such bad building blocks as human beings.

As the preceding chapters have surely demonstrated, Octavia Butler was no utopian; in fact, she tended to reject utopian thinking in the strongest possible terms. She believed human beings were biological organisms with sharp instincts for self-preservation that had been honed by evolution over innumerable millennia; she believed evolution had made us clever but mean, creative but selfish and short sighted. In the Xenogenesis books the aliens who visit the planet determine we are fundamentally broken as a species, brilliant enough to invent nuclear bombs and hierarchal enough, crazy enough, stupid enough to actually use them. In the first Parable book, the young Olamina seems like an exception to this unhappy general diagnosis, even perhaps something like a moral saint—but the other narrators of *Talents* and the redacted fragments of her middle years suggest her to be just as easily as a selfish, destructive, and extremely dangerous fanatic, a zealot willing to sacrifice anything and anyone for the Destiny. (One of my favorite never-used fragments for *Trickster* is the incredibly dark notion that Olamina's diagnosis might even be *wrong*: Butler imagines a Bow that is able to make contact with Earth, which more or less replies, *It's great to hear from you, but listen, we solved all our problems while you guys were in Hypersleep. Things are great here now; please don't come back.* [90])

What the all-important dream of the Destiny offered Olamina, offered Butler—offers *us*—is a chance not to abolish human nature but to perhaps temporarily suspend it; the extrasolar colonies are the chance to start over in circumstances whose radical hardship would offer the chance to build new practices of solidarity and collective life rather than indulge the selfish impulses the bad habits of capitalism and the bad instructions in our DNA have ingrained in us. (*"If* we survive," remember, "we have a whole solar system to grow up in." That's about as optimistic as Butler could allow herself to get.) Her cynicism led to Butler to think humans, as a species, won't behave more decently toward each other and toward our environment unless and until we have literally no other choice—and maybe not even then. But her optimism led her to believe that when push finally comes to shove we are actually capable of it, and might actually do it. Getting off the planet, achieving the Destiny, was to be the start of the hard work, not the end of it—the unfinished Parables sequels would have been Butler's chance to imagine that we might find some way to be better human beings *out there* than our bad history has ever allowed us to be *here*.

The epigram she chose for Trickster wonderfully captures this tension between optimism and pessimism, and the possibility of actually breaking through this psychic impasse into something new, quite wonderfully:

There's nothing new
under the sun,
but there are new suns.

Bow was a place where history wasn't the unhappy curse we were condemned to, a place where the tug-of-war between collective survival and collective insanity might play itself out in another way. On Bow, they can choose: either live together, work together, struggle together, and pray together, or else hoard food alone, scheme alone, lose their minds alone, break down and betray each other and die alone. And the tragedy is that Butler was never able, in her too-short life, to think through the hopeful part. Not "if this goes on," but "if only": if only she'd been able to complete that vision of better humanity, not perfect, not even perfectible, just better. If only she'd been able to finish the book.

CHAPTER 7

PARACLETE (1999–2006)

Published Works

"Amnesty" (2003)
"The Book of Martha" (2003)
Fledgling (2005)

Significant Unpublished Work

Parable of the Trickster (ca. 1989–2006)
Paraclete (alternate title: *Mortal Words*) (ca. early 2000s)
Spiritus (alternate title: *Bodhisattva*) (ca. early 2000s)
Fledgling sequel (usual title: *Asylum*) (ca. 2005)

In the last years of her career Butler had become something more than just another science fiction writer: she had become a public intellectual, particularly in the black community that had by now embraced her as one of its great and most celebrated futurists. She received fan mail and accolades from celebrities like Whoopi Goldberg, LeVar Burton, and Queen Latifah; she was a frequent visitor and guest of honor not simply at science fiction conventions but at countless colleges and universities (including Kenyon College, where she was awarded an honorary doctorate in 1997); she was an important and influential capital-A Author, with a back catalog being taken up in very different ways by the different fandoms and literary communities that had embraced her; she had become, by way of Donna Haraway, a pillar of third-wave academic feminism and someone whose work was being championed as exemplary of new ways of thinking about desire, the body, and the future. She had even become—improbably for the shy girl who had hidden in her room and for the woman who had once written and rehearsed small talk to ensure it went the way she wanted—a seasoned public speaker, giving frequent addresses that moved from reflections on her own career to sharp and funny analysis of the contemporary political moment, often utilizing beloved strips from political cartoonist Jules Feiffer and Bill Watterson, the creator of *Calvin and Hobbes*. (One *Calvin and Hobbes* cartoon was a particular favorite, often used as either an opener or a closer for her public addresses: Calvin leads Hobbes on a disastrous downhill wagon ride, right off a cliff, while proclaiming "ignorance is bliss," shutting off Hobbes's dazed attempt to analyze their misadventure with "Careful! We don't want to learn anything from this.") She was now a frequent teacher of creative writing, and a staple of the Clarion program that had helped her get started back in 1970, as well as an incredibly gener-ous mentor to the fans who wrote her asking for help with their careers; the Huntington archive is filled with the long and detailed letters of critique she would write back to them, which often included her phone number and invitations to call her at her home.

But these salad years of public fame were quite difficult for her from a creative perspective. Her inability to progress on *Parable of the Trickster* was, from Butler's perspective, the largest failure of her career, and a very worrying sign of decline—but it wasn't the only source of writerly frustration in the final years of her life. In fact, she had a long list of potential projects that she cycled through over and over, only a tiny handful of which she was ever able to bring to completion. Her journals from this period are agonizing to read: she feels she has not only grown old but also grown *sick*, with the multiple medications she was taking sapping her energy, her creativity, her sex drive (which for her was always intimately connected to her creativity),[1] her passion, and her joy. While new ideas would periodically come to her and (briefly) excite her, she felt the magic had somehow gone away, or wasn't working for her in the way it was supposed to, the way it used to. In her journals over the last five years of her life, she would list, over and over, the same half-dozen titles and story hooks as her to-do list, berating herself for being unable to move forward with any. Nearly all of them simply fizzle out in the face of disappointment or disgust. She spent her final decade trying to jumpstart a "second wind," out of skill and craft, if not passion.[2] "Enjoy this one," she reminds herself in one of her affirmative sticky notes she would place around her house as encouragement. "Love your readers. Say Yes!"[3]

Unfortunately, most of those other failed projects are as fragmentary and underdeveloped as the various *Trickster* drafts; in most cases they actually were just spinoffs or derivatives of versions of *Trickster* that Butler had abandoned. The versions of *Trickster* that contained aliens, for instance, mutated into a number of possible alien invader stories. One was an idea for a story usually called "Eden," a clever twist on the cliché of alien invasion as well as (perhaps) an allegory for her stalled creativity: the aliens arrive from outer space, burrow deep underground, and then completely disappear, seeming to die out in Earth's inhospitable soil environment. The story would have detailed the efforts of a black female historian to make some sense of this mysterious sudden arrival, which had seemed to change everything we know about philosophy, science, and religion, and yet had actually changed almost literally nothing.[4]

After many mutations, "Eden" became her published story "Amnesty," first printed at scifi.com and then in the second edition of *Bloodchild*. "Amnesty" depicts the aftermath of an alien invasion, an encounter with ineffable hive-mind Communities that arrive on the planet and integrate themselves into the social fabric of human civilization, becoming legal persons and even entering into complex employment contracts. The Communities likewise change everything and nothing—in the end they amount to just another brutal corporate employer in a broken-down world where "almost nobody else" is hiring.[5] Our heroine, Noah Cannon, is one of the people they abducted when they first arrived, who now works for them as a translator and interviewer; she grew up, like young Estelle, in lonely isolation in the "Mojave Bubble."

The workings of the Communities are somewhat inscrutable even to Noah, though she understands them better than most. She can describe the aliens only negatively: they are not like sea urchins, or beehives, or plants, or lichen, but something else entirely—the end product of a radically different evolutionary process from the one that created us.[6] Upon their arrival, we could barely even recognize each other as mutually intelligent, much less communicate.

The story is one of Butler's most direct engagements with colonization narrative, interesting to read alongside the Xenogenesis books for their shared depictions of alien invaders who, from one perspective, look completely different from all human history while, from the other, look *exactly* like human history as we sadly know it. "I'm angry because I have to be here!" rants one of Noah's job interviewees hopelessly. "I'm angry that these things, these weeds can invade us, wreck our economies, send the whole world into depression just by showing up. They do whatever they want to us, and instead of killing them, all I can do is ask them for a job!"[7] Noah is angry too; she had her entire life stolen from her, first by the Communities who kidnapped her, and second by the other human abductees within her Bubble, who raped and impregnated her during her captivity. (In a twist on Butler's more typically affirmative take on reproductive futurity, Noah views the resulting miscarriages as a blessing.[8]) But just as with the Oankali, the simple fact is the Communities are "here to stay," whether humans like it or not:

> They've settled here and they'll fight to keep the various desert locations they've chosen for their bubbles. If they do decide to fight, we won't survive. They might be destroyed too, but chances are, they would send their young deep into the ground for a few centuries. When they came up, this would be their world. We would be gone.

Now Noah, like Lilith, is forced to mediate between the two species "before one of them does something fatal," despite being an outsider to both communities.[9] Also like Lilith, she is accused of being a Judas, but she instead sees herself in terms like her namesake, saving whomever she can, as best she can.[10]

The end of the story reveals that there is absolutely no hope, even for suicidal resistance, on the part of the humans: the Communities somehow prevented the detonation of the nuclear missiles that were launched at them upon their arrival (and absconded with half of them). "It was a short, quiet war," Noah tells her interviewees. "We lost."[11] The story denies even the sort of compromised, happy resolution that seemed possible in the Xenogenesis books, as the relevant symbiotic form here is not the form of the *hybrid* but the form of the *drug*. The aliens, without planning to, have become addicted to the pleasures they derive from "enfolding" us in their weed-like tentacles; that is the job for which Noah is interviewing, the only role left for humans to participate in the future. (Humans, Noah darkly speculates, may even be brought to the stars this way: not as co-pilots, but as pets.)[12]

The story is an interesting, if extremely bleak, success, but perhaps too much a retread of the themes of the Xenogenesis books and "Bloodchild"; Butler's vague plans to expand it into a novel never went much beyond the brainstorming stage. She *could* tell the story of Noah and others "forced to endure their own separate captivity experiences," she writes in December 2005, a few months before her death; "Problem is," she says, "I feel as though I've already done that."[13] In *Strange Matings* Thomas Foster even suggests that "Amnesty" may be purposefully derivative, as a "deliberate response to the misreadings which the Xenogenesis novels generated"—another attempt on her part, he argues, to map out a vision of "necessary coexistence" that is *neither* colonialist *nor* utopian.[14]

The body-hopping versions of *Trickster* ultimately become *Bodhisattva* (sometimes *Spiritus*), a narrative about a community of people with the ability to be reincarnated as newborns after their deaths. Butler worked a bit on the earliest chapters, in which a spirit passing through her first two lives (first, a death as an old woman, then a quick death as a sexually abused and murdered child) is then enculturated into the larger Bodhisattva community over the course of her subsequent lives. The trope would have allowed Butler fresh opportunity to play with the ideas of gender and race, as the contiguity of the characters' mental identities would have been totally independent from their temporary embodiment in any particular racialized or gendered form. It would have also been an opportunity for her to continue the interest in utopian formulations: "*Spiritus*," she synopsizes in her advertising-copy mode, is the story of a "reincarnating spirit" who joins with others like itself to "take over the country and eventually the world aiming to run it without world wars, without starvation, with universal education, healthcare, and sustainable environmental stewardship so that we live more lightly on the earth."[15] But true to form, she was just as interested in the infighting and multiple desires that would inevitably exist in such a community: the difference between those who want to fix the world and those who want to rule it, versus those who simply want to pursue pleasure or who want to be left alone in obscurity. She was especially intrigued by the idea of the anti-Bodhisattva, a faction splintering off from the group that views their condition as a horrible curse, that seeks to be bring about the extinction of the human race so as to finally allow them all to die; in one fragment these self-genociders become the chief protagonists of the narrative.[16] In yet another version of the story (related to the "Frogs" fragments described below), the transmigrating souls become mixed up in a global crisis as fewer and fewer male children are born.[17] But despite these promising avenues the project was ultimately, from her perspective, another creative failure. "Can we be straight here?" she writes to herself in a late journal entry. "I feel bad about *Spiritus* because it echoes (rather feebly) *Doro*."[18] Even so, as late as January 2005 she was still including *Bodhisattva/Spiritus* on her private list of potential projects, whether as a stand-alone novel or "possibly in or as *Trickster*."[19]

The idea of a tiny group seeking to use a superhuman power to change the world also recurs in *Paraclete*, the unfinished novel Butler worked on most in the late period of her career. Around one hundred pages of *Paraclete* exist, though written across three or four incompatible narrative settings, none of which progresses very far beyond the initial "exposition" phase of the narrative. *Paraclete*, like *Spiritus*, descends from the body-hopping version of *Trickster*, a mutation of a mutation. In one version of that idea for *Trickster*, two characters inhabiting a single body are able to write letters back and forth to one another in order to explain what is happening. Butler was intrigued by this modification of the epistolary form and retained it, even after abandoning that version of *Trickster*, imagining instead an entire book written in the form of a letter handed down as a legacy from a benefactor to an inheritor. Here the legacy is another strange power, a fantasy that Butler had had intimate acquaintance with over the course of her entire life via her rituals of self-hypnosis and daily affirmation: the ability to write down *Truth*, that is, the ability to have any statement you write down magically become a fact. The epistolary form of the novel would have been Sibyl August Baldwin (perhaps borrowed from the "Aunt Sibyl" of *Blindsight*), writing down the story of her life as an elderly bearer of this strange power to the next person to possess it; the character who would have been Imara in the *Trickster* book is the off-screen recipient, the implied reader of the letters.

As befitting any of Butler's narrative situations, the power would have been much more complicated than simple wish fulfillment; in fact, Sibyl's power turns out to be as much a curse as a blessing. First there is the perhaps expected "genie's curse" or "monkey's paw" complications caused by the unforeseen consequences of inarticulate or insufficiently specific wishes, as when Sibyl writes down that a man will never again hit his wife: the man is in a horrific car accident and permanently paralyzed. How do you save a loved one from addiction—as Sibyl tries to—when you know that the wish "he never uses heroin again" could just as easily result in his sudden death as his going clean? When Sibyl is brutally attacked within her own home, in one unforgettable scene, she must write down the Truth of her own survival in her own blood before she passes out from blood loss—remembering to include careful codicils that she will heal completely and suffer no negative consequences whatsoever as a result of these events. (Surviving completely and perfectly, just as she said, she is then faced with the difficult ethical decision of whether and how to use her omnipotence to punish the people who had harmed her.)

Sibyl's power is difficult in ways that go beyond exploring the complicated rules of proper wish-making. It also makes her absolutely and radically lonely; she wields far too much power over those around her and has intervened too completely in their lives in earnest efforts to help them such that she no longer knows who they are or if their feelings for her are genuine. You can wish for a person to love you or to treat you better, or simply to make the decision you wish they'd make—but the wish is self-defeating, because when you get what you want it is no longer satisfying. You can no longer trust its authenticity. For Sibyl to be successful in helping others, she has to be a careworker rather than a dictator or a commanding God, as Butler notes in some of the earliest notes for the *Paraclete* idea, from October 2000: "She is the comforter, the intercessor, the advocate. She does not 'save' people. She enables them to save themselves."[20] This is, after all, the meaning of "paraclete" in Christian theology: the Holy Spirit.

The idea fascinated Butler; it reminded her of the *Twilight Zone* episodes she had loved in her youth.[21] She returned to it again and again. "I've been getting back into *Paraclete* because I love it and because I want so badly to make a novel of it," she writes in April 2005.[22] "I love it. I'm desperate to write it. It can be powerful. But what to do? Where does she go from discovery to . . . where? . . . I love *Paraclete* and I want to write it. *I want so badly to write it*. And to write it, I absolutely must have a story." But this problem proved in some way to be insurmountable. She considered setting the book in the present, in the recent past, in the frontier past,[23] and even the near future ("it's now 2040—USA as Cuba—worn out, shabby, but hanging on, selling the furniture"[24]), but each time period presented unique challenges that derailed the story. Setting the book in the future killed what was interesting about it to Butler; the story had no stakes unless we could see how Sibyl's well-intentioned meddling actually creates our bad history in its misguided efforts to improve it. She imagined, for instance, that Sibyl could have caused the breakup of the Soviet Union, inadvertently creating the Reagan presidency in the process. But this proved an insurmountable narrative problem; she simply saw no way that someone with Sibyl's power and political leanings would have allowed the Reagan administration to happen at all. She knew perfectly well that if she could have found a way to prevent Reagan's presidency, she would have done so, even if it just meant using her powers to cause him to "hoot like a chimp during the debates or fall dumb or weep or wet himself or any number of public gaffes that would hurt him."[25] Despite many attempts, she could find no moment in history to set *Paraclete* where the plot made sense both logically and emotionally.

In the end the only version of the *Paraclete* narrative that saw print was "The Book of Martha," a short story first published at scifi.com in 2003 (a mutation of a mutation of a mutation). In an interview with Susan Stamberg, Butler actually described "Martha" as a way of "ridding myself of the need to write" the *Paraclete* fantasy, which she says would have been a "frivolous" "break" between the grim *Talents* and the equally grim *Trickster*—though in fact she never dropped the idea of expanding *any* of the versions of the story into novels.[26] Butler's initial notes for "The Book of Martha," from August 2001, describe it as a story about utopian world-fixing very much in the *Paraclete* mode, using the veil-of-ignorance thought experiment from John Rawls as its science fictional premise: the main character would be allowed to make magical changes (without killing or changing people's outward appearances) but would then "live on the lowest rung of the resultant society."[27] But the version of "Martha" that we know reads more like a renunciation of that line of fantastic utopian thinking. Its protagonist, Martha Bes, is a childless black female science fiction writer raised in poverty by a single mother now living in Seattle (a figure that may at this point sound somewhat familiar), who is approached by God to save humanity from its reckless destruction of the environment. "You will help humankind to survive its greedy, murderous, wasteful adolescence," God says. "Help it find less destructive, more peaceful, sustainable ways to live."[28] Martha is given a taste of full omnipotence, even more powerful than Sibyl's; whatever she says simply happens immediately, exactly as she said. The constraint that she not kill is removed from the published version explicitly; Martha actually begs for this kind of constraint, but God says, "I won't fix things for you. . . . You have a free hand."[29] God even suggests that "it would be better for" Martha if she had raised a child or two, as that experience would have taught her that love can sometimes require causing pain.

Martha and God debate a minimal intervention that Martha might make—freezing the birth rate at two children—only to determine that the consequences of this change would ramify across society so completely as to be both entirely unpredictable and undesirable. In fact, God leads Martha to the anti-utopian conclusion that any change she makes to the nature of the human "will probably destroy them."[30] In the end Martha considers the possibility of giving every human being a private utopia, the one best suited for them, in their dreams. She and God—no longer looking like a white man, now with an appearance instead almost like that of Martha's sister—discuss whether the dreams could be used both to make people happier and to educate them, to push the species in the direction of maturity. God won't promise that the dreams will perfect humanity—in fact he promises they won't—but he says the dreams will do as Martha asks. She takes the deal. But Martha is mournful: she has decided, and God has confirmed, that the dreams will destroy her ability to make a living as a writer; people won't need books anymore if the dreams can give them a fully immersive, total experience designed just for them. So Martha asks God to make her forget what she's done: "I'm afraid the time might come when I won't be able to stand knowing that I'm the one who caused not only the harm, but the end of the only career I've ever cared about. I'm afraid knowing all that might drive me out of my mind someday."[31] Even if the dreams fix humanity, the price is terrible—perhaps too terrible to accept psychologically.

"I don't like utopia stories because I don't believe in them for a moment," Butler writes in the *Bloodchild* afterword for "The Book of Martha"; "It seems inevitable that my utopia would be someone else's hell."[32] So she devilishly crafts the utopia for everyone else that is *her* hell: the world where she can't write anymore, the world where there aren't any more stories to be told. Butler sometimes thought about turning "Martha" into a full novel about the human species drifting away into the utopia of sleep: "The world becomes grayer and less progressive, less productive as people are unable to resist wildly dynamic dreams. Wars peter out. Infrastructure is mostly allowed to rot. People need only a safe place to sleep, enough to eat to stay healthy, and willingness enough to produce and care for the next generation."[33] This is the very fog into which Butler felt herself slipping across the last five years of her life, as her concentration lagged and her health worsened, and her ability to write slipped further and further from her grasp. She was happy now that she had moved to Seattle, and she loved her home there—but felt just as unproductive and as tired as she had felt in California.

The *Paraclete* and "Book of Martha" narratives were ultimately versions of the dream of "fixing" of the human species that had driven (and stymied) the Parables books: "On the one hand," she writes in her journal, "I want to write fix-the-world scenarios. I seem to need to write then. The fact that I don't believe in them—don't believe humanity is fixable—does create a problem."[34] Neither the Parables version—starting over with new values on another planet—nor the *Spiritus* version—a cabal of like-minded world-healers taking action to save this one—nor the *Paraclete* version—a single, good-hearted woman given immense power—seemed able to jump the gap between today and a better future that Butler was so desperate to cross in the final years of her life. In that same journal entry she looks back to her longstanding idea of writing about a matriarchal society, an idea she'd been thinking about in various forms since the 1970s. She imagines that the only way for a "male-run humanity [to] shift to a female-run humanity" would be for men to "change in a basic, genetic way" or else for "their numbers [to be] permanently and absolutely diminished. . . . Real change, is, in this case, biological change.[35] It was an idea that was on her mind a lot in the early 2000s; one intriguing entry on the list of stories she planned is about an all-male or all-female planet, simply called "Frogs"—presumably because some frog species have the ability to switch genders spontaneously.[36] Change biology, and you could change society—but could you change society on its own? Were we as a species simply condemned to permanent misery, all because of how we have evolved?

This was the conundrum that the Oankali books had posed to her, and the Parables had been intended (but failed) to solve: How do you create a more sustainable, more benign, more *livable* society when you're stuck working with human beings? The Oankali had solved the problem by eliminating *Homo sapiens* and transforming them little by little, for better or worse, into something new—a process we saw from the largely horrified perspective of the humans being so transformed. Butler's next published book, *Fledgling*—the last published in her lifetime—would take up that same idea of biologic change but from the opposite direction, imagining a different sort of body difference that could transform (and possibly improve) society, this time written from the first-person perspective of the vampiric invader.

FLEDGLING

"I don't know how to deal with all this, Renee . . . Shori. It's like being told that extraterrestrials have arrived, and I'm sleeping with one of them."[37] Wright's offhand remark links *Fledgling* to the complex set of philosophical and existential concerns raised by the Oankali books (and never quite answered by the Parables). His interlocutor, Shori, is an Ina, a science-fictionalized, biologically rational version of the mythological vampire, who has woken with severe amnesia after a brutal attack on her home that has left her the only survivor. We meet Shori in this highly vulnerable state, looking like an eleven-year-old child even though she is actually fifty-three—though, in Ina terms, this still represents a state of young adolescence. "It was fun writing about someone who is 53, and still a child," Butler tells Vonda McIntyre in a letter—suggesting there might be some level of exuberant identification there on the part of the author, who was in her own mid-fifties when she started the book.[38]

Wright is Shori's companion, her lover, and her source of blood—and, as we eventually discover, her chemically enthralled slave.

We might note the trick borrowed from the Parables books: Shori is again a child suffering from a severe disability, in this case catastrophic, permanent memory loss. We are immediately drawn to her and made to sympathize with her, as we experience her panic and shock through first-person narration. And, as with Olamina, the pull of this identification and sympathy is sufficiently powerful that the disturbing information Shori discovers about herself as the novel progresses is never quite able to disrupt it—even as we discover that Shori's bite possesses an addictive, mind-altering venom that quite literally enslaves humans to her will, and that she even gives off pheromones that can cause other vampires to lose their sense of free choice altogether as well. Shori remains for many readers an uncomplicated heroine even as the evidence piles up that her role is much more ambiguous, and potentially much more monstrous, than that flat reading would suggest. In *Dawn*, Nikanj creepily insisted it knew Lilith and Joseph's desires and could give them the ecstatic psychosexual experiences they longed for but were unable to request directly. If anything, Shori's behavior is even more aggressively opposed to twenty-first-century norms about sex and consent—her bite overwrites her victims' desires altogether and makes them an adjunct to her own whims and commands.

A close reading of our first introduction to Wright makes this narrative tension clear. We encounter Wright as a driver who stops to help Shori when he discovers her alone by the side of the road, shortly after she has woken. Wright is concerned for this girl he has just met—who appears to be a child—and plans to take her to either a hospital or a police station in order to get her help; when Shori resists, he attempts to take her to such a place anyway against her will. She bites him—and after this he changes completely. "He tensed, almost pulling his hand way. Then he stopped, seemed to relax." He tells her that what she is doing doesn't hurt "anymore," but feels good; they begin to flirt with one another.[39] Soon Shori is on Wright's lap, asking for permission to bite him:

> "Let me bite you again," I whispered.
> He smiled. "If I do, what will you let me do?"

Shori says "I heard consent in his voice," so she begins to bite him again, now on his neck. After a long drink, she determines "he had enjoyed it—maybe as much as I had."[40] She asks to stay with him, and he agrees, not quite knowing that he can make this work but as determined as her to find a way.

The first time we read the novel, we probably believe Shori's interpretation of these events: Wright is an enthusiastic sex partner, perhaps slightly confused by the intensity of his desire for this "Jailbait. Super jailbait" but nonetheless willing to go forward with their new partnership even if it ultimately destroys his life. Yet the signs are plainly there, even as Wright agrees to all this, that something is off:

> It bothered Wright that all he wanted to do now was keep me with him, that he was taking me to his home and not to the police or to a hospital. "I'm going to get in trouble," he said. "It's just a matter of when."
>
> "What will happen to you?" I asked.
>
> He shrugged. "I don't know. Jail, maybe. You're so young. I should care about that. It should be scaring the hell out of me. It is scaring me, but not enough to make me dump you."
>
> I thought about that for a while. He had let me bite him. I knew from the way he touched me and looked at me that he would let me bite me again when I wanted to.[41]

It isn't for another sixty pages that we find out what explains the disjuncture between what Wright thinks he should believe intellectually and what he desires sexually: "We addict them to a substance in our saliva—in our venom—that floods our mouth when we feed. I've heard it called a powerful hypnotic drug. It makes them highly suggestible and deeply attached to the source of the substance. They come to need it."[42] But few readers go back to reconsider Wright's first scene in light of this new information, thinking instead that he somehow initially consented to this relationship, or (perhaps) that Shori somehow brought out pedophiliac desires that were lying latent within him. In fact, we know almost nothing about who Wright was before he fell under Shori's influence, except that his affect, demeanor, and apparent intentions toward Shori changed completely after he was bitten.

Fledgling was supposed to be Butler's "fun" novel—or at least that's how she wanted to sell it. She tells Juan Gonzalez and Amy Goodman that *Fledgling* is intended to be "lightweight," in contrast to the heavy "cautionary tales" of the Parables; she told the Science Fiction Book Club that *Fledgling* was her escape from "news burnout": "*Fledging* was me having fun."[43] But in fact we can see *Fledgling* as continuous with the line of speculation that drove Butler's work across her career, intensifying with the Oankali books: her sense that the human race was fundamentally broken on a biological level that both drove the way our culture developed and destroyed any attempts to undo the error with politics or ethics. Instead, the only viable solutions were biological, and essentially fantastic: the healing touch of the Oankali, body-swapping bodhisattvas, essentially omnipotent weed-minds who use us as a drug, words of power from a secret matriarchy of vampires hiding in plain sight. (Both the Xenogenesis books and the unfinished Parables series had flirted with her longstanding interest in a feminist utopia, especially in their earliest drafts, but *Fledgling* is the first true matriarchy she envisions.) Here the solution to our problems is found only in a kind of BDSM sex game: we might consent (or be made to consent) to fully submit to the will of those who know better, aligning human society to *their* ends rather than to our own bad self-generated ones.

The solution is no less troubled here than in the Oankali books, though the power of first-person identification seems to drag most readers into taking Shori's side uncomplicatedly. We feel bad for her, especially as we learn over the course of the novel that she is the product of genetic experimentation mixing Ina and human (specifically African American) DNA—a hybridic nature that leads her to experience extreme hate from other Ina on both speciesist and racist grounds. Shori, like so many of Butler's heroines, is another consummate survivor, enduring the impossible and coming out alive and strong—and the challenge she poses to "fixed categories and boundaries" offers, as Ali Brox has argued in *Utopian Studies*, an appealingly postcolonial vision of hybridity and difference where "agency can instigate change."[44]

Paradoxically, however, as the quote from Wright with which I opened suggests, this book can just as easily be seen as a transgenre, first-person rewrite of *Dawn*, this time from the perspective of the Oankali invaders. We don't see enough of her symbionts before she recruits them to understand how much Shori is changing them; matching the pattern established by Wright, we typically see and hear from them at length only after she has already bitten them. Their proclaimed happiness with their new situation is thus deeply suspect. Nor (we should note) do we typically hear about the Ina-symbiont relationship in objective terms: what we almost always hear is the way that the Ina speak about their symbionts *in front of other symbionts*, rather than the way they speak about them when they are alone with each other.

Three exceptions in the novel demonstrate the importance of this distinction. When the Ina Hayden tells Shori the earliest Ina legends about their origins—an Afrofuturist story of diasporic wandering in exile, sometimes framed in biological terms, sometimes religious, sometimes extraterrestrial—he uses "we" and "us" to refer only to the Ina; "we had already joined with humans ten thousand years ago"; "we were weak and sick"; and so on.[45] It is clear from the bloodless way he speaks about humans that he views Ina / not-Ina as the relevant political distinction. Likewise, as soon as Iosif sends Wright away to tell Shori the venomous secret of Ina-symbiont relations, humans immediately become a "they," a "them."[46]

Shori's conversation with the female Ina Joan, late in the book—perhaps the definitive perspective on human-Ina relations offered in the text—takes a similarly Othering stance toward the humans. Here, in private, Joan admits the extent of what symbionts give up to be with the Ina, how many come to "resent us even though they don't truly want to leave, even though they love us." Joan's description of the symbiont-Ina relationship calls to mind the addicted invaders from "Amnesty":

> We need our symbionts more than most of them know. We need not only their blood, but physical contact with them and emotional reassurance from them. Companionship. I've never known even one of us to survive without symbionts. We should be able to do it—survive through casual hunting. But the truth is that that only works for short periods. Then we sicken. We either weave ourselves a family of symbionts, or we die. Our bodies need theirs. But human beings who are not bound to us, who are bound to other Ina, or not bound at all . . . they have no protection against us except whatever decency, whatever morality we choose to live up to. You see?

Here, at least to me, it becomes clear: the Ina are predators after all, surviving off both the blood and the (at least partially unwilling) companionship of the human beings to whom they are addicted—even when they grow genuinely attached to their prey. Here—as with Xenogenesis, "Bloodchild," and "Amnesty"—we again find Butler advancing a biological model of "love" in which affection (however earnest) cannot be disaggregated from exploitation and domination, even literal consumption. Discussions among the Ina about the proper ethical stance to take toward humans thus amount, from this perspective, to debates about animal cruelty in slaughterhouses—they are important debates, yes, but bracket much larger ethical questions about speciesism and dominance. The relationship between Ina and humans is not a mutually beneficial symbioticism, as the Ina suggest, so much as it is a one-sided parasitism: the humans give far more than the Ina and derive far fewer benefits, while being the only party to the relationship that could survive independently from the other. Shori, for her part, seems to have had her eyes opened by this exchange; she underlines its importance in the narrative by saying, "[Joan] had just told me more about the basics of being Ina than anyone else ever had."[47]

When I have taught *Fledgling* to my students, I have been struck by their widespread sense, despite enjoying the novel, that the ending is abrupt, or that the book even seems unfinished. The ending is also deeply unexpected: what begins as a vampire fantasy novel ends, weirdly, in an Ina courtroom, hashing out the peculiarities of Ina legal traditions and the complex nature of Ina citizenship. Butler herself was very aware of, and extremely frustrated by, the book's flaws. She wrote in her journal that the book "isn't very good"—and not the book it could have been if she were well and unmedicated. She even compares herself to Shori, "forced to re-educate myself, relearn my art, my craft, the thing I love and need most."[48] When the proofs come back, she is despondent: "I wish I had never sent it out."[49]

Nevertheless, Butler's papers reveal (multiple) plans for possible sequels for the book that would have fleshed out, expanded, or even significantly complicated the existing narrative of *Fledgling*. The idea filled her with her characteristic mix of excitement and dread. "I don't want to spend the last years of my life writing Shori stories," Butler writes in her journal in December 2005. "But a Shori story is what I have now."[50] Some of the most interesting existing pages of the *Fledging* sequel focus on a new character, Darya, who would have been Shori's newest symbiont. Darya suffers from terrible nightmares, unbidden memories of an unhappy childhood with a stepfather who had brutally abused her both violently and sexually, both individually and with groups of likeminded perverts.[51] (Another version has Darya abused by an adult lover rather than a stepfather, again as a child of only fourteen; in this version Darya is sold into sexual slavery and only rescued much later.[52]) Darya believes herself to be irreparably damaged by her experiences: "Everything good in me has been scraped away and wasted for the pleasure of others. . . . You should throw me back like a fish half-eaten by disease."[53] Darya's predicament is the occasion for a radical revision of our attitude for Shori's power, which as we have seen is typically framed in *Fledgling* in quite sinister terms. She experiences her chemical attachment to Shori, however artificial, as the "miracle" that allows her to trust people for the first time in her adult life. Her love for Shori will similarly be the basis for a novel sort of therapy: her loss of volition at the hands of Shori's venom will not only provide Darya with the sense of security she has lacked since being betrayed by her stepfather, but it will actually help her to eliminate the dreams altogether. The power of Shori's commands goes this far; over time she will be able to "talk" Darya out of her nightmares.[54]

At the same time, the more sinister reading of Shori's power can still be heard even in this revision. Darya is a lawyer—providing an obvious source of value to Shori—and someone who seems to have been attracted to Shori precisely *because* of her previous trauma. Shori can be seen as much a predator as a partner here. The chapter ends with Darya twice offering her blood to Shori, first as a meal and then as "dessert," but Shori turns her down both times. "I laughed. 'Sleep, Darya. You know I'll come to you in two days'"[55]— suggesting that what Shori has built is a polyandrous marriage requiring a regularized sex schedule, as in male-led polygamy, with her at the center and with each of her symbionts having only a fraction of a partner.

This interest in the happiness or unhappiness of the symbionts can be seen on a meta level in the multiple versions of the text Butler began in the way Wright passes in and out of different versions of the sequel narrative. In some versions he has come to terms completely with his status as one symbiont among many; in others he barely appears, having left the group for a time, perhaps with the intention to stay away permanently. It seems significant, in focusing on the ambiguities of the Ina fantasy, that the very first sentence of some versions of the *Fledgling* sequel is "I've never had a dream"; whatever Ina are, however like humans they may superficially appear, that is the extremity of the gulf that separates them from us.[56]

As with the myriad versions of *Parable of the Trickster*, Butler's creativity pulled her in multiple trajectories at once for what she assumed would be "at least"[57] a trilogy. (The usual titles she gives for these books are *Asylum* and *Flight*.) The plot for *Asylum* typically involved Shori's uneasy wandering with her symbionts as she searched for a place where she could not only be safe but thrive; Butler imagined that Shori would try living with other Ina, and even try living miserably in Seattle before being driven out by the chaos of so many people, before finally settling with her symbionts in a place where they could live together in relative isolation. One version she speculates might have ended with her purchasing a farm in tiny Snohomish or Skagit County in Washington.[58] Another version, imagined in 2005, ends with Shori owning a hotel. Here Shori would be able to practice both the self-interested and the beneficent aspects of her power: she could "use" the travelers who visit for her own purposes ("get stock tips") but also help them ("learn about crimes," provide "therapy").[59] This version of Shori lends itself to a new version of the *Paraclete* word-of-power plot Butler could never quite make work in that context: as the manager of an exotic, out-of-the-way supernatural hotel, Shori could "do a lot of good very quietly."[60] It's this hotel version perhaps that lent itself in Butler's mind to something more ambitious than a trilogy; it could easily be the story engine for a long, open-ended series of Shori adventures.

Other versions of the *Fledgling* plot end much less happily. Alongside the story of Shori's wanderings in search of a new home, Butler was developing an alternative version wherein Shori is kidnapped by two surviving members of the Silk brood and subjected to brutal torture. The template for *this* version of Shori's future narrative is synopsized on the first page of a manuscript titled "Shadow Rise" or "Shadow Memory," describing a brutal abduction involving drugging, starvation, torture, and abuse.[61] The genre wires have now once again short-circuited; Shori has somehow unhappily slipped from her blend of science fiction and vampire horror to something more like a slasher movie, or torture porn.

Some existing fragments blend the wandering "Asylum" version with the "Shadow Rise" version, giving Shori the difficult task of figuring out what to do with Silk survivors who have been stalking her in contravention of the judgment of the Council at the end of *Fledgling* and all the laws of their society. Do the Silk want to kill her, or torture her—or do they really want to force her to *bite* them, thereby forcing her in accordance with Ina law to accept them as her mates and thereby ensure the continuation of their bloodline? Other nascent versions suggest the real story is Shori's search for her sisters—the only people, given the pheromonic realities of Ina life, who could be truly equal partners to her—and her attempts to combat her amnesia by researching facts about her lost life.

In yet another version, Shori is forced to contend against a Dracula-like Super-Ina who wants to mate with her and gain her powers for his descendants. Still other versions eliminate the Dracula angle and focus instead on Shori's own agency as a kind of Lilith power-figure, the originator of a new "brood," and imagines the race of Ina who might descend from her unique talents. While these narratives exist only in very brief sketches, they threaten to turn the entire logic of *Fledgling* on its head: What if Shori's enemies are *right*, and she really is an existential threat to the world? Shori's daywalking children would be free to do what the Ina never could, rule openly—a disruption of a once-stable symbiosis that would threaten to throw the world into complete chaos.[62] The Ina and the humans have evolved in delicate but stable equilibrium, dependent in part on the Ina's key weakness: their inability to act during the day. From this ecological mindset, it turns out that Shori's critics may have been correct to see her as a very dangerous experiment: she is a genetically engineered invasive predator species whose descendants will overrun their niche and eat too much of their prey. This future for Shori's world looks suspiciously like the world of *Patternmaster*: total power for a privileged few, and total enslavement for the rest of us. There's even a suggestion in the journal entry that Shori herself might realize this fact and therefore choose to sterilize herself or die—a final, muted vision of a character who refuses to say YES, another maximum-NO story of suicide on the species scale.

The last few months of Butler's life were extremely hard for her. Her health began to decline quite rapidly; she was lethargic constantly, unable to write, let alone keep up on her correspondence or errands. She felt "flat," and worried she might never write again. She was terrified by the prospect of retiring on her current savings and felt she needed to write at least two more books in order to survive. In fact, she wanted to write many more books—she hoped to write until she died—but she felt she needed at least two more.[63] She experimented: new dosages, new diets, avoiding caffeine or certain types of detergents, always having protein on hand.[64] But her health worsened. She was pleased to be nominated for an NAACP Image Award in January 2006, looking forward to potentially feeling "human again by the end of February,"[65] and, as February 2006 neared its end, she described in her journals her hope that her situation might improve in the coming spring.

But instead, on February 24, 2006, she died.

In her final bound commonplace book, on one of the last journal pages we have from her—it is, I think, literally the last page in the Huntington archive that she wrote on before she died—we find her brainstorming titles for the omnibus version of the Patternist series that would eventually be released under the title *Seed to Harvest*.[66] In a strange way, Butler's career had come full circle. Of course, as always, she came up with too many: The Pattern, Doro and His Children, Doro's Garden, Doro's Clay, Doro's Kiln, Doro's Bane, Eden to Armageddon, Genesis, Sun Children, Sunrise.

UNEXPECTED STORIES

Published Works

"A Necessary Being" (2014)

"When I began writing science fiction," Butler once told an interviewer, "when I began reading, heck, I wasn't in any of this stuff I read. [. . .] The only black people you found were occasional characters or characters who were so feeble-witted that they couldn't manage anything, anyway. I wrote myself in, since I'm me and I'm here and I'm writing."[1] Butler's act of writing herself in transformed the science fiction genre in ways that are still being felt today. When she began her career she was (with Samuel R. Delany and Stephen Barnes) one of only a handful of African American authors writing science fiction, and for the bulk of her career she was the only black woman anywhere earning her living doing so. But since her career began, the genre has been utterly transformed, in her image: now there are many African and

African American writers in the field, including such famous female names as Nalo Hopkinson, Tananarive Due, Nisi Shawl, Nnedi Okorafor, and Sofia Samatar, many of whom were inspired by Butler's fiction or even directly mentored by her during her life. It is perhaps fitting that in the wake of the controversy following Okorafor's winning of the 2011 World Fantasy Award—which is memorialized by a bust of notorious racist H. P. Lovecraft—a petition began circulating to change the award to a bust of Butler instead. Since 2007 the Carl Brandon Society—named after a famous fan hoax regarding an apocryphal black fan of the 1950s, and devoted to the promotion of inclusion and diversity in SF—has offered an "Octavia E. Butler Memorial Scholarship" for a writer of color to attend the Clarion Writers' Workshop, in honor of the place where Butler got her start. Online fan-scholar projects like the Octavia E. Butler Legacy Network founded by Ayana Jamieson promote her legacy through Tumblr and blog posts, while myriad academic gatherings and conferences continue to be dedicated to both studying and celebrating her work. When Ytasha L. Womack named the three members of the holy trinity of Afrofuturism, it is Butler (above even Samuel R. Delany) who stands in for black science fiction literature, alongside Sun Ra and George Clinton in music.[2] And—if the entertainment rumors are true—some of her work is finally being adapted for film and television, at long last.

The "Black Futures" anthology finally happened, in the end, and then some—Butler's idea was just a decade or two too early. *Dark Matter: A Century of Speculative Fiction from the African Diaspora* (edited by Sheree R. Thomas) was published in 2000, with a successor volume (*Dark Matter: Reading the Bones*) coming out in 2004 and a planned third volume, *Dark Matter: Africa Rising*, forthcoming. "The Evening and the Morning and the Night" [II] appears in the collection, as does Butler's brief essay "The Monophobic Response," reprinted from a PEN speech she gave about the persistence of racism in science fictional speculations. We write about aliens, she says, because we can't stop creating them out of each other. We want aliens to be real so that we are not "alone in a universe that cares no more for us than it does for stones or suns or any other fragments of itself. And yet we are unable to get along with those aliens who are closest to us, those aliens who are of course ourselves."[3]

Similar volumes, like *So Long Been Dreaming: Postcolonial Science Fiction and Fantasy*, *The Apex Book of World SF*, *AfroSF*, *Long Hidden: Speculative Fiction from the Margins of History,* and *Terra Incognita: New Short Speculative Stories from Africa* have shown that both the talent and a hungry publishing market exist for science and speculative fiction that does not originate in or pander to the white male perspective that for so long was imagined as the ideal fan of science fiction. Not all of these writers and editors have read Butler, but most of them have, and the presence of this Afrofuturist turn within the science fiction publishing industry has to be credited in large part to the way she broke through, refashioning the assumptions of sometimes unwilling publishers, critics, and readers to include previously marginalized voices like hers. Alongside her books, interviews, and essays, the flourishing of diversity in science fiction from the 1990s onward is another part of her literary and cultural legacy. To so many, she has been hero and inspiration.

One of these anthologies deserves, I think, special attention: *Octavia's Brood: Science Fiction Stories from Social Justice Movements*, edited by Adrienne Maree Brown and Walidah Imarisha and published in 2015. The book, plainly, takes its name from the rebranding of the Xenogenesis books as "Lilith's Brood" and is dedicated to Butler:

> . . . who serves as a north star for so many of us. She told us what would happen—"all that you touch you change"—and then she touched us, fearlessly, brave enough to change us. We dedicate this collection to her, coming out with our own fierce longing to have our writing change everyone and everything we touch.[4]

Originating in and devoted to advancing social justice movements from a science fictional register, Imarisha writes in her introduction that "this is what it means to carry on Butler's legacy of writing visionary fiction." She cites Butler's visit to a retreat for women writers in 1988, where Butler says she wants to be not "the solitary Black female sci-fi writer" but one of many, "one of thousands of folks writing themselves into the present and into the future"—and calls upon the group of black writers who were and are inspired by Butler, and who chose to write themselves in, too, to work together to make the world more like our collective dreams.[5] The project speaks to the highest call of Butler's fiction, and is perhaps even more unabashedly utopian than she ever allowed herself to be—but I think she would have liked it.

Butler's work continues to be promoted by scholars and fans, with countless conference papers, panels, special events, and special issues devoted to her work. And she continues to be deeply mourned, both by her fans and by those who were close to her. A remarkable 2010 special issue of *Science Fiction Studies*, the flagship journal of that scholarly subfield, contains a special section memorializing Butler, not simply through the usual sort of literary criticism but through ten pages of reflections from admirers, scholar-fans, editors, and friends. Vonda McIntyre writes for the issue, remembering Butler as the "Estelle" she first met at the Clarion Workshop in 1970; others wrote movingly and mournfully of her work, her legacy, the tribute we can pay to her now that she is gone, even the time they were privileged, once, to simply sit with her at dinner.[6]

Similarly, *Strange Matings: Science Fiction, Feminism, African American Voices, and Octavia E. Butler* (edited by Rebecca J. Holden and Nisi Shawl) is a collection unlike any other scholarly work I have encountered, with interviews, poems, testimonials, and other personal remembrances alongside traditional criticism. The inescapable sense of real grief is palpable across the book; reading it, one has a sense that for the writers of *Strange Matings*—both for those who knew Butler personally and those who were touched by her only through her work—this loss still feels very raw, as if it somehow happened only yesterday. "The last Christmas card Octavia sent me had a photo of Mt. Rainier on the front," Nisi Shawl writes in her own contribution to the volume. "Not only did she love that mountain, she resembled it. She towered over everything ordinary; she made her own weather."[7] Even the more academic essays in the book frequently find themselves slipping into the rhetoric of personal witnessing, as one can see simply from scanning the titles: "The Impact of Octavia Butler's Early Work on Feminist Science Fiction as a Whole (and on One Feminist Science Fiction Scholar in Particular)"; "How a Young Feminist Writer Found Alternatives to White Bourgeois Narrative Models in the Early Novels of Octavia Butler"; "Growing (Up) with Octavia E. Butler"; "Octavia Butler, 'Speech Sounds,' and Me"; "Goodbye My Hero." As Holden herself admits in the introduction, she and other writers in the book find themselves unable to hold to the staid academic convention that would call her only "Butler" after the first use of her name (a convention I have struggled with myself throughout this book); she is somehow always "Octavia." Scholarly literary criticism, even of science fiction, is supposed to be objective and detached, Serious Business—one *enjoys* reading these stories, perhaps, but that's not something you necessarily go around talking about. But it is never that way with Octavia, for whom even the most disciplined critics frequently find themselves gushing with enthusiasm, with love, and, following her too-soon death, with a sense of permanent regret and loss. Her fandom is ecstatic and devotional; even her critics are evangelists.

As discussed in the introduction to this book, for those who did not know Butler (but wish they had), the opening of the Huntington Library archives marks a tremendous opportunity to commune with Butler's life, almost as a kind of reliquary. A self-confessed "packrat," Butler kept everything—*everything*—dating back to the original composition notebooks in which she journaled and fantasized and dreamed as a child. The *finding aid* for the collection is five hundred pages long; the number of pages contained within boxes at the Huntington numbers in the tens of thousands (at least).

The Huntington Library makes possible an entirely new era in Butler scholarship by giving us unprecedented access to her unfinished work, to altered and expurgated drafts, to her copious correspondence with many of the best-loved science fiction writers of her generation, as well as (of course) her personal notebooks, journals, and private thoughts. The Huntington made this book possible—and it is my hope that the *Octavia E. Butler* of the Modern Masters of Science Fiction series is only at the very beginning of a long second renaissance in Butler scholarship that makes use of the material in the archive to cast new light both on her existing published work and on the work few have thus far seen. There's much more to her career than the dozen or so books we know; out of the spirit of brutal perfectionism that drove her, she held a lot of interesting and worthy work back. I've talked a lot about the treasures of the Huntington in these pages: the unpublished *Blindsight*, "Evening" [I], and *Paraclete*; the many *Tricksters*; the alternative Xenogenesis; the lost short stories and essays and sequels and interviews and plays. This material should not be left only to the small number of scholars who are able to make their way to the Huntington; much of it can see, and deserves to see, publication. These are not discarded scraps or abandoned, embarrassing mistakes; it's just *more*.

Butler's incredible productivity, coupled with her intense self-criticism, self-censorship, and perfectionism, has conspired to create a vast intertextual hidden archive of alternative versions and lost tales that will, I hope, reinvigorate the study of her work as more scholars are able to get to the Huntington and as more of it trickles out in published form. And, in fact, the publication of the unseen additional material found among her papers has already begun. Open Road Media's 2014 publication of *Unexpected Stories* contains two stories that had previously not been seen: the long lost "Childfinder" (discussed in chapter 1) and the novella "A Necessary Being," depicting a crucial background event in *Survivor*. "Reading these tales," writes Walter Mosley, "is like looking at a photograph of a child whom you only knew as an adult. In her eyes you can see the woman that you came to know much later; a face, not yet fully formed, that contains the promise of something that is now a part of you: the welcomed surprise of recognition in innocent eyes."[8] But what we have in these stories is actually something less like a childhood photograph, or juvenilia, or apocrypha, and more like the miraculous discovery that the beloved book you've read a dozen times has an extra chapter you've somehow never noticed. These stories don't feel different; they feel like just her. (And having spent some cherished months in the Huntington archives, I must say again that these two stories are really only the start.) "A Necessary Being" is an especially fascinating inclusion for this volume, as it quietly suggests that even the famous prohibition against republishing *Survivor* could itself someday fall; why else publish a prequel to a novel that Butler not only disliked but also ensured most of her fans would never read unless they could hunt down a very old, very used copy on Amazon or eBay or in a university library?

The novella takes place years before the humans arrive on the planet; it explains how the "good tribe" (the Tehkohn) formed as a merger of two smaller, weaker tribes in order to fight the bad one, the Garkohn (an important historical event that is described in *Survivor* only very briefly). The two tribes each have a Hao, who decide unexpectedly to take a chance on trusting each other rather than fighting, as tradition suggests they must; the unusual merger will allow both tribes to survive and successfully oppose the bad tribe, driving the Garkohn almost to defeat until the arrival of the humans destabilizes the situation and gives the "bad tribe" a chance to recover. "A Necessary Being," taken on its own terms, therefore seems to suggest a very traditional sort of "happy ending," in which the Hao of the now-merged tribe will mate and have children who will renew the kingdom and perhaps even begin to restore the faded glory of the fallen Empire. It's only those few who have actually read *Survivor* who will recognize the characteristically Butlerian sour note in all this: we know from the pages of *Survivor* that this union will actually prove to be barren and that each of the two Hao have taken many other lovers in order to try (unsuccessfully) to produce some heir. We similarly learn that humans and Kohn can mate—the extreme biological improbability of this is at the core of Butler's unhappiness with the novel—but we learn this only retrospectively after the infant offspring has already been brutally murdered during a Garkohn raid. The suggestion at the end of *Survivor* is that the human woman and her Hao husband will try to get pregnant again—but the scene on which the novel actually ends is of her trying to persuade her hopelessly speciesist human father to accept her choice and of him then steadfastly refusing, rejecting her and casting her away.

In "Childfinder," the retrospective doom cast down by the encyclopedic *Psi: History of a Vanished People* interrupts the surface optimism of the main narrative, calling back to us from an unhappy future and reminding us not to have any hope. The pessimism of *Survivor* actually performs much the same function for "A Necessary Being," insofar as the full novel indicates the novella's seemingly restorative "happy ending" does not bear fruit, or, indeed, stay "happy" for very long. And yet *Survivor* is a story, like so many of Butler's stories, about, well, *survivors*—and unlike the final doom of the "vanished people" cast down by the end of "Childfinder," both *Survivor* and its prequel "A Necessary Being" imagine lives that do go on—lives that change, of course, but go on nonetheless. "I've given you back your life," says the Hao Tahneh to her young partner and lover, Diut, at the end of "A Necessary Being." "That's enough. What you do with it is up to you." (An older Diut, in turn, goes on to play much the same role of teacher-master-captor-lover to Alanna in the pages of *Survivor*.) And then, "as much warningly as affectionately, she reached over and caressed his throat."[9] So much of the delicious ambiguity of Butler's fiction, across her career, is tied up in that little moment: the intertwining of optimism and pessimism, hope and threat; violent caress and caressing violence; the miracle of survival, and of love, if not always exactly how we'd like it.

Butler once said of *Survivor*: "I thought, oh well, you can't really erase embarrassing early work, but you don't have to repeat it."[10] But really she never sought to erase her early work (which was never, despite her modesty, all that embarrassing); she kept it all for us, every page, but made us wait a very long time to read it. The throwing open of her personal archives and the surprise publishing of *Unexpected Stories* can only invite us to continue to expect the unexpected from Butler; like so many of her fans, I have to hope there are more and more unexpected stories to come.

"LOST RACES OF SCIENCE FICTION" (1980)
by Octavia E. Butler

Fourteen years ago, during my first year of college, I sat in a creative writing class and listened as my teacher, an elderly man, told another student not to use black characters in his stories unless those characters' blackness was somehow essential to the plots. The presence of blacks, my teacher felt, changed the focus of the story—drew attention from the intended subject.

This happened in 1965. I would never have expected to hear my teacher's sentiments echoed by a science fiction writer in 1979. Hear them I did, though, at an SF convention where a writer explained that he had decided against using a black character in one of his stories because the presence of the black would change his story somehow. Later, this same writer suggested that in stories that seem to require black characters to make some racial point, it might be possible to substitute extraterrestrials—so as not to dwell on matters of race.

Well, let's do a little dwelling.

Science fiction reaches into the future, the past, the human mind. It reaches out to other worlds and into other dimensions. Is it really so limited, then, that it cannot reach into the lives of ordinary, everyday humans who happen not to be white?

Blacks, Asians, Hispanics, Amerindians, minority characters in general have been noticeably absent from most science fiction. Why? As a black and a science fiction writer, I've heard that question asked often. I've also heard several answers given. And, because most people try to be polite, there have been certain answers I haven't heard. That's all right; they're obvious.

Best, though, and most hopeful from my point of view, I've heard from people who want to write SF, or who've written a few pieces, perhaps, and who would like to include minority characters, but aren't sure how to go about it. Since I've had to solve the same problem in reverse, maybe I can help.

But first some answers to the question, Why have there been so few minority characters in science fiction?

Let's examine my teacher's reason. Are minority characters—black characters in this case—so disruptive a force that the mere presence of one alters a story, focuses it on race rather than whatever the author had in mind? Yes, in fact, black characters can do exactly that if the creators of those characters are too restricted in their thinking to visualize blacks in any other context.

This is the kind of stereotyping, conscious or subconscious, that women have fought for so long. No writer who regards blacks as people, human beings, with the usual variety of human concerns, flaws, skills, hopes, etc., would have trouble creating interesting backgrounds and goals for black characters. No writer who regards blacks as people would get sidetracked into justifying their blackness or their presence unless such justification honestly played a part in the story. It is no more necessary to focus on a character's blackness than it is to focus on a woman's femininity.

Now, what about the possibility of substituting extraterrestrials for blacks—in order to make some race-related point without making anyone . . . uncomfortable? In fact, why can't blacks be represented by whites who are not too thoroughly described, thus leaving readers free to use their imaginations and visualize whichever color they like?

I usually manage to go on being polite when I hear suggestions like these, but it's not easy.

All right. Let's replace blacks with tentacled beings from Capella V. What will readers visualize as we describe relations between the Capellans and the (white) humans? Will they visualize black humans dealing with white humans? I don't think so. This is science fiction, after all. If you tell your readers about tentacled Capellans, they're going to visualize tentacled Capellans. And if your readers are as touchy about human races as you were afraid they might be when you substituted the Capellans, are they really likely to pay attention to any analogy you draw? I don't think so.

And as for whites representing all of humanity—on the theory that people will imagine other races; or better yet, on the theory that all people are alike anyway, so what does it matter? Well, remember when men represented all of humanity? Women didn't care much for it. Still don't. No great mental leap is required to understand why blacks, why any minority, might not care much for it either. And apart from all that, of course, it doesn't work. Whites represent themselves, and that's plenty. Spread the burden.

Back when *Star Wars* was new, a familiar excuse for ignoring minorities went something like this: "SF is escapist literature. Its readers/viewers don't want to be weighted down with real problems." War, okay. Planet-wide destruction, okay. Kidnapping, okay. But the sight of a minority person? Too heavy. Too real. And, of course, there again is the implication that a sprinkling of blacks, Asians, or others could turn the story into some sort of racial statement. The only statement I could imagine being made by such a sprinkling would be that among the white, human people; the tall, furry people; the lumpy, scaly people; the tentacled people, etc., were also brown, human people; black, human people, etc. This isn't such a heavy statement—unless it's missing.

From my agent (whose candor I appreciate), I heard what could become an even stronger reason for not using black characters in particular—not using them in film, anyway. It seems that blacks are out of fashion. In an industry that pays a great deal of attention to trends, blacks have had their day for a while. How long a while? Probably until someone decides to take a chance, and winds up making a damn big hit movie about blacks.

All right, forget for a moment the fadishness of the movie industry. Forget that movies about blacks are out. Movies, SF and otherwise, with a sprinkling of minority characters, but no particular minority theme, seem to do well. Yaphet Kotto certainly didn't do *Alien* any harm. In fact, for me, probably for a good many blacks, he gave the movie an extra touch of authenticity. And a monster movie—even a good monster movie—needs all the authenticity it can get.

That brings me to another question I hear often at SF conventions. "Why are there so few black SF writers?" I suspect for the same reason there were once so few women SF writers. Women found a certain lack of authenticity in a genre that postulated a universe largely populated by men, in which all the power was in male hands, and women stayed in their male-defined places.

Blacks find a certain lack of authenticity in a genre which postulates a universe largely populated by whites, in which the power is in white hands, and blacks are occasional oddities.

SF writers come from SF readers, generally. Few readers equal few writers. The situation is improving, however. Blacks are not as likely as whites to spend time and money going to conventions, but there is a growing black readership. Black people I meet now much more likely to have read at least some science fiction, and are not averse to reading more. My extra copy of *Dreamsnake* (by Vonda McIntyre) had reached its fifth reader, last I heard. Movies like *Alien*, *Star Wars* (in spite of its lack), and *Close Encounters of the Third Kind*, plus the old *Star Trek* TV series, have captured a lot of interest, too. With all this, it's been a pleasantly long time since a friend or acquaintance has muttered to me, "Science fiction! How can you waste your time with anything that unreal?"

Now to those reasons people aren't as likely to give for leaving minorities out of SF: The most obvious one, and the one I feel least inclined to discuss, is conscious racism. It exists. I don't think SF is greatly afflicted with it, but then, racism is unfashionable now, and thus is unlikely to be brought into the open. Instead, it can be concealed behind any of the questions and arguments I've already discussed. To the degree that it is, this whole article is a protest against racism. It's as much of a protest as I intend to make at the moment. I know of too many bright, competent blacks who have had to waste time and energy trying to reason away other people's unreasonable racist attitudes: in effect, trying to prove their humanity. Life is too short.

A more insidious problem than outright racism is simply habit, custom. SF has always been nearly all white, just as until recently, it's been nearly all male. A lot of people had a chance to get comfortable with things as they are. Too comfortable. SF, more than any other genre, deals with change—change in science and technology, social change. But SF itself changes slowly, often under protest. You can still go to conventions and hear deliberately sexist remarks—if the speaker thinks he has a sympathetic audience. People resent being told their established way of doing things is wrong, resent being told they should change, and strongly resent being told they won't be alone any longer in the vast territory—the universe—they've staked out for themselves. I don't think anyone seriously believes the present world is all white. But custom can be strong enough to prevent people from seeing the need for SF to reflect a more realistic view.

Adherence to custom can also cause people to oppose change by becoming even more extreme in their customary behavior. I went back to college for a couple of quarters a few years ago and found one male teacher after another announcing with odd belligerence, "I might as well tell you right now, I'm a male chauvinist!"

A custom attacked is a custom that will be defended. Men who feel defensive about sexist behavior may make sexist bigots of themselves. Whites who feel defensive about racist behavior may make racist bigots of themselves. It's something for people who value open-mindedness and progressive attitudes to beware of.

A second insidious problem is laziness, possibly combined with ignorance. Authors who have always written of all-white universes might not feel particularly threatened by a multicolored one, but might consider the change too much trouble. After all, they already know how to do what they've been doing. Their way works. Why change? Besides, maybe they don't know any minority people. How can they write about people they don't know?

Of course, ignorance may be a category unto itself. I've heard people I didn't consider lazy, racist, or bound by custom complain that they did not know enough about minorities and thus hesitated to write about them. Often, these people seem worried about accidentally giving offense.

But what do authors ordinarily do when they decide to write about an unfamiliar subject?

They research. They read—in this case recent biographies and autobiographies of people in the group they want to write about are good. They talk to members of that group—friends, acquaintances, coworkers, fellow students, even strangers on buses or waiting in lines. I've done these things myself in my reverse research, and they help. Also, I people-watch a lot without talking. Any public situation offers opportunities.

Some writers have gotten around the need for research by setting their stories in distant egalitarian futures when cultural differences have dwindled and race has ceased to matter. I created a future like this in my novel, *Patternmaster*, thought I did not do it to avoid research. *Patternmaster* takes place in a time when psionic ability is all that counts. People who have enough of that ability are on top whether they're male or female, black, white, or brown. People who have none are slaves. In this culture, a black like the novel's main woman character would, except for her coloring, be indistinguishable from characters of any other race. Using this technique could get a writer accused of writing blacks as though they were whites in Coppertone, and it could be a lazy writer's excuse for doing just that. But for someone who has a legitimate reason for using it, a story that requires it, it can be a perfectly valid technique.

More important than technique, however, is for authors to remember that they are writing about *people*. Authors who forget this, who do not relax and get comfortable with their racially different characters, can wind up creating unbelievable, self-consciously manipulated puppets; pieces of furniture who exist within a story but contribute nothing to it; or stereotypes guaranteed to be offensive.

There was a time when most of the few minority characters in SF fell into one of these categories. One of the first black characters I ran across when I began reading SF in the fifties was a saintly old "uncle" (I'm not being sarcastic here. The man was described as saintly and portrayed asking to be called "uncle") whom Harriet Beecher Stowe would have felt right at home with. I suspect that like the Sidney Poitier movies of the sixties, Uncle was daring for his time. That didn't help me find him any more believable or feel any less pleased when he and his kind (Charlie Chan, Tonto, that little guy who swiped Fritos . . .) were given decent burials. Times have changed, thank heavens, and SF has come a long way from Uncle. Clearly, though, it still has a long way to go.

FICTION

Novels, Series, and Story Collections (original publication)

Patternist Series

Patternmaster. New York: Doubleday, 1976.
Mind of My Mind. New York: Doubleday, 1977.
Survivor. New York: Doubleday, 1978.
Wild Seed. New York: Doubleday, 1980.
Clay's Ark. New York: St. Martin's, 1984.
Seed to Harvest (Patternist series omnibus edition, minus *Survivor*). New York: Hachette, 2007.

Xenogenesis Series

Dawn. New York: Warner, 1987.
Adulthood Rites. New York: Warner, 1988.
Imago. New York: Warner, 1989.
Lilith's Brood (Xenogenesis trilogy omnibus edition and rebranding). New York: Warner, 2000.

Parables Series

Parable of the Sower. New York: Four Walls Eight Windows, 1993.
Parable of the Talents. New York: Seven Stories, 1998.

Standalone Novels

Kindred. New York: Doubleday, 1979.
Fledgling. New York: Seven Stories, 2005.

Story Collections

Bloodchild and Other Stories. New York: Four Walls Eight Windows, 1995. Expanded 2nd edition. New York: Seven Stories, 2005.
Unexpected Stories (e-book). Foreword by Walter Mosely. New York: Open Road Media, 2014.

Short Stories (original publication)

"Amnesty." scifi.com (2003).
"The Book of Martha." scifi.com (2003).
"Bloodchild." Isaac Asimov's Science Fiction Magazine (June 1984).
"Childfinder." *Unexpected Stories* (e-book). New York: Open Road Media, 2014.
"Crossover." *Clarion Journal*. Edited by Robin Scott Wilson. New York: Signet, 1971.
"The Evening and the Morning and the Night." *Omni* (May 1987).
"Near of Kin." *Chrysalis* 4. Edited by Roy Torgeson. New York: Zebra, 1979.
"A Necessary Being." *Unexpected Stories* (e-book). New York: Open Road Media, 2014.
"Speech Sounds." Isaac Asimov's Science Fiction Magazine (December 1983).

Significant Uncompleted and Unpublished Works

Blindsight (ca. 1981, ca. 1984)
Canaan (alternate version of *Kindred*, set in Patternist universe) (ca. 1975–1976)
Doro-Jesus (ca. 1970s)
"The Evening and the Morning and the Night" [I] (ca. 1970–1975)
Fledgling sequel (usual title: *Asylum*) (ca. 2005)
God of Clay (alternate and fragmentary versions of *Parable of the Sower*) (ca. 1989–1993)
Parable of the Talents (abandoned sketches, scenes, and drafts from original versions) (ca.
    1993–1996)
Parable of the Trickster (many versions and fragments) (ca. 1989–2006)
Paraclete (alternate title: *Mortal Words*) (ca. early 2000s)
Spiritus (alternate title: *Bodhisattva*) (ca. early 2000s)

These works are available in manuscript form in the Octavia E. Butler Collection at the Huntington Library in San Marino, California, near Pasadena. References to these and other unpublished Butler manuscripts in this text use the Huntington Library's catalogue system (codes beginning with OEB).

NONFICTION AND ESSAYS

"Birth of a Writer." *Essence* 20 (May 1989). (Reprinted as "Positive Obsession" in *Bloodchild and Other Stories*.)
"Brave New Worlds: A Few Rules for Predicting the Future." *Essence* (May 2000): 165–66, 264.
"*Devil Girl from Mars*: Why I Write Science Fiction." MIT "Media in Transition" Forum (February 19, 1998). Available at http://web.mit.edu/comm-forum/papers/butler.html.
"Essay on Racism: A Science-Fiction Writer Shares Her View of Intolerance" (September 1, 2001). NPR.org. Available at http://www.npr.org/programs/specials/racism/010830. octaviabutler.html.
"Eye Witness: Octavia Butler's A-Ha! Moment." *O: The Oprah Magazine* 3, no. 5 (May 2002): 79–80.
"Free Libraries: Are They Becoming Extinct?" *Omni* 15 (August 1993): 4.

"Furor Scribendi." *L. Rob Hubbard Presents Writers of the Future*. Vol. 9. Los Angeles: Bridge, 1993. (Also reprinted in *Bloodchild and Other Stories*.)

"How I Built Novels Out of Writer's Blocks." *Writer's Digest* (June 1999): 12–15.

"Lost Races of Science Fiction." *Transmission* (Summer 1980): 17–18. Reprinted herein.

"The Monophobic Response." In *Dark Matter: A Century of Writing from the African Diaspora*, edited by Sheree R. Thomas, 415–16. New York: Warner, 2000.

SELECTED INTERVIEWS, PANEL APPEARANCES, AND PUBLISHED LETTERS

Starred interviews are reprinted in *Conversations with Octavia E. Butler*, edited by Conseula Francis (Jackson: University Press of Mississippi, 2010). My page references are to the reprint of the interview, unless otherwise indicated.

* "Big Thinker." By Susan Stamberg. *Weekend Edition*, December 29, 2001.

"Black Women and the Science Fiction Genre." By Frances Beal. *Black Scholar* 17, no. 2 (March / April 1986): 14–18.

"butler8star@qwest.net." Emails to Nnedi Okorafor. In *Strange Matings: Science Fiction, Feminism, African American Voices, and Octavia E. Butler*, edited by Rebecca J. Holden and Nisi Shawl, 216–20. Seattle: Aqueduct, 2013.

"Charlie Rose." By Charlie Rose. PBS. June 1, 2000.

* "'Congratulations! You've Just Won $295,000': An Interview with Octavia E. Butler." By Joan Fry. *Poets and Writers* 25, no. 2 (March 1, 1997): 58.

* "A Conversation with Octavia Butler." By Nick DiChario. *Writers and Books* (wab.org). February 2004.

"A Conversation with Octavia E. Butler." By Nisi Shawl. In *Strange Matings: Science Fiction, Feminism, African American Voices, and Octavia E. Butler*, edited by Rebecca J. Holden and Nisi Shawl. Seattle: Aqueduct, 2013.

"A Conversation with Octavia E. Butler." *Parable of the Sower* (2007 Hachette edition).

* "Essay on Racism." By Scott Simon. NPR. September 1, 2001.

"Fun, Fun, Fun." Letters to Merrilee Heifetz. In *Strange Matings: Science Fiction, Feminism, African American Voices, and Octavia E. Butler*, edited by Rebecca J. Holden and Nisi Shawl, 173–81. Seattle: Aqueduct, 2013.

"Future Forum." By Jeffrey Eliot. *Future Life* 17 (1980): 60.

"Futurist Woman: Octavia Butler." By Veronica Mixon. *Essence* 9 (April 1979): 12, 15.

"Going to See the Woman: A Visit with Octavia E. Butler." *Obsidian III: Literature in the African Diaspora* 6.2 / 7.1 (2005–2006): 14–39.

"Having Her Say: Octavia Butler Talks with Evette Porter about *Fledgling*." By Evette Porter. *Essence* 35, no. 6 (October 2005): 96.

"The Interplay of Science and Science Fiction." NPR. June 18, 2004. Available at http:// www.npr.org / templates / story / story.php?storyId=1964371.

* "Interview: Octavia E. Butler." By John C. Snider. Scifidimensions.com, June 2004.

* "Interview with Octavia Butler." By Jelani Cobb. Jelanicobb.com (1994).

"Interview with Octavia Butler." By Jeffrey Eliot. *Thrust* 12 (Summer 1979): 19–22.

"An Interview with Octavia Butler." By Joan Fry. *Poets and Writers* 25 (March-April 1997): 58–69.

"An Interview with Octavia Butler." By Joshunda Sanders. *In Motion*, March 14, 2004. Available at www.inmotionmagazine.com/ac04/obutler.html.

* "An Interview with Octavia E. Butler." By Randall Kenan. *Callaloo* 14, no. 2 (1991): 495–504.

* "An Interview with Octavia E. Butler." By Larry McCaffery and Jim McMenamin. In *Across the Wounded Galaxies: Interviews with Contemporary American Science Fiction Writers*, edited by Larry McCaffery, 54–70. Urbana: University of Illinois Press, 1990.

* "An Interview with Octavia E. Butler." By Charles Rowell. *Callaloo* 20, no. 1 (1997): 47–66.

* "Interviewing the Oracle: Octavia Butler." By Kazembe Balagun. *The Indypendent*, January 13, 2006.

* "The Lit Interview: Octavia Butler." By Daniel Burton-Rose. *San Francisco Bay Guardian*, December 2005.

* "Nebula Award Nominee Octavia Butler Is Expanding the Universe of Science-Fiction Readers." By Jane Burkitt. *Seattle Times*, May 9, 2000.

"New Frontier Panel Discussion: Butler, Barnes, Due, and Hopkinson." By Gregory Jerome Hampton. In *Changing Bodies in the Fiction of Octavia Butler: Slaves, Aliens, and Vampires*, 135- 46. New York: Lexington, 2014.

* "Octavia Butler." By Mike McGonical. IndexMagazine.com, 1998.

* "Octavia Butler." By Juan Williams. *Talk of the Nation*, May 8, 2000.

"Octavia Butler: A Hermit Living in a Big City." By Nibir K. Ghosh. In *Multicultural America: Conversations with Contemporary Authors*, 73–79. Chandigarh, India: Unistar, 2005.

"Octavia Butler: Science Future, Science Fiction." With Arthur Cover. Excerpt from UCLA Panel Discussion 2002. Available at https://www.youtube.com/watch?v=IgeyVE3NHJM.

* "Octavia Butler's *Kindred* Turns Twenty-Five." By Allison Keyes. *Tavis Smiley Show*, 2004.

* "Octavia E. Butler: Persistence." By Charles N. Brown. *Locus* 21, no. 10 (October 1988).

"Octavia E. Butler Plants an Earthseed." By Therese Littleton. Amazon.com. Available at http://www.amazon.com/exec/obidos/tg/feature/-/11664.

"On the Phone with Octavia Butler." By Gregory Jerome Hampton. In *Changing Bodies in the Fiction of Octavia Butler: Slaves, Aliens, and Vampires*, 133–38. New York: Lexington, 2014.

* "PW Interviews: Octavia E. Butler." By Lisa See. *Publishers Weekly* 240 (December 13, 1999): 50–51.

* "'Radio Imagination': Octavia Butler on the Politics of Narrative Embodiment." By Marilyn Mehaffy and AnaLouise Keating. *MELUS: Multi-Ethnic Literature of the United States* 26, no.1 (2001): 45–76.

"The Science Fiction of Octavia Butler." By Carolyn S. Davidson. *Sagala* 2, no. 1 (1981): 35.

* "Science Fiction Writer Octavia Butler on Race, Global Warming, and Religion." By Juan Gonzalez and Amy Goodman. *Democracy Now* (November 11, 2005): n.p.

* "Sci-Fi Tales from Octavia E. Butler." By H. Jerome Jackson. *Crisis* 101, no. 3 (April 1994): 4.

* "Sci-Fi Visions: An Interview with Octavia Butler." By Rosalie G. Harrison. *Equal Opportunity Forum* 8, no. 2 (1980): 30–34.

* "The Value of Literacy." With Samuel R. Delany and Henry Jenkins. *MIT Communications Forum* (February 19, 1998). Available at http://web.mit.edu/m-i-t/science_fiction/transcripts/butler_delany.html.

"Visions: Identity; 'We Tend to Do the Right Thing When We Get Scared.'" By Michel Marriott. *New York Times*, January 1, 2000. Available at http://www.nytimes.com/2000/01/01/books/visions-identity-we-tend-to-do-the-right-thing-when-we-get-scared.html.

* "'We Keep Playing the Same Record': A Conversation with Octavia E. Butler." By Stephen W. Potts. *Science Fiction Studies* 23 (November 1996): 331–38.

INTRODUCTION: BEGINNING AT THE END

1. See "A Brief Conversation with Octavia Butler," OEB 236–70, as well as the versions she published as her "about the author" endnotes in her books.

2. Qtd. in Dery, "Black to the Future," 208.

3. "Lost Races of Science Fiction," 18 and republished herein.

4. "Black Women" (Beal interview), 18.

5. "Science Fiction of Octavia Butler" (Davidson interview), 35.

6. "Monophobic Response," 415–16.

7. "Interview with Octavia E. Butler" (McCaffery and McMenamin), 18.

8. OEB 95, an "autobiographical fragment."

9. See "Positive Obsession" and "Furor Scribendi," both in *Bloodchild*.

10. OEB 2717, one of her unfinished memoirs.

11. OEB 1556, journal entry dated July 1983.

12. Ibid. While brainstorming new ideas for stories, she expresses a desire to finally get away from the Pattern and explore something new.

13. References to bestsellerdom and YES- and NO-BOOKS are frequent in the archives, but see especially OEB 107 and 1595. She writes about her desire for *Parable of the Trickster* to be a YES-BOOK in OEB 2037; a failed version of the 1970s "The Evening and the Morning and the Night" [I] is described, in contrast, as a NO story (OEB 503).

14. See, for instance, the seemingly hastily scribbled note to her mother dated February 5, 1991 (OEB 3832).

CHAPTER 1: CHILDFINDER (1947–1971)

1. "Interview with Octavia E. Butler" (Rowell), 52–53. This citation and all following are from the *Callaloo* edition of the interview. Butler's age of death at the time of her father's passing is reported by different scholars as ranging from infancy to age seven, but in the Rowell interview she says she was a toddler when he died and that she has no real memories of him.

2. "Interview with Octavia E. Butler" (McCaffery and McMenamin), 15.

3. OEB 4443, letter dated April 7, 1990.

4. "Lit Interview" (Burton-Rose), 197. See also "Octavia E. Butler: Persistence" (Brown interview), 182–83, and "Interview with Octavia E. Butler" (Rowell), 50–51, as well as my discussion of *Kindred* in chapter 3 of this book.

5. "Devil Girl from Mars," n.p.

6. "A Conversation with Octavia E. Butler" (*Sower* 2007), 334.

7. "Interview with Octavia Butler" (Elliott), 19.

8. "Devil Girl from Mars," n.p.

9. "Interviewing the Oracle" (Balagun), 226.

10. "Conversation with Octavia E. Butler" (*Sower* 2007), 334.

11. "Devil Girl from Mars," n.p.

12. The codename was "Gelly," as revealed in OEB 928.

13. See OEB 379, which contains several unfinished and fragmentary ideas for *Star Trek* plots alongside the sketched-out plot for an episode called "Darkside."

14. OEB 95.

15. For more on the influence of comics on her early work, see chapter 2 of this book, as well as my article "Bred to Be Superhuman."

16. "Interview with Octavia E. Butler" (McCaffery and McMenamin), 16.

17. OEB 2424 (also 3902), letters dated March 24, 1977. This anecdote appears in their correspondence but does not appear in the short published profile.

18. OEB 2311.

19. See "butler8star@qwest.net" (Okorafor).

20. OEB 439.

21. OEB 2717.

22. OEB 2806; OEB 814.

23. To take but one example, see one of the private poems she used in her practice of self-affirmation, found amid her notes for *Adulthood Rites*, where she describes a successful novel as an intense sexual exchange between writer and reader. OEB 13.

24. OEB 533–35.

25. OEB 298, entries dated October 26 and 27, 1972.

26. OEB 825.

27. OEB 826.

28. OEB 1515 and elsewhere. Notably, in the OEB 1515 version she cuts out a line from the original self-help text about living "in harmony with the overall purpose of the Creator," reflecting her move away from her Baptist upbringing.

29. "Positive Obsession" (in *Bloodchild*), 131.

30. Ibid., 127.

31. Ibid., 131.

32. "Interview with Octavia E. Butler" (Kenan), 36–37.

33. "Conversation with Octavia E. Butler" (Fry), 127.

34. "Positive Obsession" (in *Bloodchild*), 127–28.

35. OEB 1632.

36. "Positive Obsession" (in *Bloodchild*), 128.

37. OEB 6735, letter to Warner Books dated February 12, 2006.

38. "An Interview with Octavia E. Butler" (McCaffery and McMenamin), 14.

39. See, for instance, OEB 3823–25 and OEB 4256, letters to her mother and childhood best friend, from Clarion.

40. "Childfinder," loc. 736.

41. Ibid., loc. 747.

42. Ibid., loc. 761.

43. Ibid., loc. 789.

44. Ibid., loc. 844.

45. Ibid., loc. 872.

46. The term is borrowed from Lee Edelman's influential work of queer theory, *No Future: Queer Theory and the Death Drive*. For more in particular on this subject with regard to Butler's fictions, see the other chapters in this book.

47. "Childfinder," loc. 872.

48. Ibid., loc. 886.

49. OEB 4977, letter dated September 8, 1970.

50. OEB 295.

51. See letters to *The Magazine of Fantasy and Science Fiction* and to Donald A. Wollheim, OEB 4987 and 4988.

52. See OEB 375 and following.

53. "On the Phone with Octavia Butler" (Hampton), 137.

54. "We Keep Playing the Same Record" (Potts interview), 66.

55. OEB 3724, letter dated 1988.

56. See his *Race and American Science Fiction*.

57. She referred to this crush in her diaries frequently but only obliquely, typically calling Ellison by the code names "Elyano" or "Yano." OEB 494 even features an erotic fantasy centered on Ellison, in which her first TV sale becomes the occasion for the consummation of their relationship.

58. OEB 4583, undated letter, presumably to her mother, as it is signed "June."

59. OEB 2042.

CHAPTER 2: PSYCHOGENESIS (1971–1976)

1. OEB 2608. As with so many of Butler's personal journal entries from her teens and twenties, I am reluctant to declare with confidence when she is describing actual experiences as opposed to imagined or fantasized ones.

2. "Interview with Octavia Butler" (Sanders).

3. OEB 805.

4. OEB 2289.

5. OEB 4166, letter dated November 16, 1971.

6. The aborted Thomas and Aaor narratives, discussed in chapter 5.

7. OEB 1253.

8. See also OEB 939 (entry dated September 28, 1971) and following. See also OEB 4169 (letter dated August 3, 1972).

9. OEB 2400.

10. OEB 9.

11. See for instance OEB 3174.

12. See for instance OEB 993, entry dated December 10, 1974, in which she looks forward to another imminent layoff.

13. OEB 945, entry dated August 20, 1972.

14. OEB 4162.

15. OEB 4167.

16. Ibid., entry dated October 6, 1972.

17. OEB 983, entry dated April 6, 1974. A journal entry from two years earlier, OEB 927, has an equally depressive and disturbing mood: she calls herself a coward because she doesn't "have the guts" to kill herself.

18. OEB 1002, entry dated June 6, 1976.

19. OEB 102.

20. OEB 929 and following.

21. OEB 1183, entry dated May 8, 1976.

22. "Positive Obsession" (in *Bloodchild*), 129.

23. Ibid., 133.

24. "Furor Scribendi" (in *Bloodchild*), 143.

25. OEB 1583.

26. OEB 3878, letter dated December 4, 1975.

27. OEB 3876, letter dated October 23, 1975.

28. "Lost Races of Science Fiction," 18, and republished herein.

29. OEB 3883, letter dated February 24, 1977.

30. *Patternmaster*, 4.

31. Ibid., 3.

32. Ibid., 5.

33. Ibid., 191.

34. Jameson, "World Reduction in Le Guin," 269 (in *Archeologies*).

35. Ibid., 271–72.

36. "Interview with Octavia E. Butler" (McCaffery and McMenamin), 15.

37. *Patternmaster*, 5.

38. OEB 4444.

39. "Interview with Octavia E. Butler" (McCaffery and McMenamin), 16–17.

40. "Interview with Octavia Butler" (Sanders).

41. OEB 3884, letter dated March 4, 1976.

42. "Value of Literacy."

43. Qtd. in Glickman, "Octavia Butler," 40.

44. See Reynolds, *Super Heroes*, 16.

45. *Patternmaster*, 7.

46. *Mind of My Mind*, 185–86.

47. "Interview with Octavia E. Butler" (McCaffery and McMenamin), 18.

48. Jameson, "World Reduction in Le Guin," 275 (in *Archeologies*).

49. *Patternmaster*, 64.

50. A similar inversion happened within the pages of *Fantastic Four* comics themselves, when Sue Storm's purely defensive power of invisibility was rewritten as a power to create and manipulate force fields, giving her an offensive capability more powerful than any other member of the team. See *Fantastic Four* #22 (October 1963) for the start of this shift.

51. *Patternmaster*, 68.

52. Ibid., 75–76.

53. Ibid., 20–22.

54. Ibid., 79–80.

55. Ibid., 198.

56. Ibid., 79.

57. Ibid., 76.

58. Ibid., 202.

59. *Mind of My Mind*, 4.

60. Ibid., 8.

61. Ibid., 19.

62. Ibid., 22.

63. Tal, "That Just Kills Me," 66–67.

64. *Mind of My Mind*, 87.

65. Ibid., 88.

66. Ibid., 8–9.

67. Fawaz, "Where No X-Man Has Gone Before!" 357.

68. Govan, "Connections," 84.

69. See for instance OEB 2703.

70. *Mind of My Mind*, 215.

71. Lavender, "Critical Race Theory," 192.

72. *Patternmaster*, 63–64.

73. Ibid., 78.

74. Ibid., 41.

75. Ibid., 24–35.

76. Marriott, "Visions," n.p.

77. "Congratulations!" (Fry) 129–30.

78. "Congratulations!" (Fry), 129.

79. "Interview with Octavia E. Butler" (Rowell), 63.

80. "Interview with Octavia E. Butler" (McCaffery and McMenamin), 15.

81. This equation between survival and murder is foregrounded in a conversation between Doro and Anyanwu late in *Wild Seed* (213).

82. *Mind of My Mind*, 87–89.

83. OEB 3842, letter dated January 27, 1987.

84. OEB 523.

85. OEB 520.

86. Ibid. Ellipsis in original.

87. OEB 503.

88. See OEB 505.

89. Edelman, *No Future*, 2–3.

90. OEB 3896, letter dated December 14, 1976.

91. OEB 4101, letter dated June 19, 1978.

92. OEB 993, entry dated June 6, 1976. This is only a few weeks after she sends the book to Doubleday.

93. Shawl, "Third Parable," 209.

94. "Interview with Octavia E. Butler" (Kenan), 32–33.

95. "Octavia E. Butler Plants an Earthseed" (Littleton). Mr. Spock, one of the most famous characters from the original *Star Trek*, was the product of a human-Vulcan marriage, while Captain Kirk would frequently romance alien women on the planets the starship would visit.

96. "Octavia Butler" (McGonigal), 135; "Conversation with Octavia E. Butler" (Shawl), 49.

1. "Interview with Octavia E. Butler" (Rowell), 51.
2. Ibid.
3. "The Lit Interview" (Burton-Rose), 196.
4. "Octavia E. Butler" (Brown), 182.
5. Ibid.
6. "The Lit Interview" (Burton-Rose), 197.
7. The story's original title was, in fact, "Kindred." See OEB 4346, letter dated November 17, 1978.
8. OEB 4275.
9. OEB 4105.
10. See the afterword to "Near of Kin" in *Bloodchild* (85). The title of the story, "Near of Kin," originates in the prohibition against incest in Leviticus 18:6.
11. OEB 1183, notes dated April 26, 1976.
12. "Interview with Octavia Butler" (Eliot), 20.
13. "Sci-Fi Tales from Octavia E. Butler" (Jackson), 43. "There are limits to what people will put up with when they're reading a novel." See also "Octavia Butler" (McGonigal), 134–35.
14. "Octavia Butler" (McGonigal), 135–36.
15. OEB 3177.
16. *Kindred*, 184.
17. *Kindred*, 264.
18. OEB 274, entry dated October 17, 1975.
19. OEB 275.
20. OEB 1197.
21. The quoted text is from OEB 2489, but it was an observation she made quite often.
22. OEB 4536, letter dated November 23, 1992.
23. OEB 3913.
24. OEB 3930.
25. OEB 4305, letter dated September 5, 1998; see also OEB 4270.
26. OEB 4039, letter dated August 8, 2005.
27. OEB 4481, letter dated July 2, 1982.
28. OEB 4236, letter dated April 20, 1982.
29. Thaler, *Black Atlantic Speculative Fictions*, 27.
30. Ibid., 35–37.
31. Goodison, "Negrocity," 625.
32. *Wild Seed*, 215.
33. As noted above, such violations of the incest taboo are fully normalized by the time of *Patternmaster's* future.
34. See his essay "The Myth of Superman."
35. OEB 3181.
36. *Wild Seed*, 178.
37. Ibid., 9.
38. Ibid., 288, 283.
39. Ibid., 276–78.

40. Thaler, *Black Atlantic Speculative Fictions*, 40.

41. Ibid., 41.

42. Ibid., 41.

43. *Wild Seed*, 86.

44. Ibid., 80–81.

45. Ibid., 140–41.

46. "Conversation with Octavia E. Butler" (*Sower* 2007), 334.

47. Butler highlights this facet of the dolphin sequence with a brief callback in *Clay's Ark*, in which a character describes the trove of religious movies in the library of the place where they are staying: "Some were religious, some antireligious, some merely exploitive—Sodom-and-Gomorrah films. Some were cause-oriented—God arrives as a woman or a dolphin or a throwaway kid. And some were science fiction. God arrives from Eighty-two Eridani Seven" (179).

48. *Wild Seed*, 83.

49. Ibid., 84.

50. Ibid., 91.

51. Ibid., 196.

52. Ibid., 198.

53. Sands, "Octavia Butler's Chiastic Cannibalistics," 7.

54. *Wild Seed*, 215.

55. See Shawl, "The Third Parable," 210.

56. Vint, "Becoming Other," 288.

57. A number of these clippings still exist in the Huntington in OEB 329.

58. OEB 819.

59. OEB 1556, entry dated July 1983.

60. "Eye Witness: Octavia Butler's A-Ha Moment."

CHAPTER 4: BLINDSIGHT (1980–1987)

1. "Lost Races," 17.

2. Ibid.

3. "Lost Races," 18.

4. OEB 5181, letter dated September 5, 1980.

5. OEB 4005, letter dated September 15, 1980.

6. OEB 3783, letter dated October 9, 1980.

7. OEB 4005, letter dated September 15, 1980.

8. OEB 4007, letter dated November 1, 1980.

9. OEB 4005, letter dated September 15, 1980.

10. OEB 4008, letter dated February 19, 1981.

11. OEB 4010, letter dated April 21, 1982.

12. "Positive Obsession" (in *Bloodchild*), 134–135.

13. Many of the references to King in Butler's journals use the code name "Stako."

14. OEB 121.

15. OEB 122, entry dated January 25, 1979.

16. OEB 118.

17. See, for instance, OEB 122.

18. OEB 123.

19. OEB 126.

20. In one version of the novel Aaron and Davis briefly replace Kyna with Aaron's own mother as the third member of the sexual triad. See OEB 199A-B.

21. OEB 167.

22. OEB 199B.

23. OEB 5291.

24. OEB 4483.

25. Vonda M., September 6, 1983.

26. OEB 4492, letter dated September 21, 1984.

27. OEB 1011, journal February 25, 1984.

28. OEB 4492, letter dated September 21, 1984.

29. "Fun, Fun, Fun" (Heifetz letters in *Strange Matings*), 176.

30. OEB 1008, July 24, 1982.

31. OEB 1094, entry dated July 26, 2000.

32. OEB 1021, entry dated July 27, 1990.

33. OEB 4266, letter dated May 19, 1983.

34. "Speech Sounds," afterword, 110.

35. "Speech Sounds," 98.

36. Ibid., 106–7.

37. Ibid., 108.

38. "Bloodchild," 25.

39. Ibid., 28.

40. "Bloodchild," afterword, 30–32.

41. I am able to discuss the ambiguous utopia of this "kingdom of the sick" in "Evening" [II] in much more detail in my article "Life without Hope?"

42. OEB 519.

43. OEB 518.

44. OEB 505.

45. OEB 2423.

46. OEB 3588, letter dated January 6, 1987.

47. OEB 3139, entry dated June 4, 1998.

48. OEB 4119, letter dated November 12, 1984.

49. See *Doro-Jesus*, OEB 453 and following.

50. See OEB 1556, entry dated July 1983.

51. OEB 1556, entry dated July 1983.

52. OEB 4572, letter dated July 9, 1984.

53. OEB 3175, entry dated September 9, 1980.

CHAPTER 5: THE TRAINING FLOOR (1987–1989)

1. OEB 2917.

2. OEB 809.

3. OEB 2887 entry dated August 11, 1974.

4. OEB 1004 entry dated August 18, 1977. A few days later, in an entry dated August 20, she rejects the idea, saying that although writing another Patternist novel would be "fun,"

what she really needs to do is write a "realistic fantasy of the kind people like Stephen King are selling for huge amounts of money." "I want financial security for myself and my mother," she says.

5. OEB 2993.

6. OEB 2460.

7. "Octavia E. Butler: Persistence" (Brown), 188. She talks about this in more detail in an unfinished essay on "World Making" in the Huntington archive (OEB 2967), which describes her practice of using scrap paper to record her ideas as part of "the chaos that eventually forms my worlds."

8. See OEB 391 for a character list of this version of the Oankali books, which includes key plot details about the prospects for life in the tiny, eventually all-woman colony.

9. The capital-A stylization is borrowed from the novel.

10. OEB 395.

11. OEB 396. The same list that describes Lilith as a Moses also amusingly describes her as a Lou Grant, from the *Mary Tyler Moore Show*: "Competent, manipulative, a hell of a bullshitter (sometimes it works, sometimes it doesn't)." See Wood, "Subversion through Inclusion," for an extended reading of the relationship between Butler's Lilith and the Judaic Lilith, the legendary first wife of Adam.

12. "Interview with Octavia E. Butler" (Rowell), 58.

13. *Dawn*, 14.

14. OEB 3179, which also suggests another intriguing alterative title for *Dawn: Carcenogenesis*.

15. OEB 3181.

16. Butler's notes indicate that Derrick's plot in particular—essentially reduced to a handful of sentences in the published novel—was once intended to be a more substantial part of the story. See OEB 13.

17. *Dawn*, 36.

18. "We couldn't survive as a people if we were always confined to one ship or one world." *Dawn*, 34.

19. Kathryn Hendrickson pointed out to me one reason this might be an evolutionarily rational adaptation, as opposed to a mere boast: if the Oankali could not remember their own full history of division, one group of Oankali might inadvertently assimilate another, in a kind of species-level cannibalism.

20. Haraway, "Biopolitics," 227.

21. Haraway, *Primate Visions*, 379.

22. Belk, "Certainty of the Flesh," 376.

23. "Conversation with Octavia Butler" (DiChario).

24. Not all critics take the Oankali side, of course, as I note below; see Frances Bonner's "Difference and Desire, Slavery and Seduction" in particular for a strong denunciation of the Oankali as rapists, as well as Holden, "High Costs"; Zaki, "Future Tense"; Johns, "Becoming Medusa" and "Time Had Come"; and Stein, "Bodily Invasions." While a full articulation of the critical debate about the Oankali is beyond the scope of this book, I would recommend the works listed in the bibliography as a good starting place for further reading.

25. "Octavia Butler" (Williams), 178–79.

26. Vint, *Bodies of Tomorrow*, 65.

27. *Dawn*, 41–42.

28. Ibid., 93–95. Titus says "They said I could do it with you," though the Oankali claim they "didn't know" Titus would behave that way.

29. Ibid., 96, 246. Thomas D. Moore suggested during one of our class discussions on the novel that the rebranding of the series as "Lilith's Brood" may have at least partially been intended to let the Oankali "off the hook" for this extreme violation by making the revelation of the pregnancy less a surprise for the reader.

30. Ibid., 223.

31. Ibid., 163–64.

32. Ibid., 188–89.

33. Ibid., 183–91.

34. See Tate's subplot in *Adulthood Rites*.

35. OEB 2980.

36. OEB 1016, entry dated December 30, 1988.

37. "The Oankali enforce their point of view, like groups of humans throughout history, with essentialist definitions. Again and again, they point to the genetic flaw in humanity in order to justify their colonization and virtual erasure of this species." Holden, "High Costs," 52.

38. On this point see, for instance, Stein, "Bodily Invasions."

39. *Adulthood Rites*, 261.

40. "Interview with Octavia E. Butler" (McCaffery and McMenamin), 23.

41. OEB 4084.

42. OEB 4085.

43. OEB 2707.

44. OEB journal entry May 2, 1997.

45. OEB 3150.

46. "Interview with Octavia E. Butler" (McCaffery and McMenamin), 23.

47. "Octavia Butler" (Ghosh), 77.

48. *Dawn*, 122.

49. OEB 13.

50. *Dawn*, 242.

51. Ibid., 227.

52. Ibid., 240.

53. Ibid., 14.

54. Ibid., 15.

55. Ibid., 16.

56. Thank you to Tony Manno for planting the seeds of this observation.

57. See for instance OEB 13.

58. *Adulthood Rites*, 41.

59. *Dawn*, 85.

60. OEB 4429, letter dated January 6, 1988.

61. For more on this point, see again my article "Life without Hope?" on the use of Huntington's disease in the trilogy and in "The Evening and the Morning and the Night."

62. *Adulthood Rites*, 199.

63. OEB 2464.

64. OEB 1143, entry dated May 21, 2003.

65. Zaki, "Future Tense," 249.

66. *Imago*, 9.

67. Ibid., 57.

68. Zaki, "Future Tense," 249n7.

69. *Imago*, 104–5.

70. Ibid., 136–39.

71. Ibid., 82.

72. Ibid., 112.

73. Ibid., 105.

74. Ibid., 214–15.

75. OEB 34.

76. OEB 2994.

77. "Congratulations!" (Fry), 130.

78. Slonczewski, "Octavia Butler's Xenogenesis Trilogy," n.p.

79. *Dawn*, 246–48.

80. *Adulthood Rites*, 24–25.

81. *Imago*, 137. She says it "quietly," denoting some internal conflict—but she says it.

82. Ibid., 147.

83. Tucker, "Human Contradiction," 174.

84. Beal, "Black Women," 14.

85. OEB 1143, entry dated May 21, 2003.

86. "Radio Imagination" (Mehaffy and Keating interview), 105.

87. "We Keep Playing the Same Record" (Potts interview), 67.

88. OEB 803, an early draft of *Parable of the Sower*.

89. "U.N. Racism Conference," n.p.

90. "Lit Interview" (Burton-Rose), 201.

CHAPTER 6: GOD OF CLAY (1989–2006)

1. OEB 1017. An excerpted version of this letter (and OEB 1018 and 4522) was read by Merrilee Heifetz at a 2006 "Tribute to Octavia Butler" at the New York Public Library and can be found online at http://www.nypl.org/sites/default/files/events/butler6506.pdf. It can also be found in its entirety in "Fun, Fun, Fun," in *Strange Matings*, 173–78.

2. OEB 1018.

3. OEB 1017.

4. Ibid.

5. Ibid.

6. OEB 1018.

7. OEB 4522.

8. OEB 4525, letter dated March 21, 1990.

9. "Interview with Octavia E. Butler" (McCaffery and McMenamin), 26.

10. OEB 2056.

11. "Octavia E. Butler: Persistence" (Brown), 182–83.

12. *Sower*, 22.

13. See OEB 801, among other places she discusses her move in both her private journals and her public speeches.

14. *Sower*, 68.

15. OEB 3982.

16. OEB 1824, letter dated August 11, 1994.

17. OEB 4536, letter dated November 23, 1992.

18. OEB 3193.

19. OEB 1518. She says as much explicitly in a handwritten note in OEB 835, imagining the transition from "sincere religious mystic to hard-nosed manipulator."

20. OEB 803.

21. See "Interview with Octavia Butler" (Cobb), 63, especially for some thoughts about the way Lauren's position as a black woman complicated her power-seeking.

22. OEB 2426. See also "Interview with Octavia Butler" (Cobb), 63.

23. *Sower*, 1. References are to the Warner edition, not the 2007 re-release.

24. *Talents*, 8.

25. "Devil Girl from Mars." After exhaustively searching for the origin of this quote, I have concluded Butler was misremembering, and it was actually Asimov who said this in his preface to *More Soviet Science Fiction* (8). Heinlein's typical list of the basic science fictional story types was structured rather differently.

26. See "Octavia E. Butler: Persistence" (Brown), 182.

27. "Interview with Octavia Butler" (Cobb), 54–55.

28. Nilges, "We Need the Stars," 1333.

29. Nilges, "Neoliberalism," 372.

30. *Sower*, 137.

31. *Sower*, 295.

32. OEB 381.

33. Thaler, *Black Atlantic Speculative Fictions*, 69–97.

34. "We Keep Playing the Same Record" (Potts interview), 65.

35. *Sower*, 4.

36. *Sower*, 15.

37. *Talents*, 150.

38. Ibid., 170.

39. Ibid., 145.

40. "Interview with Octavia Butler" (Cobb), 58.

41. "Radio Imagination" (Mehaffy and Keating), 121–22.

42. Lavender, *Black and Brown Planets*, 23.

43. Curtis, *Postapocalyptic*, 161.

44. Moylan, *Scraps of the Untainted Sky*, 243.

45. Stillman, "Dystopian Critiques," 32.

46. "Free Libraries."

47. "A Few Rules for Predicting the Future." The full letter to the White House can be found at OEB 3850.

48. OEB 3131. Butler had precisely this paradox of education in mind; she made the remark in the context of her pressing need to learn about "investment, business, business law" while she was in "Uncle Boisie's window." Recall her thoughts on the Patternists, too, and the difference between good teachers and bad.

49. *Talents*, 430–31.

50. *Talents*, 444.

51. See Allen, "Octavia Butler's Parable Novels."

52. *Talents*, 445.

53. OEB 1823.

54. OEB 1839.

55. OEB 1889.

56. OEB 5450, letter dated April 10, 2005.

57. OEB 3196, entry dated June 10, 1995.

58. In practice, however, she simply soon began to think about how she might get more money: whereas she wrote that she needed to find a way to come up with a million dollars in 1993 (OEB 3127), by 1999 she needed five million: "Two million for me, and three million as a base for very quiet giving and helping" (OEB 1045, entry dated August 16, 1998).

59. OEB 4121, letter dated May 20, 1997.

60. OEB 1842.

61. OEB 3139. She quite commonly expressed the notion that Earthseed was close to the truth; in OEB 3193 she talks about coming to peace with religion after some time as a "hostile atheist" and concludes that "very probably God is Change."

62. OEB 3139. This letter is republished in Heifetz, *Strange Matings*, 179.

63. OEB 2426.

64. See her essay "The Third Parable" in *Strange Matings*.

65. In some versions it is named "Ola," after Olamina, or even sometimes "Trickster."

66. OEB 601, entry dated October 13, 2003.

67. OEB 2055.

68. Some of the blindness versions of the narrative take a name she should have known better than to invoke: *Blindsight*.

69. OEB 2078.

70. OEB 2214.

71. OEB 2070.

72. *Talents*, 1.

73. OEB 601, entry dated October 13, 2003.

74. OEB 2043.

75. "Octavia E. Butler: Persistence" (Brown), 183.

76. OEB 1055.

77. OEB 2037.

78. OEB 1091.

79. OEB 2047, entry dated September 21, 2001.

80. "butler8star@qwest.net" (Okorafor), 219.

81. Shawl, "Conversation," 170.

82. OEB 1864.

83. *Sower*, 22.

84. Matthew 25:14–30, as quoted in *Parable of the Talents*, 447–48.

85. Luke 6:8–13.

86. Her personal journals show her wrestling with this question, listing many alternative biblical parables that might fit the bill (see OEB 1045, 1046, 1055). In some documents she seems attracted to the Parable of the Mustard Seed instead, which suggests a happier resolution to *Trickster* than most of her notes (OEB 2081).

87. OEB 2078.

88. OEB 3279.

89. OEB 3279, entry dated May 17, 2005. The observation takes the form of one of Olamina's poems.

90. OEB 601, entry dated October 13, 2003.

CHAPTER 7: PARACLETE (1999–2006)

1. See OEB 3149: "I've always written with my sex drive as much as with my mind. What can I do now with my mind alone—such as it is."

2. OEB 601, entry dated October 13, 2003.

3. OEB 2059.

4. See, for instance, the plot synopsis for "Eden" she gives in OEB 2224, though this draft is confusingly labeled "Paraclete." Butler's tendency toward reusing the same titles over and over reaches its absolute apex in this period of her career, making it at times very difficult to pull ideas apart or identify which idea is which.

5. "Amnesty," 156.

6. "Amnesty," 162–63.

7. Ibid., 160.

8. Ibid., 166.

9. Ibid., 167.

10. Ibid., 168.

11. Ibid., 184.

12. Ibid., 180–82.

13. OEB 1169, entry dated December 1, 2005.

14. Foster, "We Get to Live," 140–41.

15. OEB 2498.

16. OEB 2513. Here, too, we see a connection to Doro, who in Butler's private notes sometimes expressed a similar longing for death that was the secret cause of all his other actions; see *Doro-Jesus*, OEB 453–59.

17. OEB 2514.

18. OEB 2500.

19. OEB 3279, entry dated January 18, 2005.

20. OEB 1110.

21. OEB 1134, entry dated November 16, 2001. *The Twilight Zone* reference was a double-edged sword, however; it could just as easily refer to the tired form of the "twist." When a version of "The Book of Martha" mutation of *Paraclete* is published as a short story, it references *The Twilight Zone*. See "The Book of Martha," *Bloodchild* (2nd edition), 187–214 (207).

22. OEB 1161, entry dated April 21, 2005.

23. OEB 2225, ca. 2001.

24. OEB 2116, dated to May 29, 2003.

25. OEB 1106. "I thought of it then," Butler writes mysteriously. "So would she."

26. "Big Thinker" (Stamberg interview), 194. The story actually goes unnamed, but "Martha" fits the description, while "Amnesty" does not.

27. OEB 1125, entry dated August 17, 2001.

28. "Book of Martha," 192.

29. Ibid., 196.

30. Ibid., 200.

31. Ibid., 213.

32. Ibid., 214.

33. OEB 1158, entry dated February 13, 2005.

34. OEB 1143, entry dated May 21, 2003.

35. Ibid.

36. OEB 2500.

37. *Fledgling*, 67.

38. OEB 4126.

39. *Fledgling*, 11.

40. Ibid., 12.

41. Ibid., 16.

42. Ibid., 73.

43. OEB 4286. Though see again the letter to Okorafor: "With the most recent presidential elections, I was depressed for a long time; this was way before the hurricanes. I'd think about the war and watch as corruption became a more normal thing—so I wrote a vampire story" (219).

44. Brox, "Every Age," 392–93.

45. *Fledgling*, 187–90.

46. Ibid., 73–74.

47. Ibid., 269–70.

48. OEB 1149.

49. OEB 3257, entry dated March 30, 2005.

50. OEB 3279.

51. OEB 77. This is the first page of the first chapter of this version of the book.

52. OEB 83.

53. OEB 77.

54. OEB 77.

55. Ibid.

56. OEB 77.

57. OEB 75. Handwritten addendum.

58. Ibid.

59. OEB 3155.

60. Ibid. See note 58 of chapter 6 for a close replication of this language of doing good quietly as part of Butler's personal fantasies about the future.

61. OEB 78, p. 2.

62. OEB 601, entry dated Friday, August 1, 2003.

63. OEB 3279, entry dated July 9, 2005.

64. Ibid., entries dated July 4, 2005, and February 7, 2006.

65. OEB 6385, letter dated January 13, 2006.

66. Ibid., pages after entry dated February 11, 2006.

CONCLUSION: UNEXPECTED STORIES

1. "Visions: Identity" (Marriott), n.p.
2. Womack, *Afrofuturism*, 109.
3. "Monophobic Response," 415–16. See also her "Essay on Racism," at NPR.
4. Brown and Imarisha, *Octavia's Brood*, dedication.
5. Imarisha, "Introduction," in ibid., 5.
6. "Reflections on Octavia Butler," 433–39.
7. Holden and Shawl, *Strange Matings*, 2.
8. Preface, *Unexpected Stories*, loc.14.
9. "A Necessary Being" loc. 722.
10. Kenan 32–33.

BIBLIOGRAPHY OF SECONDARY SOURCES

Ackerman, Erin. "Becoming and Belonging: The Productivity of Pleasures and Desires in Octavia Butler's 'Xenogenesis' Trilogy." *Extrapolation* 49, no. 1 (2008): 24–43.

Agusti, Clara Escoda. "The Relationship between Community and Subjectivity in Octavia E. Butler's *Parable of the Sower*." *Extrapolation* 46, no. 3 (Fall 2005): 351–59.

Alaimo, Stacy. "Displacing Darwin and Descartes: The Bodily Transgressions of Fielding Burke, Octavia Butler, and Linda Hogan." *Isle: Interdisciplinary Studies in Literature and Environment* 3, no. 1 (Summer 1996): 47–66.

Allen, Marlene D. "Octavia Butler's Parable Novels and the Boomerang of African American History." *Callaloo* 32, no. 4 (Fall 2009): 1353–65.

Allison, Dorothy. "The Future of Female: Octavia Butler's Mother Lode." In *Reading Black, Reading Feminist*, edited by Henry Louis Gates Jr., 471–78. New York: Meridian, 1990.

Anderson, Crystal S. "'The Girl Isn't White': New Racial Dimensions in Octavia Butler's *Survivor*." *Extrapolation* 47, no. 1 (Spring 2006): 35–50.

Armitt, Lucie. *Contemporary Women's Fiction and the Fantastic*. Houndsmill, Eng.: Macmillan, 1999.

Asimov, Isaac. *More Soviet Science Fiction*. New York: Collier, 1982.

Attebery, Brian. *Decoding Gender in Science Fiction*. New York: Routledge, 2002.

Baccolini, Raffaella. "Gender and Genre in Feminist Critical Dystopias of Katharine Burdekin, Margaret Atwood, and Octavia Butler." In Barr, *Future Females*, 13–34.

———. "The Persistence of Hope in Dystopian Science Fiction." *PMLA* 119 (2004): 518–21.

Barr, Marleen. *Afro-Future Females: Black Writers Chart Science Fiction's Newest New-Wave Trajectory*. Columbus: Ohio State University Press, 2008.

———. "Octavia Butler and James Tiptree Do Not Write about Zap Guns: Positioning Feminist Science Fiction within Feminist Fabulation." In *Lost in Space: Probing Feminist Science Fiction and Beyond*, edited by Marleen S. Barr, 97–107. Chapel Hill: University of North Carolina Press, 1993.

Barr, Marleen S., ed. *Future Females: The Next Generation*. Lanham, Md.: Rowman and Littlefield, 2000.

Becker, Jennifer. "Octavia Estelle Butler." In *Voices from the Gap: Women Artists and Writers of Color*, edited by Laura Curtright. Available at umn.edu (August 2004, updated 2006).

Bedore, Pamela. "Slavery and Symbiosis in Octavia Butler's *Kindred*." *Foundation* 84 (Spring 2002): 73–81.

Belk, Nolan. "The Certainty of the Flesh: Octavia Butler's Use of the Erotic in the *Xenogenesis* Trilogy." *Utopian Studies* 19, no. 3 (2008): 369–90.

Birns, Nicholas. "Octavia Butler: Fashioning Alien Constructs." *Hollins Critic* 38, no. 3 (2001): 1–6.

Bogstad, Janice. "Octavia E. Butler and Power Relations." *Janus* 4, no.4 (1978–79): 28–31.

Bollinger, Laurel. "Placental Economy: Octavia Butler, Luce Irigaray, and Speculative Subjectivity." *LIT: Literature Interpretation Theory* 18, no. 4 (October 2007): 325–52.

———. "Symbiogenesis, Selfhood, and Science Fiction." *Science Fiction Studies* 37, no. 1 (March 2010): 34–53.

Bonner, Francis. "Difference and Desire, Slavery and Seduction: Octavia Butler's Xenogenesis." *Foundation* 48 (1990): 58–62.

Bould, Mark. "The Ships Landed Long Ago: Afrofuturism and Black SF." *Science Fiction Studies* 34, no. 2 (2007): 177–86.

Boulter, Amanda. 1996. "Polymorphous Future: Octavia Butler's Xenogenesis Trilogy." In *American Bodies: Cultural Histories of the Physique*, edited by Tim Armstrong, 170–85. New York: NYU Press, 1996.

Burwell, Jennifer. "Speaking Parts: Internal Dialogic and Models of Agency in the Work of Joanna Russ and Octavia Butler." In *Notes on Nowhere: Feminism, Utopian Logic, and Social Transformation*, 87–130. Minneapolis: University of Minnesota Press, 1997.

Braid, Christina. "Contemplating and Contesting Violence in Dystopia: Violence in Octavia Butler's Xenogenesis Trilogy." *Contemporary Justice Review* 9, no. 1 (March 2000): 47–65.

Brataas, Delilah Bermudez. "Becoming Utopia in Octavia E. Butler's Xenogenesis Series." *Foundation* 96 (Spring 2006): 84–101.

Broad, Katherine R. "Body Speaks: Communication and the Limits of Nationalism in Octavia Butler's *Xenogenesis* Trilogy." In *The Postnational Fantasy: Essays on Postcolonialism, Cosmopolitics, and Science Fiction*, edited by Masood Ashraf Raja, Jason W. Ellis, and Swaralipi Nandi, 141–55. Jefferson, N.C.: McFarland, 2011.

Brown, Adirenne Maree, and Walidah Imarisha. *Octavia's Brood: Science Fiction Stories from Social Justice Movements*. Oakland, Calif.: AK, 2015.

Brox, Ali. "Every Age Has the Vampire It Needs: Octavia Butler's Vampiric Vision in *Fledgling*." *Utopian Studies* 19, no. 3 (2008): 391–409.

Buckman, Alyson. "'What Good Is All This to Black People?': Octavia Butler's Reconstruction of Corporeality." *FEMSPEC* 4, no. 2 (2004): 201–18.

Call, Lewis. "Structures of Desire: Erotic Power in the Speculative Fiction of Octavia Butler and Samuel Delany." *Rethinking History* 9, no. 2–3 (2005): 275–96.

Calvin, Ritch. "An Octavia E. Butler Bibliography (1976–2008). *Utopian Studies* 19, no. 3 (2008): 485–516.

Canavan, Gerry. "Bred to Be Superhuman: Comic Books and Afrofuturism in Octavia Butler's Patternist Series." *Paradoxa* 25 (Fall 2013): 253–87.

———. "Life without Hope? Huntington's Disease and Genetic Futurity." In *Disability in Science Fiction: Representations of Technology as Cure*, edited by Kathryn Allan, 169–87. New York: Palgrave MacMillan, 2013.

Caputi, Jane. "Facing Change: African Mythic Origins in Octavia Butler's *Parable* Novels." In *Goddesses and Monsters: Women, Myth, Power, and Popular Culture*, 366–69. Madison: University of Wisconsin Press, 2004.

Curtis, Claire P. *Postapocalyptic Science Fiction and the Social Contract*. New York: Lexington, 2010.

———. "Theorizing Fear: Octavia Butler and the Realist Utopia." *Utopian Studies* 19, no. 3 (2008): 411–31.

———. "Utopian Possibilities: Disability, Norms, and Eugenics in Octavia Butler's *Xenogenesis*." *Journal of Literary and Cultural Disability Studies* 9, no. 1 (2015): 19–33.

DeGraw, Sharon. "'The More Things Change, the More They Remain the Same': Gender and Sexuality in Octavia Butler's Oeuvre." *FEMSPEC* 4, no. 2 (2004): 219–38.

Deman, J. Andrew. "Taking Out the Trash: Octavia E. Butler's *Wild Seed* and the Feminist Voice in American SF." *FEMSPEC* 6, no. 2 (2005): 6–14.

Dery, Mark. "Black to the Future: Interviews with Samuel R. Delany, Greg Tate, and Tricia Rose." In *Flame Wars: The Discourse of Cyberculture*, edited by Mark Dery, 179–222. Durham, N.C.: Duke University Press, 1995.

Donadey, Anne. "African American and Francophone Postcolonial Memory: Octavia Butler's *Kindred* and Assia Djebar's *La feeme sans sepulture*." *Research in African Literatures* 39, no. 3 (Fall 2008): 65–81.

Donawerth, Jane. *Frankenstein's Daughters: Women Writing Science Fiction*. Syracuse, N.Y.: Syracuse University Press, 1997.

———. "Utopian Science: Contemporary Feminist Science Theory and Science Fiction by Women." *NWSA Journal* 2, no. 4 (Autumn 1990): 535–57.

Dubey, Madhu. "Contemporary African American Fiction and the Politics of Postmodernism." *Novel* 35, no. 2–3 (Spring/Summer 2002): 151–68.

———. "Folk and Urban Communities in African-American Women's Fiction: Octavia Butler's *Parable of the Sower*." *Studies in American Fiction* 27, no. 1 (1999): 103–24.

———. "Speculative Fictions of Slavery." *American Literature* 82, no. 4 (December 2010): 779–805.

Eco, Umberto. "The Myth of Superman." *Diacritics* 2, no. 1 (Spring 1972): 14–22.

Edelman, Lee. *No Future: Queer Theory and the Death Drive*. Durham, N.C.: Duke University Press, 2004.

Ephick, Keith. "Discursive Transgressions and Ideological Negotiations: From Orwell's *1984* to Butler's *Parable of the Sower*." In *Environments in Science Fiction: Essays on Alternative Spaces*, edited by Susan M. Bernardo, 171–90. Jefferson, N.C.: McFarland, 2014.

Fawaz, Ramzi. "Where No X-Man Has Gone Before! Mutant Superheroes and the Cultural Politics of Popular Fantasy in Postwar America." *American Literature* 83, no. 2 (2011): 355–88.

Federmayer, Éva. "Octavia Butler's Maternal Cyborgs: The Black Female World of the Xenogenesis Trilogy." In *Anatomy of Science Fiction*, edited by Donald E. Morse, 95–108. Newcastle-upon-Tyne, Eng.: Cambridge Scholars, 2006.

Ferreira, Maria Aline. "Symbiotic Bodies and Evolutionary Tropes in the Work of Octavia Butler." *Science Fiction Studies* 37, no. 3 (November 2010): 401–15.

Fink, Marty. "AIDS Vampires: Reimagining Illness in Octavia Butler's *Fledgling*." *Science Fiction Studies* 37, no. 3 (November 2010): 416–32.

Flagel, Nadine. "'It's Almost Like Being There': Speculative Fiction, Slave Narrative, and the Crisis of Representation in Octavia Butler's *Kindred*." *Canadian Review of American Studies* 42, no. 2 (2012): 216–45.

Foster, Frances S. "Octavia Butler's Black Female Future Vision." *Extrapolation* 23, no. 1 (1982): 37–49.

Foster, Thomas. "'We Get to Live, and So Do They': Octavia Butler's Contact Zones." In Holden and Shawl, *Strange Matings*, 140–67.

Francis, Conseula, ed. *Conversations with Octavia E. Butler.* Jackson: University Press of Mississippi, 2010.

Friend, Beverly. "Time Travel as a Feminist Didactic in Works by Phyllis Eisenstein, Marlys Nillhiser, and Octavia Butler." *Extrapolation* 23, no. 1 (1982): 50–55.

Glickman, Simon. "Octavia Butler (1947–): Science Fiction Writer." In *Contemporary Black Autobiography* 8, edited by L. Mpho Mabunda. New York: Gale, 1994.

Goodison, Camille. "Negrocity: An Interview with Greg Tate." *Callaloo* 35, no. 3 (2012): 621–37.

Gordon, Joan. "Two SF Diaries at the Intersection of Subjunctive Hopes and Declarative Despair." *Foundation: The International Review of Science Fiction* 72 (Spring 1998): 42–48.

Goss, Theodora. "The Gothic Technological Imaginary in Mary Shelley's *Frankenstein* and Octavia Butler's Xenogenesis." *Modern Fiction Studies* 53, no. 3 (Fall 2007): 434–59.

Govan, Sandra Y. "Connections, Links, and Extended Networks: Patterns in Octavia Butler's Science Fiction." *Black American Literature Forum* 18 (1984): 82–87.

———. "*Fledgling* by Octavia Butler." *Obsidian III: Literature in the African Diaspora* 6, no. 2 / 7, no. 1 (2005–2006): 40–43.

———. "Homage to Tradition: Octavia Butler Renovates the Historical Novel." *MELUS* 13, nos. 1 and 2 (Spring/Summer 1986): 79–96.

Grayson, Sandra M. *Visions of the Third Millennium: Black Science Fiction Novelists Write the Future.* Trenton, N.J.: Africa World, 2003.

Green, Michelle Erica. "'There Goes the Neighborhood': Octavia Butler's Demand for Diversity in Utopias." In *Utopian and Science Fiction by Women: Worlds of Difference,* edited by Jane L. Donawerth and Carol A. Kolmerten, 166–89. Syracuse, N.Y.: Syracuse University Press, 1994.

Grewe-Volpp, Christa. "Octavia Butler and the Nature/Culture Divide: An Ecofeminist Approach to the Xenogenesis Trilogy." In *Restoring the Connection to the Natural World: Essays on the African American Environmental Imagination,* edited by Sylvia Mayer, 149–73. Münster: LIT, 2003.

Gumbs, Alexis Pauline. "When Goddesses Change." *Hooded Utilitarian,* July 7, 2015. Available at http://www.hoodedutilitarian.com/2014/07/when-goddesses-change.

Hairston, Andrea. "'The Evening and the Morning and the Night,' Octavia E. Butler, 1987." In *Daughters of the Earth: Feminist Science Fiction in the Twentieth Century,* edited by Justine Larbalestier, 265–86. Middletown, Conn.: Wesleyan University Press, 2006.

———. "Octavia Butler—Praise Song to a Prophetic Artist." In *Daughters of the Earth: Feminist Science Fiction in the Twentieth Century,* edited by Justine Larbalestier, 287–304. Middletown, Conn.: Wesleyan University Press, 2006.

Hampton, Gregory Jerome. *Changing Bodies in the Fiction of Octavia Butler: Slaves, Aliens, and Vampires.* New York: Lexington, 2014.

———. "In Memoriam: Octavia E. Butler." *Callaloo* 29, no. 2 (Spring 2006): 245–48.

———. "Migration and Capital of the Body: Octavia Butler's *Parable of the Sower.*" *CLA Journal* 49, no. 1 (September 2005): 56–73.

Haraway, Donna. "The Biopolitics of Postmodern Bodies: Constitutions of Self in Immune System Disease." In *Simians, Cyborgs, and Women: The Reinvention of Nature,* 203–30. New York: Routledge, 1991.

———. "A Cyborg Manifesto: Science, Technology, and Socialist-Feminism in the Late Twentieth Century." In *Simians, Cyborgs, and Women: The Reinvention of Nature*, 149–82. New York: Routledge, 1991.

———. *Primate Visions: Gender, Race, and Nature in the World of Modern Science*. New York: Routledge, 1990.

Harper, Amie Breeze. "The Absence of Meat in Oankali Dietary Philosophy: An Eco-Feminist-Vegan Analysis of Octavia Butler's *Dawn*." In *The Black Imagination: Science Fiction, Futurism, and the Speculative*, edited by Sandra Jackson and Julie E. Moody-Freeman, 111–29. New York: Peter Lang, 2011.

Helford, Elyce Rae. "'Would You Really Rather Die than Bear My Young?': The Construction of Gender, Race, and Species in Octavia E. Butler's 'Bloodchild.'" *African American Review* 28, no. 2 (Summer 1994): 259–71.

Holden, Rebecca J. "The High Costs of Cyborg Survival: Octavia Butler's Xenogenesis Trilogy." *Foundation* 72 (1998): 49–56.

Holden, Rebecca J., and Nisi Shawl, eds. *Strange Matings: Science Fiction, Feminism, African American Voices, and Octavia E. Butler*. Seattle, Wash.: Aqueduct, 2013.

Holloway, Karla F. C. *Moorings and Metaphors: Figures of Culture and Gender in Black Women's Literature*. New Brunswick, N.J.: Rutgers University Press, 1992.

Hopkinson, Nalo. "Writing Ourselves In: Report on the Octavia E. Butler Celebration of the Fantastic in the Arts." *Science Fiction Studies* 40, no. 2 (2013): 399–401.

Jablon, Madelyn. "Metafiction as Genre: Walter Mosley, *Black Betty*; Octavia E. Butler, *Parable of the Sower*." In *Black Metafiction: Self-Consciousness in African American Literature*, 139–65. Iowa City: University of Iowa Press, 1997.

Jacobs, Naomi. "Posthuman Bodies and Agency in Octavia Butler's Xenogenesis." In *Dark Horizons: Science Fiction and the Dystopian Imagination*, edited by Raffaella Baccolini and Tom Moylan, 91–112. New York: Routledge, 2003.

Jameson, Fredric. "World Reduction in Le Guin: The Emergence of Utopian Narrative." *Science Fiction Studies* 2, no. 3 (November 1975): 221–30. Republished in *Archaeologies of the Future*, by Fredric Jameson, 267–80. New York: Verso, 2005.

Jenkins, Alice. "Knowing and Geography in Octavia Butler, Ursula K. Le Guin and Maureen McHugh." *Journal of the Fantastic in the Arts* 16, no. 4 (Winter 2006): 320–34.

Jesser, Nancy. "Blood, Genes, and Gender in Octavia Butler's *Kindred* and *Dawn*." *Extrapolation* 43, no. 1 (Spring 2002): 36–61.

Johns, J. Adam. "Becoming Medusa: Octavia Butler's 'Lilith's Brood' and Sociobiology." *Science Fiction Studies* 37, no. 3 (November 2010): 382–400.

———. "The Time Had Come for Us to Be Born: Octavia Butler's Darwinian Apocalypse." *Extrapolation* 51, no. 3 (2010): 395–413.

Jos, Philip. "Fear and the Spiritual Realism of Octavia Butler's Earthseed." *Utopian Studies* 23, no. 2 (2012): 408–29.

Kilgore, De Witt Douglas, and Ranu Samantrai. "A Memorial to Octavia E. Butler." *Science Fiction Studies* 37, no. 3 (November 2010): 353–62.

Knickerbocker, Dale. "Apocalypse, Utopia, and Dystopia: Old Paradigms Meet a New Millennium." *Extrapolation* 51, no. 3 (2010): 345–57.

Lacey, Lauren J. "Octavia E. Butler on Coping with Power in *Parable of the Sower, Parable of the Talents*, and *Fledgling*." *Critique* 49, no. 4 (Summer 2008): 379–94.

Lavender, Isiah, III. *Black and Brown Planets: The Politics of Race in Science Fiction*. Jackson: University Press of Mississippi, 2014.

———. "Critical Race Theory." In *The Routledge Companion to Science Fiction*, edited by Mark Bould, Andrew Butler, Adam Roberts, and Sherryl Vint, 185–193. New York: Routledge, 2009.

———. *Race in American Science Fiction*. Bloomington: Indiana University Press, 2011.

Lefanu, Sarah. *Feminism and Science Fiction*. Bloomington: Indiana University Press, 1988.

Levecq, Christine. "Power and Repetition: Philosophies of (Literary) History in Octavia E. Butler's *Kindred*." *Contemporary Literature* 41, no. 3 (Fall 2000): 525–53.

Levy, Michael M. "Ophelia Triumphant: The Survival of Adolescent Girls in Recent Fiction by Butler and Womack." *Foundation* 72 (Spring 1998): 34–41.

Link, Eric Carl, and Gerry Canavan, eds. *The Cambridge Companion to American Science Fiction*. New York: Cambridge University Press, 2015.

Long, Lisa A. "A Relative Pain: The Rape of History in Octavia Butler's *Kindred* and Phyllis Alesia Perry's *Stigmata*." *College English* 64, no. 4 (March 2002): 459–83.

Luckhurst, Roger. "'Horror and Beauty in Rare Combination': The Miscegenate Fictions of Octavia Butler." *Women: A Cultural Review* 7, no. 1 (1996) 28–38.

Magedanz, Stacy. "The Captivity Narrative in Octavia E. Butler's *Adulthood Rites*." *Extrapolation* 53, no. 1 (2012): 45–59.

Melzer, Patricia. "'All That You Touch You Change': Utopian Desire and the Concept of Change in Octavia Butler's *Parable of the Sower* and *Parable of the Talents*." *FEMSPEC* 3, no. 2 (2002): 31–52.

Menne, Jeff. "'I Live in This World, Too': Octavia Butler and the State of Realism." *Modern Fiction Studies* 57, no. 4 (2011): 715–37.

Michaels, Walter Benn. "Political Science Fictions." *New Literary History* 31, no. 4 (Autumn 2000): 649–64.

Miller, Jim. "Post-Apocalyptic Hoping: Octavia Butler's Dystopian/Utopian Vision." *Science Fiction Studies* 25, no. 2 (1989): 336–60.

Mitchell, Angelyn. "Not Enough of the Past: Feminist Revisions of Slavery in Octavia E. Butler's *Kindred*." *MELUS* 26, no. 3 (Autumn 2001): 51–75.

Morris, Susanna. "Black Girls Are from the Future: Afrofuturist Feminism in Octavia E. Butler's *Fledgling*." *Women's Studies Quarterly* 40, nos. 3–4 (Spring 2012): 146–66.

Moylan, Tom. *Scraps of the Untainted Sky: Science Fiction, Utopia, Dystopia*. Boulder, Colo.: Westview, 2000.

Nilges, Mathias. "Neoliberalism and the Time of the Novel." *Textual Practice* 29, no. 2 (2015): 357–77.

———. "'We Need the Stars': Change, Community, and the Absent Father in Octavia Butler's *Parable of the Sower* and *Parable of the Talents*." *Callaloo* 32, no. 4 (Fall 2009): 1333–52.

Obourn, Megan. "Octavia Butler's Disabled Futures." *Contemporary Literature* 54, no. 1 (2013): 109–38.

"Octavia Butler Special Issue." *Utopian Studies* 19, no. 3 (2008).

Osherow, Michele. "The Dawn of a New Lilith: Revisionary Mythmaking in Women's Science Fiction." *NWSA Journal* 12, no. 1 (Spring 2000): 68–83.

Outterson, Sarah. "Diversity, Change, Violence: Octavia Butler's Pedagogical Philosophy." *Utopian Studies* 19, no. 3 (2008): 433–56.

Paulin, Diana R. "De-Essentializing Interracial Representations: Black and White Border-Crossings in Spike Lee's *Jungle Fever* and Octavia Butler's *Kindred*." *Cultural Critique* 36 (1997): 165–93.

Penley, Constance. "Time Travel, Primal Scene, and the Critical Dystopia." In *Liquid Metal*, edited by Sean Raymond, 126–35. New York: Wallflower, 2004.

Peppers, Cathy M. "Dialogic Origins and Alien Identities in Butler's Xenogenesis." *Science Fiction Studies* 22, no. 1 (March 1995): 47–62.

Pfeiffer, John R. "Butler, Octavia E(stelle)." In *Twentieth-Century Science-Fiction Writers* (3rd ed.), edited by Noelle Watson and Paul E. Schellinger, 109–10. Chicago: St. James, 1991.

———. "Octavia Butler Writes the Bible." In *Shaw and Other Matters: A Festschrift for Stanley Weintraub on the Occasion of the Fifty-Second Anniversary at The Pennsylvania State University*, edited by Susan Rusinko, 140–52. Selinsgrove, Penn.: Susquehanna University Press, 1998.

Phillips, Jerry. "The Intuition of the Future: Utopia and Catastrophe in Octavia Butler's *Parable of the Sower*." *Novel* (Spring/Summer 2002): 299–311.

Plisner, Andrew. "Arboreal Dialogics: An Ecocritical Exploration of Octavia Butler's *Dawn*." *African Identities* 7, no. 2 (2009): 145–59.

Raffel, Burton. "Genre to the Rear, Race and Gender to the Fore: The Novels of Octavia E. Butler." *Literary Review* 38 (Spring 1995): 453–61.

Ramírez, Catherine S. "Cyborg Feminism: The Science Fiction of Octavia Butler and Gloria Azaldúa." In *Reload: Rethinking Women and Cyberculture*, edited by Mary Flanagan and Austin Booth, 374–402. Cambridge, Mass.: MIT Press, 2002.

Reed, Brian K. "Behold the Woman: The Imaginary Wife in Octavia Butler's *Kindred*." *CLA Journal* 47, no. 1 (September 2003): 66–74.

"Reflections on Octavia Butler." *Science Fiction Studies* 37, no. 3 (November 2010): 433–42.

Reynolds, Richard. *Super Heroes: A Modern Mythology*. Jackson: University Press of Mississippi, 1992.

Richard, Thelma Shinn. "Defining Kindred: Octavia Butler's Postcolonial Perspective." *Obsidian III: Literature in the African Diaspora* 6, no. 2 / 7, no. 1 (2005–2006): 118–34.

Robertson, Benjamin J. "'Some Matching Strangeness': Biology, Politics, and the Embrace of History in Octavia Butler's *Kindred*." *Science Fiction Studies* 37, no. 3 (November 2010): 362–81.

Rutledge, Gregory. "Futurist Fiction and Fantasy: The 'Racial' Establishment." *Callaloo* 24, no. 1 (Winter 2001): 236–52.

Salvaggio, Ruth. "Octavia Butler." In *Suzy McKee Charnas, Octavia Butler, and Joan D. Vinge*, edited by Marleen S. Barr, Ruth Salvaggio, and Richard Law, 1–44. Mercer Island, Wash.: Starmont House, 1986.

———. "Octavia Butler and the Black Science Fiction Heroine." *Black American Literature Forum* 18, no. 2 (1984): 78–81.

Sands, Peter. "Octavia Butler's Chiastic Cannibalistics." *Utopian Studies* 14, no. 1 (2003): 1–14.

Sargent, Lyman Tower. "The Three Faces of Utopianism Revisited." *Utopian Studies* 5, no. 1 (1994): 1–37.

Schell, Heather. "The Sexist Gene: Science Fiction and the Germ Theory of History." *American Literary Theory* 14, no. 4 (Winter 2002): 805–27.

Schwab, Gabriele. "Ethnographies of the Future: Personhood, Agency, and Power in Octavia Butler's Xenogenesis." In *Accelerating Possession: Global Futures of Property and Personhood*, edited by Bill Maurer and Gabriele Schwab, 204–28. New York: Columbia University Press, 2006.

Seed, David. "Posthuman Bodies and Agency in Octavia Butler's Xenogenesis." In *Dark Horizons: Science Fiction and the Dystopian Imagination*, edited by Raffaella Baccolini and Tom Moylan, 91–111. New York: Routledge, 2003.

Shawl, Nisi. "The Third Parable." In Holden and Shawl, *Strange Matings*, 208–13.

Shinn, Thelma J. "Signifyin(g) Science Fiction: Octavia E. Butler." In *Women Shapeshifters: Transforming the Contemporary Novel*, 73–85. Westport, Conn: Greenwood, 1996.

———. "The Wise Witches: Black Women Mentors in the Fiction of Octavia Butler." In *Conjuring: Black Women, Fiction, and Literary Traditions*, edited by Marjorie Pryse and Hortense J. Spillers, 203–15. Bloomington: Indiana University Press, 1985.

Slonczewski, Joan. "Octavia Butler's Xenogenesis Trilogy: A Biologist's Response." Presented at the Science Fiction Research Association (Cleveland, June 2000). Available at http://biology.kenyon.edu/slonc/books/butler1.html.

Smith, Rachel Greenwald. "Ecology beyond Ecology: Life after the Accident in Octavia E. Butler's Xenogenesis Trilogy." *Modern Fiction Studies* 55, no. 3: 545–65.

Smith, Stephanie. "Octavia Butler: A Retrospective." *Feminist Studies* 33, no. 2 (Summer 2007): 385–94.

Smith, Stephanie A. "Morphing, Materialism, and the Marketing of Xenogenesis." *Genders* 18 (Winter 1993): 67–86.

"Special Section on Octavia E. Butler." *Science Fiction Studies* 37, no. 3 (November 2010): 353–442.

Stein, Rachel, ed. "Bodily Invasions: Gene Trading and Organ Theft in Octavia Butler and Nalo Hopkinson's Speculative Fiction." In *New Perspectives on Environmental Justice: Gender, Sexuality, Activism*, 209–24. New Brunswick, N.J.: Rutgers University Press, 2004.

Steinberg, Marc. "Inventing History in Octavia Butler's Postmodern Slave Narrative." *African American Review* 38, no. 3 (2004): 467–76.

Stillman, Peter G. "Dystopian Critiques, Utopian Possibilities, and Human Purpose in Octavia Butler's Parables." *Utopian Studies* 14 (2003): 15–35.

Strong, Melissa. "The Limits of Newness: Hybridity in Octavia E. Butler's *Fledgling*." *FEMSPEC* 11, no. 1 (2010): 27–43.

Tal, Kali. "That Just Kills Me: Black Militant Near-Future Fiction." *Social Text* 71 (Summer 2002): 65–91.

Talbot, Mary M. "'Embracing Otherness': An Examination of Octavia Butler's Xenogenesis Trilogy." *Kimota* 5 (Winter 1996): 45–49.

Texter, Douglas W. "Of Gifted Children and Gated Communities: Paul Theroux's *O-Zone* and Octavia Butler's *The Parable of the Sower*." *Utopian Studies* 19, no. 3 (2008): 457–85.

Thaler, Ingrid. *Black Atlantic Speculative Fictions: Octavia E. Butler, Jewelle Gomez, and Nalo Hopkinson*. New York: Routledge, 2010.

Thibodeau, Amanda. "Alien Bodies and a Queer Future: Sexual Revision in Octavia Butler's 'Bloodchild' and James Tiptree Jr.'s 'With Delicate Mad Hands.'" *Science Fiction Studies* 39, no. 2 (2012): 262–82.

Thiess, Derek. "Care Work, Age, and Culture in Butler's Parable Series." *FEMSPEC* 15, no. 2 (2015): 63–99.

Thomas, Sheree Renée. "Praisesong on the Passage of a Brilliant Star, from a Dreamer Below." *Callaloo* 29, no. 2 (Spring 2006): 249–53.

Thompson, Carlyle Van, ed. "Moving Past the Present: Racialized Sexual Violence and Miscegenous Consumption in Octavia Butler's *Kindred*." In *Eating the Black Body: Miscegenation as Sexual Consumption in African American Literature and Culture*, 107–44. New York: Peter Lang, 2006.

Troy, Maria Holmgren. "Negotiating Genre and Captivity: Octavia Butler's *Survivor*." *Callaloo* 33, no. 4 (2010): 1116–31.

Tucker, Jeffrey A. "'The Human Contradiction': Identity and/as Essence in Octavia Butler's Xenogenesis Trilogy." *Yearbook of English Studies* 37, no. 2 (2007): 164–81.

Turner, Stephanie S. "'What Actually Is': The Insistence of Genre in Octavia Butler's *Kindred*." *FEMSPEC* 4, no. 2 (2004): 259–80.

Vint, Sherryl. "Becoming Other: Animals, Kinship, and Butler's *Clay's Ark*." *Science Fiction Studies* 32, no. 2 (2005): 281–300.

———. *Bodies of Tomorrow: Technology, Subjectivity, Science Fiction*. Buffalo, N.Y.: University of Toronto Press, 2007.

———. "'Only by Experience': Embodiment and the Limitations of Realism in Neo-Slave Narratives." *Science Fiction Studies* 34, no. 2 (2007): 241–61.

Wald, Priscilla. "Cognitive Estrangement, Science Fiction, and Medical Ethics." *Lancet* (North American Edition) 371 (June 7–13, 2008): 1908–9.

Wallace, Molly. "Reading Octavia Butler's *Xenogenesis* after Seattle." *Contemporary Literature* 50, no. 1 (2009): 94–128.

Warfield, Angela. "Reassessing the Utopian Novel: Octavia Butler, Jacques Derrida, and the Impossible Future of Utopia." *Obsidian III: Literature in the African Diaspora* 6, no. 2 / 7, no. 1 (2005–2006): 61–71.

West, C. S'Thembile. "The Competing Demands of Community Survival and Self-Preservation in Octavia Butler's *Kindred*." *FEMSPEC* 7, no. 2 (2006): 72–86.

White, Eric. "The Erotics of Becoming: Xenogenesis and *The Thing*." *Science Fiction Studies* 20, no. 3 (1993): 394–408.

Wolmark, Jenny. *Aliens and Others: Science Fiction, Feminism, and Postmodernism*. New York: Hervester-Wheatsheaf, 1994.

Womack, Ytasha L. *Afrofuturism: The World of Black Sci-Fi and Fantasy Culture*. Chicago: Lawrence Hill, 2013.

Wood, Sarah. "Subversion through Inclusion: Octavia Butler's Interrogation of Religion in Xenogenesis and *Wild Seed*." *FEMSPEC* 6, no. 1 (2005): 87–99.

Yaszek, Lisa. "'A Grim Fantasy': Remaking American History in Octavia Butler's *Kindred*." *Signs* 28, no. 4 (Summer 2003): 239–51.

Zaki, Hoda M. "Future Tense." *Women's Review of Books* 9, nos. 10–11 (1994): 37–38.

———. "Utopia, Dystopia, and Ideology in the Science Fiction of Octavia Butler." *Science Fiction Studies* 17, no. 2 (July 1990): 239–51.

Burton, LeVar, 153
Bush, George W., 146
Butler, Laurice (father), 13–14, 193n1
Butler, Octavia E.: birth and childhood of, 13–14; career struggles of, 30–31, 80, 83–84; celebrity of, 152–53; and children, 90–91; and comic books, 40–46, 50; and commercial fiction, 34–35; commercial success of, 66; depression and self-criticism of, 11–12, 35–36; dyslexia of, 21; early career of, 5–6, 20–21; early interest of, in fantasy and SF, 14–15, 32; early writings of, 7, 16–21; favorite authors of, 16–17; formal education of, 36, 58–59; international travel by, 92; last months and death of, 2, 170–71; on libraries and reading, 138–39; literary legacy of, 2, 175–78; loneliness of, 22, 31; parents of, 13–14, 59–60, 142, 193n1; politics and, 28–29, 109–10; and power, 3–4, 43–46; preference of, for novel writing, 37–38; professional frustrations of, 35, 36–37, 153–54; scholarly works on, 10–11; social anxiety of, 21–22; world reduction and, 40. *See also* autobiographical writing by Butler; Earthseed, Butler and; honors/awards for Butler; thought, development of Butler's; *and entries for specific works*
Butler, Octavia M. (mother), 13–14, 59–60, 142

California State University at Los Angeles, 36
Calvin and Hobbes (comic strip), Butler's use of, in speeches, 153
Campbell, John W., 35, 42
Canaan (Butler), 64–65
Capricorn One (film), black character in, 77
Carl Brandon Society, 174
Carrie (film), and concern with perceived plagiarism, 81
Celestine Prophecy, The (Redfield), and potential of New Age audience, 129
Charnas, Suzy McKee, 16

"Childfinder" (Butler), 7, 9, 23–29, 31, 33, 52, 56, 178, 179
Clarion Journal, 23
Clarion science fiction writers' workshop, 23, 30–31, 174, 176
Clarke, Arthur C., 79
Clay's Ark (Butler), 7–8, 10, 60, 91, 199n47; animal themes in, 73, 74; Butler's hopes for selling, 66–67; Oankali and, 95, 99; in Patternist series, 32, 33, 34; writing of, 85–87
Close Encounters of the Third Kind (film), influence of, 184
Cold War, the, 100
comic books, 16, 26–27, 32, 40–46, 50, 69, 194n15, 196n50
"Cyborg Manifesto" (Haraway), 3, 102

Dark Matter anthologies (ed. Thomas), and SF market, 79, 174
Davidson, Carolyn S., 3
Dawn (Butler), 6, 37, 54, 74, 95–96, 116, 119–20, 163, 165; Butler's views on nuclear war in, 108–15; Oankali character and ideology in, 98–108
Delany, Samuel R., 3, 23, 41, 79, 80, 173
Devil Girl from Mars (film), impact of, on Butler, 15, 16, 95
Dispossessed, The (Le Guin), impact of, on Butler, 40
Divergent (Roth), and Parables series, 133
Doro (character): as critique of power, 44, 50, 69; in *Doro-Jesus*, 91, 145; in early stories, 17; importance of, to Butler, 8, 48, 69, 171; in *Mind of My Mind*, 32, 44, 48–50, 52–53; other characters as similar to, 82, 90, 130, 157; in Patternist series, 17, 44, 48–49, 91–92; and reproductive futurity, 56; and survival, 52; in versions of *Kindred*, 64; in versions of *Blindsight*, 81, 82, 84; in *Wild Seed*, 32, 44, 49, 67–72
Doro-Jesus (Butler), 6, 91

Doubleday Books, 38–39, 56–57, 66, 67, 79, 129

Dreaming Jewels, The (Sturgeon), as model, 42

Dreamsnake (McIntyre), 77, 184

Due, Tananarive, 174

Dune (Herbert), as model, 17, 42, 81

dyslexia, 21

Earthseed, Butler and, 127–29, 133, 138–39, 145–46

Earthseed: The Books of the Living (Butler), 133–36. See also *Parable of the Sower; Parable of the Talents; Parable of the Trickster*

Eco, Umberto, 69

Edelman, Lee, 56, 195n46

editors, Butler's relationship with, 38–39, 66–67, 129–30

Eliot, Jeffrey M., 15, 63

Ellison, Harlan, 7, 23, 28–29, 32, 57, 195n57

Empire Strikes Back, The (film), black character in, 77

Encyclopedia Galactica (Asimov), and "Childfinder," 24

ESP, 19, 42. *See also* psychic superman stories; telepathy

Essence (magazine): essay in, 138; interview in, 17

Eth, Felicia, 67

"Evening and the Morning and the Night, The" (Butler), 4, 7, 55, 60, 174, 202n61; early drafts of, 89–90; plot of, 95–97; rejected by Ed Ferman, 35; Xenogenesis series and, 117–18

"Evolution" (Butler), 19

Fantastic (magazine), 16

Fantastic Four (comic), 196n50

Feiffer, Jules, 153

Ferman, Ed, 35

"Few Rules for Predicting the Future, A" (Butler), 138

Flash series (Butler), 18–19, 95

Fledgling (Butler), 1, 5, 8, 10, 54, 147; alternate versions of, 169–70; ending of, 167; as a "fun" novel, 164–65; plot of, 162–64, 166–68; possible sequels to, 6, 167–68

Fledgling II (Asylum) (Butler), 6, 167–69

Fossey, Dian, 108

"Four-Hour Fugue" (Bester), 79

Four Walls, Eight Windows, 129

Fry, Joan, 52, 118

Gaia hypothesis, 124

Galaxy (magazine), 16

genocide, 106–8

Ghosh, Nibir K., 110

Gingrich, Newt, 146

Giver, The, and Parables series, 133

Godfather, The (Puzo), and *Blindsight*, 81

God of Clay (Butler), 126–31, 143. See also *Parable of the Trickster*

Goldberg, Whoopi, 153

"Gone Fishin'" (Wilson), 79

Gonzalez, Juan, 164–65

"Good-by" (Butler), 9, 33

Goodman, Amy, 164–65

Govan, Sandra, 51

Greenberg, Martin H., 78–79

Griggs, Sutton, 49

Guy, Lynn (Butler pseudonym), 35

Haraway, Donna, 3, 153

Heifetz, Merrilee, 124, 203n1

Heinlein, Robert A., 16, 34, 132

Henderson, Zenna, impact of, on Butler, 16–17, 42

Hendrickson, Kathryn, 201n19

Herbert, Frank, 16, 42, 81

Hill, Napoleon, 20

Hitler, Adolf, 81

Holden, Rebecca J., 108, 176

"Holdout" (Sheckley), 79

honors/awards for Butler, 2, 75, 143, 152–53; MacArthur Foundation grant, 2, 14, 37, 142

Moore, Alan, 44
Moore, Thomas D., 202n29
More than Human (Sturgeon), as model, 42
Morrison, Toni, 67, 79–80
Moylan, Tom, 137–38

National Public Radio, 103, 104
"Near of Kin" (Butler), 60–61, 198n10
Nebula Award for Best Novel, 143
"Necessary Being, A" (Butler), 68, 173, 178–80
Negro History Bulletin (journal), interview for, 15
New York Times (newspaper), interview in, 52
Nilger, Mathias, 132
No Future (Edelman), and reproductive futurity, 195n46
nuclear war, Butler's views on, 108–15

O (magazine), 74
Oankali, the, 5, 36, 98–100, 201n8, 201n19, 201n24, 202nn28–29, 202n37; animal themes and, 75; beneficence of, 107–8; character and ideology of, 97–108; in *Dawn*, 98–115, 120; fallibility of, 115–19; first mention of, 93–94; as flawed like humans, 121–22; *Fledging* and, 165; as fugitive race, 94; genocide by, 106–7; in *Imago*, 115–22; influence of Patternist stories on, 7; nuclear war and, 108–15; sexual practices of, 8–9; slavery and, 93–95
Octavia E. Butler Legacy Network, 174
Octavia's Brood (ed. Brown and Imarisha), 79, 175
Odd John (Stapledon), as model, 42, 81
Okorafor, Nnedi, 174
Omni (magazine), essay for, 138
Open Road Media, 178
Orwell, George, 27

Parable of the Sower (Butler), 6, 66, 126, 129, 143; plot of, 131–40; as post-apocalyptic, 132–33, 137–38

Parable of the Talents (Butler), 126, 131, 132, 135–37, 143; as a mother-daughter story, 142; plot of, 140–43; unfairness of God's justice in, 147–48
Parable of the Trickster (Butler), 5, 6, 29, 55, 115, 126, 205n86; alternate versions of, 144–47; biblical inspiration for, 148–49; as Butler's largest failure, 153–54; false starts for, 144; influence of Zenna Henderson on, 16–17; *Spiritus* and, 156–57; versions of, 8
Parables series (Butler), 5, 8, 10, 37, 147, 149
Paraclete (Butler), 6, 8, 110, 206n4, 206n21; plot of, 157–58; similarities of, to "The Book of Martha," 161–62; time setting of, 159
Paradoxa (journal), 40
Pasadena City College, 36, 58–59; Literacy Contest of, 19
Patternist series (Butler), 2, 4–5, 6, 10, 17, 91–92, 201–2n4; categorization of stories in, 32–33; comic book influence on, 41–46; influence of, on other Butler works, 7–8, 31–32; as trilogy, 56–57. *See also entries for specific books in series*
Patternmaster (Butler), 2, 31–32, 56–57, 67, 81; general plot of, 39–40; narrative crisis of, 46–48; power theme in, 43–46; race in, 186; sold to Doubleday, 38–39; world reduction in, 40
Penley, Constance, 62
Pilgrimage (Henderson), Butler's love of, 17
Poets and Writers (magazine), interview in, 52, 118
politics, 28–29; Black Power movement and, 28, 58–59; Cold War, 100; Indian removal and, 107–8; nuclear war and, 108–10
"Positive Obsession" (Butler), 21, 37, 80
power themes, 3–4, 43–46
"Principles of Newspeak" (Orwell), 27
Psi: History of a Vanished People (invented work quoted in "Childfinder"), 27, 179

GERRY CANAVAN is an assistant professor of twentieth- and twenty-first-century literature at Marquette University in Milwaukee, Wisconsin. He has published widely on the subject of science fiction and other fantastic literatures and is a co-editor at *Extrapolation* and *Science Fiction Film and Television*. He is also the co-editor of two recent critical anthologies on science fiction: *Green Planets: Ecology and Science Fiction* (with Kim Stanley Robinson) and *The Cambridge Companion to American Science Fiction* (with Eric Carl Link).

MODERN MASTERS OF SCIENCE FICTION

John Brunner   *Jad Smith*

William Gibson   *Gary Westfahl*

Gregory Benford   *George Slusser*

Greg Egan   *Karen Burnham*

Ray Bradbury   *David Seed*

Lois McMaster Bujold   *Edward James*

Frederik Pohl   *Michael R. Page*

Alfred Bester   *Jad Smith*

Octavia E. Butler   *Gerry Canavan*

THE UNIVERSITY OF ILLINOIS PRESS

is a founding member of the

Association of American University Presses.

Designed by Kelly Gray

Composed in 10.75/14.5 Dante

with Univers display

by Lisa Connery

at the University of Illinois Press

Manufactured by Cushing-Malloy, Inc.

Cover image: *Xenon* by Debra Lowman

University of Illinois Press

1325 South Oak Street

Champaign, IL 61820-6903

www.press.uillinois.edu